HOW WAS I SUPPOSED TO KNOW?

The Adventures of a Girl Whose Name Means Lost

By

Lorna Lee

How Was I Supposed to Know? A Memoir

All photographs, including the cover photograph, were provided by the personal collection of the author and her family.

ISBN 978-0-9888468-0-7

Published by Early Girl Enterprises on CreateSpace

Praise for How Was I Supposed to Know?

"I couldn't stop laughing. I didn't want it to end." My mom, who wouldn't want my life story to end for obvious reasons.

"Just hysterical. I laughed until I cried and then I laughed some more. But I think you were too nice to Victor [my ex-husband]." Tina, my older sister, who is very protective of me and never approved of my mate choices, except for Philip.

"Besides the fact that it's very funny and extremely well-written, I admire your courage, Lorna. You put your life out there—warts and all—so that other people might be inspired by how you handled some pretty tough challenges." Lisa, my younger sister, who always idolized me and is a very good judge of character. (Just to be clear, I don't have warts.)

"It was a quick read." Philip, the man of my dreams, a man of few words, and a man who appreciates an author that doesn't blather on and on and on.

"I was afraid that it was going to be boring and was really surprised that I enjoyed reading it. I found myself laughing out loud at the same old stories I've heard a million times. Good job." Alex, my son. I must have over-emphasized the honesty thing with him when he was growing up.

"I can't remember laughing so much while reading a book...or doing anything for that matter. My husband

wondered what was so funny and I told him I found the next Erma Bombeck." Emily, a former librarian who remembers Erma Bombeck and was apparently looking for her.

NOTE: When I get reviewers who don't already know and love me to say nice things about this book, I'll be sure to add their comments in the next edition.

Dedication

For Phil, who found me, over and over and over again
.

Note to Readers (Or anyone who refuses to read this book but wants to know what I said about you)

Extraordinary events happen to ordinary people every day. I have examined my life and tallied up the number of remarkable events that pushed and pulled me (an ordinary person) to places I never expected to go. How was I supposed to know that I—a girl whose name, Lorna, as in "forlorn," means lost—could find the security I always craved by walking blithely through a minefield of fluky experiences? If there were warning signs, I missed them.

Well, maybe I ignored them.

This is the story of my journey told from my perfectly imperfect and idiosyncratic perspective. It is based on my recollections of the facts of my life as they happened, keeping in mind that time and experience have shaped my memories. My having consumed a small pond of vodka in my early years may have affected a few of my recollections. Blacking out tends to make you forget details you wish you could recover when writing a memoir or trying to find your underwear.

I fully understand that others involved in my life would write a different account of the same events that we experienced together. Truth, like beauty or how spicy that "mild" chili was, is subjective. My memoir is as true as my recollections about the events of my life and my feelings about those events.

I name names in this book, but when I use names, I use only first names or cleverly fashioned pseudonyms to protect the privacy of those involved in my journey. If I use a real-sounding name, either I obtained permission from the very real person, or I made up a name very different from the person's true name. Only those very close to me or those who are psychic will know the real from the phony names.

I also gave myself creative license to break up long pages of prose with snappy, witty dialogue that captures the feeling of what transpired. I cannot swear that everything—or even anything—in the dialogue you will read is a verbatim transcription of a real conversation. The essence of what transpired in the conversations is what I attempted to capture.

Everything that I am about to reveal to you happened to me in the sequence in which I present it. I am omitting many events of my life, however, because they didn't add to this particular exploration of my life. This does not mean that what I choose to exclude was not important to me; it just means that I have material for other books or that I wish to keep those memories for my heart only.

Table of Contents

How Was I Supposed to Know? A Memoir

CHAPTER 1: PERFECT STORMS

I'm the one on the right. Do I look as if I'm prepared for the tough realities of life?

I never expected any of it to happen, especially not to me—maybe to a reality TV drama queen, but certainly not to ordinary me. But it did. All of it. Most of it wasn't the kind of thing a person would plan for herself if she had any sense. But I'm not a planner. And my "sense" could never have been deemed "common." I just wandered naively into the events that piled up and became my life.

*****

If Someone Up There has been gunning for me, that Someone Up There has dreadfully bad aim. I've almost been struck by lightning. Twice. So far.

The first time was in 1967, when I was about ten years old. I was with my two sisters and some other kids at a family friend's lake cabin. A storm was brewing, and Mrs. Really Old herded us inside the small, rustic structure. I wanted to stay outside to watch the dark clouds roll in, feel the rain pelt me, and maybe see some bolts of lightning. I loved storm watching. But Mrs. Really Old went all "safety first" on us, so we had to wait out the storm in the only room in the cabin that could contain all of us kids—one bedroom packed with a combination of bunk beds and single beds.

I sat propped against the wall on the bunk-bed positioned directly opposite a half-open window. The middle of my back was against the room's electrical outlet. An instant after I lay down on my left and propped myself up on my elbow because that electrical socket was digging into my back, a fiery red-yellow ball whizzed over my shoulder and into the electrical outlet. *Bam! Crack! Sizzle!* The outlet and a big piece of the pink, flowery wallpaper around the outlet were black—burned to a crisp. I'm pretty sure the electricity in the cabin went off.

"Did you see that?" my older sister Tina asked.

There was a lot of wide-eyed nodding.

Mrs. Really Old rushed into the bedroom, which was only about two feet from the kitchen, to see what happened. She seemed winded from her sprint. "What happened?" she asked, her voice just a little too high-pitched for an Adult In Charge.

Tina, our fearless twelve-year-old leader, spoke for us all. "A ball of lightning came through the open window..." she pointed at the open window, "...and flew into that electrical socket. Right after Lorna laid down."

2

She pointed toward me and then at the charred wall. Our heads all rotated on cue.

Mrs. Really Old gasped, then said, "Lord have mercy!" After some hand-wringing and the kind of muttering that adults do right before they either tell you what to do or start yelling at you, she finally added, "After the rain stops, you girls need to go home." She looked at me like I was some kind of devil-child, as if I'd known exactly when the fireball from Satan was coming and when to dodge it. The rest of the kids were her grandchildren so she had to keep them around, but I think she really wanted to be alone to pray and de-Satanize the place.

The camp was four miles from our home, and our walk back was pretty quiet, as if we had just borne witness to some holy (or unholy) event that we needed to honor with silence. Maybe we were in a state of disbelief or shock, but it's more likely none of us wanted to talk about the fact that I had missed being part of the charred remains of that lightning ball by seconds. I sure didn't want to dwell on my near-demise. Tina, who felt responsible for her sisters, didn't want one of them dying on her watch. My other sister, eight-year-old Lisa, adored me, and the thought of her idol reduced to a black splotch on the wallpaper was more than she could probably bear. Like me, she was a sensitive girl.

*****

The odds of being struck by lightning are almost one in a million. That made me pretty special. I was so close to being hit that I count myself among the almost one in a million. Plus, ball lightning is really rare, which only strengthened my case that I was one super-special, lucky kid. How many kids live to tell that kind of story? Only one that I know of. If I hadn't been uncomfortable and plopped down, that ball lightning would have actually whizzed through my heart and killed me dead. Then I would have been *super* special. Imagine the hullabaloo and the obituary. I would have been legendary.

I don't know if Mrs. Really Old ever recovered from the incident, but I didn't give it much thought until my next run-in with lightning in 2010, forty-two years later. I guess Someone Up There had been taking target practice lessons. The odds of being hit by lightning twice in a lifetime are about forty million to one. My guess is that Someone Up There wanted me to be Certifiably Special.

*****

The afternoon in question, I was walking my terrier-mix, Scrappy, along a tree-lined dirt road that followed a babbling mountain brook. While this sounds relaxing and idyllic, and would be for most people under most circumstances, it was not. I'm not "most people," and my life situation at that time was not idyllic and didn't fall under the category of "most circumstances."

The reason I was taking a solo walk with my pooch, Scrappy, was because my twenty-six-year marriage had ended when my husband decided he'd misplaced himself and needed to go on a search and rescue mission. Without me. What I didn't understand, since I was the one always helping him find his keys or wallet, was *why couldn't I help him find himself?* I could have remained in our isolated 200-plus-year-old farm house that I'd called home for nearly twenty years, but it needed more work than my failed marriage did. (Besides, I was never particularly handy or prudent with power tools.) Once I accepted that my husband wanted to find himself without my help, I opted to buy a condo in a nearby city. Unfortunately for me, the mortgage I was promised kept getting held up, so I was a squatter at my younger sister's vacation home for much longer than the two weeks I'd intended. I had six weeks of "vacation" with no Internet, no TV or radio, and lots of time to ponder homelessness if I lost the contract on my condo because the mortgage company was being picky about my simple finances, which were all tied up with my looking-for-happiness-elsewhere husband's complicated finances.

Since I had no high-tech access to weather forecasts, I relied on "Eyewitness Weather." I looked up at the sky. It seemed clear. My plan was to walk Scrappy, then stop by the local library for my fix of civilization. Driving to a secluded spot on a road along a babbling brook, I parked my car and let Scrappy romp without his leash. The trees obscured the sun, or so I thought. They were luscious trees and gave abundant shade. We were about two tenths of a mile from my car when I felt a big *splat* hit my head. I was sure some bird had "done the dirty" from mid-air. But then I noticed more *splats* all around me. *Oh great,* I thought, *rain with attitude.* I looked up through the canopy of trees and saw charcoal skies that should have been blue.

Scrappy, being a fast and smart dog, ran back to the car while I stood there thinking about summer rain washing over my face and what a wonderful entry that observation would make for my Gratitude Journal, something I kept religiously to keep me from misplacing myself. When the clouds released Niagara Falls on me, however, I figured it was time to join Scrappy. Unless you count the time I fell into a lake fully clothed, I'd never been so thoroughly drenched so quickly in public.

Just as I turned to run back to the car, two of my senses were simultaneously assaulted, common sense not being among them. First, I heard an ear-splitting *crack,* then, over my left shoulder, I saw a blinding spray of light.

5

This all seems vaguely familiar, I thought to myself right before I bolted for the car. Soggie Doggie and Drenched Driver got into the car and slowly made our way to the library. By then, the sheets of rain had stopped and the skies were blue again. I made quick work of my business at the library, feeling self-conscious in my *squish-squashing* sneakers and looking like I'd just come from a wet-T-shirt contest.

Returning to my temporary shelter, the beautiful mountain lodge, I lay down on a couch to read. Two hours later, I woke up. (Napping is highly unusual for me.) Scrappy's nose was about two inches from mine. It was an hour past his dinner time. When I tried to get up, I noticed that my legs weren't cooperating. They felt like lead weights. My arms did, too. It was like I woke up but my body didn't. Ever so slowly I was able to coax my extremities to move so I could feed Scrappy. I moved like a barely animated zombie. *No wonder zombies seem so cranky in the movies,* I thought. *Moving dead limbs is very hard work.*

Exhausted from the dog-dinner preparation, I dragged myself back to the couch and fell asleep again. When I woke up after another hour, I knew something was wrong. *Two naps in one afternoon?* I hadn't eaten much that day, but that was typical at the time, so I tried to get up to get something to eat. But that was too much work. Scrappy knew a few tricks, but "Fetch the cashews" wasn't one of them.

"What's wrong with me, Scrap?" Since we'd begun living alone, Scrappy and I had developed quite a close relationship. He was my main confidant and advisor. His listening skills often proved very illuminating when I needed answers to compelling questions.

He looked up from licking his groin area and gave me his bright-eyed, cocked-head, *I'm listening* look, and then continued grooming his privates.

The only odd thing I could think of that day was our walk. *Lightning? Could it be?* I did what I always did when I needed answers and didn't have access to the Internet: I called Tina.

Jim, my brother-in-law, answered. "Hello?"

"Jim? Ish me. Lor…na." I was very groggy.

"Hi, Lorn. What's up?"

"Hi, Jim. Ish me. Um. Can you do some tings for me?" My tongue was cooperating about as well as my arms and legs.

"Lorn, are you okay?"

"Hi, Jim. Ish me. Um, sure. Um, fine. Can you look up on the, um, um, com-u-ter, what happens to me if, um, light-zing gets me?"

Suddenly he sounded alarmed. "What? You got hit by lightning? I'm coming up there now!" (It's an hour and a half drive.)

"Nah, nah, nah…jus' look up, um, heavy legs." I knew what I wanted to say, but the properly constructed sentences in my head wouldn't come out properly.

"Lorn, you don't sound good. I'm looking up the symptoms now." He paused, then, "Do you have heart palpitations?"

I slapped my chest. "Ouch. Um. Nope."

"Burns anywhere?"

I looked around the room, "Don't know. Um, don't see any tings."

"Oh, God. It says here confusion is a symptom."

"Might have dat."

"You need to go to a hospital."

"Really? A hostible? No. Ish me. Jus real tired."

"Hang tight," he said. "I'll call Tina and call you right back, okay?"

"'K. Jim. Ish me. Tanks."

I hung up and fell back asleep until the phone ringing awakened me. It was Tina. "Lorn, can you call 911."

"Hi, Teen. Ish me."

"Yes. Yes. Can. You. Call. 911?" She spoke slowly and deliberately, like she was talking to a child. Or someone with a brain injury.

"Yup." I started dialing with a heavy finger while she was still on the phone. I heard her call my name.

"No, Lorn! Stop dialing. Use the land line so they find you in their system."

"They who? Teen...you comin'?"

"Yes, I'm coming, but you call 911 first. On Lisa's phone. An ambulance will come. The people will help you and get you to a hospital. Then call us back to tell us which hospital they're taking you to. We're on our way. Can you do all that?"

"Yup. No prolem. Sir, um, Teen. Ish me. Um fine."

After Tina hung up, all I had were Scrappy and my wits, and neither were any help in emergency situations unless barking or behaving like the zombie poster girl for lobotomies could summon magical help. I could have used some major magic at that moment. And at many other moments in my life, come to think of it.

The trip from the couch to my sister Lisa's phone was excruciating. I felt like I was dragging a dead body, not that I had any direct experience with that kind of thing. I felt disoriented, too. Taking a deep "cleansing breath" (others often interpret these breaths as "sighs") with each arduous step, I dragged myself closer to the phone. The lodge is spacious, and my progress was excellent...for a disabled sloth. When finally I got to the phone, I was relieved that I only had to push three numbers: 9-1-1.

"What is your emergency?"

"Um, I tink I wash hit by lightzing."

"You believe you were hit by lightning, Ma'am? Is that correct?"

"Yup."

"When did this happen?"

"Um. Probly two clock?" I hoped she knew the answer because I wasn't sure.

"Two p.m. today? Ma'am? It's now 6:15 p.m."

"Okay." I liked this woman. She seemed to know a lot.

She had another question for me. "Ma'am, are you experiencing any symptoms?"

"Real tired an', um, heavy."

"Are you alone?"

"No. Scrappy's here."

"Can Scrappy take you to the hospital?"

"Haha. No. He's a dog. Haha. That'd be funny."

"We're going to send someone to help you. What's your address?"

"I don know." (I really didn't know their formal address) "On a big hill."

"Can you be more specific?" the patient 911 operator asked.

"Um. A real big hill near a road with lotsa trees?"

There was a pause during which I heard a clear cleansing breath. Then she asked, "What's your name?"

"Lorna. Bud I don' liff here."

"Okay, Lorna. Where do you live?" Her voice was taking on the tone of a kindergarten teacher.

"Um…nowhere. My husban' leff me so I leff my house 'cuz it was all really broken, ya know?"

"Have you had any alcohol or other substances?"

9

"No. Jus' normal pills for my dizzy head." I have Chronic Fatigue Syndrome, and most of my symptoms are neurological. Constant dizziness, hypersensitivity to auditory and visual stimuli, and the inability to focus when stressed are my major challenges. But I didn't tell her all that. (With my zombie brain and zombie mouth, I couldn't have pronounced the words.) Instead, I said, "Um, my sisser owns her house. She let me liff here for a lil while."

Then I gave them my brother-in-law's name, and she found the address. "Okay, Lorna, we found you in the system. I've just dispatched an ambulance. I'm going to stay on the phone with you until they get there."

"Oh, thas nice."

Before too long, I heard several large pickup trucks in the driveway and then I heard knocking on the door. I told the 911 operator I had visitors and hung up, then slowly shuffled to the hallway and waved some rather handsome men inside. They looked so friendly. When Scrappy started barking, one of them asked me to put Scrappy in one of the bedrooms because there would be a lot of activity. *Activity? Hmm?* That sounded good to me, so Scrappy got sequestered.

The local Volunteer Rescue Squad was kind enough to send Mr. May, Mr. June, Mr. July, and Mr. August from their 2010 Hunk Calendar. They came in and started assessing my situation while I assessed them. I wished I'd put on some eyeliner and done something with my pillow-hair. After hearing my story (as best I could tell it) and taking my "vitals," they decided I'd been hit by "side-splash lightning." A tree twenty feet away from me had been directly hit by a bolt of lightning, the current had traveled into the ground, and, because there was so much water on the ground and in the air, the current had then "splashed" into the atmosphere, supercharging everything in the vicinity, including me.

"Tha' happen?" I asked as they were trying to listen for any irregularities in my heart.

"Yes, ma'am. It's rare, but it happens."

"Oh. Iz not ma'am. Iz Lorna. Getting diforced. Husban' leff me. But thas okay. I can take care off mysef."

They tried not to smile but couldn't help themselves when I flashed then a wide grin. I may have winked, too.

When I heard the ambulance arrive, sirens and all, I prepared myself for the second ambulance ride of my life. I asked the Hunky Calendar Guys where they were taking me so I could let Tina know. Before they put the oxygen mask on me, I called Tina and Jim and told them to meet me at the smallest hospital in the state. As it turned out, it was also the best hospital in the state for me under the circumstances. They had a two-bed emergency room. One was occupied by an unfortunate man who'd combined alcohol with the wrong drugs and was puking out his spleen. The other room was vacant, just waiting for me, along with two nurses and the attending physician. This tiny hospital didn't get many lightning-strike victims, so my case was way more medically—and aesthetically— attractive than Puking Guy. As long as I was there, the medical staff doted on me.

I kept drifting off to sleep and I felt paralyzed, both of which scared me. I felt as if all my blood was draining from my body. But since I wasn't bleeding, it was my energy that was pouring out of me. I was sure I would sink into a coma and die if they let me fall asleep. Thankfully, the nurse kept asking me questions and making me try to move my now seemingly phantom limbs.

After checking my feet for burns (there were none) and my vitals (there were some), they recorded me as a perfectly healthy fifty-ish woman whose main symptom was a bad case of loopiness.

"Pease," I begged the nurse, "don' let me die or go to bed."

She patted my arm. "You need to rest, Sweetie. Don't worry. We're all here to make sure you don't die. We haven't lost anyone so far this month." She was having a hard time suppressing a smile.

"Thas good. Jus' don' let me shleep mysef 'to a coma. I don wanna wake up dead. My life hash ta start gettin' good soon. I wanna be here when it does. Ya know?"

"I know, Honey. Are you hungry? Have you eaten anything today?"

"No. Nuthin'."

"Well, that just might be part of your problem. What can I bring you?" She was a portly woman and I could tell the topic of food delighted her. I really didn't have the energy to tell her about my ultra-restrictive vegan diet, which excluded everything normal people eat (gluten, sugar, or anything that had a shelf life longer than an hour).

When Tina and Jim finally arrived, I asked them to call my "new-old flame," a man who recently had come back into my life but was out of town on business. He was upset and wanted to fly back to be with me, but I somehow convinced him not to by telling him I was in "goo' hans" and was "jus gate." Tina filled him in on the details that she knew, reassured him, and hung up. She then went into Big Sister Mode, making sure everyone was making me the Number One Emergency that evening. If I get hit by lightning again, I sure hope Tina's on duty again for triage.

While she was issuing instructions, Jim stayed by my side, comforting me. "Don't worry, Lorn, we'll take care of you."

In an attempt to appear self-reliant, I said, "Tanks, Jim. Ya know...but I c'n take care uff mysef. Ya know?" I'd been homeless for the last six weeks, was still unsure about my mortgage, and was lying in the ER, having just been struck by side-splash lightning...my slurry self-confidence must have seemed a bit ironic to him, but he just nodded and lovingly stroked my hand for what seemed like hours. That kind of thing makes him feel better and a love-abrasion on my hand was the least of my worries.

The physician was positively charged with enthusiasm about my case and actually looked a bit disappointed when she told me my heart was fine and all blood work looked normal. Her chance to shine came when she announced her diagnosis: my extreme lethargy was due to Post Traumatic Stress Disorder. Because my immune system was already compromised by Chronic Fatigue Syndrome, the super-charge from the side-splash lightning had sent my body into temporary hyper-mode. My current stupor was the ultimate "crash." She said I should expect more dizziness and possibly a lot of headaches. I couldn't be left on my own for several days, she went on, because I wasn't capable of making good decisions. *Did she know me, or what?*

Scrappy and I stayed with Tina and Jim for a couple of days, and then I returned to the lodge in the mountains for another week. I was determined to be an autonomous single woman who could take care of herself as long as wild electricity wasn't involved. But my independent single womanhood days had to wait. I still didn't have an approved mortgage, and my condo contract was expiring, and now that it was summer, my younger sister and her family needed their summer vacation home. I looked into short-term rentals, but:

1. Landlords of nice apartments didn't allow pets.

2. Attendants of motels that allowed animals of all kinds only rented rooms by the hour.

3. The Budget Rent-A-Car people only had subcompacts, which would've made sleeping arrangements for Scrappy and me cozier than either of us were willing to attempt.

Since I wasn't willing to abandon Scrappy and the other two options were risky to my finances or reputation, I started to worry about being single and homeless at the same time. I worried for about an hour before Tina came to my rescue again. Scrappy and I packed up our few belongings and accepted her invitation to squat at her house until my housing situation became clearer. I think she wanted to keep an eye on me and didn't want to have to engage in any future search and rescue missions if I got lost.

All my life, just when I least expect it, miracles find me. I escaped a direct hit from lightning twice. If that wasn't enough of a miracle for one lifetime, an even less likely miracle occurred next: the mortgage company came through just in time. I was able to purchase my condo on the very last day the contract was valid. Since I had left behind almost everything from the house that held my married life, I had a lot of shopping to do before my condo resembled a proper home. So I stayed with Tina and Jim a few more weeks while we painted the condo and waited for the new furniture to arrive, piece by piece by piece. The last time I'd moved into my own place had been when I was eighteen years old. Except for having new furniture rather than hand-me-downs, moving thirty years later wasn't all that different. I was excited and scared, but I knew I was right where I needed to be.

*****

Good decisions have never been my forte. Maybe lightning knocks more than the energy out of a person;

maybe it knocks the common sense out, too. I never thought that my close call with ball-lightning all those years ago had any lasting effects, but might it explain the string of blunders that I collectively (and endearingly) call "my life"? Nature may have given me the equivalent of electroshock therapy. Twice. No wonder my judgment was a bit off on some of my life choices—the same life choices that have led me to this brand new life of a dizzy, independent, fifty-five year-old, single woman.

But, no, I can't lay all the blame on Mother Nature's fireworks. My decisions about which way to turn when there was a fork in the road were often, if not always, made without knowing some pretty important information that was, for some reason or another, withheld from me. Would I have made the same choices if I had known the — a truth I discovered only after I had traveled too far down the path I had chosen?

I'll never know.

Maybe that's the point. Does the truth set you free, or does it just make you wonder? I can only look at my own life to try to figure that one out.

CHAPTER 2: C PLACES

This is one of those C places I lived in. A Creepy forest where our mobile home landed.

I lived my childhood in C places.

I don't mean C like the grade teachers give on the first essays of the school year just to make the points that (a) your mind melts in summer and (b) how critical school is to keeping the distinction between kids and apes as clear as possible. And I don't mean "C" as in "average," although anybody could look at where we lived and see that there was room for improvement.

I lived in places that started with the letter C.

Long before I could remember anything, I lived in a trailer in rural Chazy, New York. People affiliated with trailers tend to call them *mobile homes*, making them seem exceptional. And they are. They are homes that accompany a family wherever it chooses to go. Now that's special. Plus, the kind of trailer I lived in back then, according to old-time black and white photographs, had wing-like edges on all the corners and resembled a rocket ship. That's double-special.

Our trailer was parked next to Mémé and Pépé's little house in Chazy farm country. Mémé and Pépé were my mother's parents and Mom was their only child. It's not like they had to worry that a whole bunch of other children would ask to park a rocket ship next to them, so they let us land there for a while. Mémé spoke mostly French, plus her special kind of broken English that my two sisters and I came to understand. But she could also speak Finnish. Since only Finns can speak Finnish—because it's a tortuous language that doesn't play nicely with any other language except maybe Siberian—I knew she must *be* Finnish. Mémé was something of a mystery woman to me, what with all those languages floating inside her. And that wasn't the only thing about Mémé that confused me. She also told us that Mom was *her* daughter, but she was not Pépé's daughter. (I wasn't able to solve that puzzle until I was nearly ten years old and started caring about such things.) Mémé was also the boss of Pépé and everyone else, and she was very suspicious of anyone who was American, including Pépé. When I got old enough to notice all of this, I felt sorry for Pépé, who was just a simple, honest, hard-working man with a fondness for fart jokes. I let him adopt me as his trusty sidekick.

I guess we were on better terms with Mom's side of the family than my other grandparents, who probably didn't want a rocket ship parked next to their home in the middle of West Chazy, which was not a booming metropolis, but at least they had both sidewalks and dignity. My father's family was more like a collection of proper ladies and gentlemen in a country manor. A big collection. Daddy was one of nine children. His father was a popular dentist, so I don't know when he had time to make such a big family. His mother was a stern, quiet woman who prayed as her major form of entertainment. I don't know if she was always that way, or having all those children changed her into a holy sour-puss.

The six of us—my mother, Mémé, Pépé, my father, toddling Tina and me—all lived in the middle of a corn field. It was a two-acre plot carved out of a dairy farm and cow poop dumping ground. The only sign of civilization was a two-lane paved road with lines that somebody had painted but those lines were barely visible under all of the dirt and cow poop.

*****

True to its fancy name, our home got mobile and we moved to Cadyville, which was about fifteen miles from Mémé and Pépé's house. This was sometime before Lisa was born. Being not yet two years old, I didn't know the reason why we launched the rocket ship, nor do I remember the move. I remember Cadyville, though, because we lived there until I was four-going-on-five. If Chazy was *nowhere* in 1959, Cadyville was *the other side of nowhere*. It was like our rocket ship time traveled backwards into the back woods and landed on a hill with nothing but trees all around us and creepy things that lived in the trees. A black bear regularly shopped in our garbage cans, whereas the dense population of cows and one major roadway were behind us.

I just can't believe my parents actually *chose* to raise us in the woods. We were *girls*, not *squirrels*.

We had electricity and running water, though, so we were somewhat better off than our only human neighbors, whose house we couldn't see because of all the trees. Eventually, someone hacked a path to their house. Those neighbors were as close to hillbillies as I ever saw in person. They were really, really nice hillbillies, though. Except for Mr. Hillbilly.

There were six Hillbillies in all: the two parents, three older sons (who I didn't know very well) and one daughter. I knew the two females in the clan best. Mrs. Hillbilly was the strongest woman I ever met. If she hadn't worn dresses and cooked, I would have bet she was a man. She smoked as if the source of life itself came from those white sticks with the glowy tips. And she didn't smoke lady-like, either. She let the cigarette hang from the corner of her mouth while she talked, then she'd suck in real hard and blow smoke out of the other side of her mouth and her nose at the same time. It was breathtaking to see. Her hands were unforgettable, too, in that they were always busy doing chores. They also bore a striking resemblance to the bark on the old twisted trees in the wilderness that passed as our yard. Mrs. Hillbilly always smelled of the most peculiar concoction of cigarette smoke and bacon.

Bee was her teenage daughter and the only babysitter my mother ever trusted with us girls. Bee looked like Tina's Midge doll. She was so pretty. Her hair was shiny-dark and swayed when she sashayed. I tried to walk like she did, but I just looked like I needed corrective shoes. She was the most stylish of the clan in her tight pants and tops, and she masked the signature cigarette/bacon Hillbilly smell with sweet perfume.

Mrs. Hillbilly and Bee were like family—no, they were *better than family*. They didn't have to love us or do nice things for us, but they did anyway. When Mrs. Hillbilly made us bologna sandwiches, she drew a smiley face with yellow mustard on the round bologna and made sure we saw it before she covered it up with the slice of Wonder bread. She wanted us to eat a happy sandwich. That's how nice she was.

But then there was Mr. Hillbilly. For reasons beyond all comprehension, we called him Uncle Al. He was as much like family to me as that big, creepy bear that stole our garbage just about every night. Uncle Al was the scariest man I hoped ever to meet. He never left his chair in their dark cave of a living room. On the few occasions I caught a glimpse of him, I saw a skinny old man with a long, pointy nose like the Wicked Witch of the West. But he wasn't green. He was gray. And so was his stringy hair. He smoked so much that it looked like a thick fog had settled into the living room. Plus, he was remarkably fluent in cuss words and used them with his family, their dog, people on the TV, and the Lord Himself.

"Git me another beer, goddammit," he always bellowed at Mrs. Hillbilly. And…

"What the hell kind of nonsense is that bastard talkin' about?" he shouted at Walter Cronkite. And…

"Git the hell over here, you stupid bastard," he commanded any two- or four-legged creature when he wanted company, which was rare. And…

"Jee-zus H. Christ!" This was one of his favorite outbursts. The emphasis was always on the "Jee" part of Jesus. I'd be sitting in the kitchen, watching Mrs. Hillbilly and Bee do some form of heavy labor, and all of a sudden we'd hear him yell, "Jee-zus H. Christ!" We'd all stop and listen. Nothing. Then things would proceed as before. That happened a lot. I never knew Jesus had a middle name. *What did the "H" stand for?* I always wondered if it meant "Holy," but I never dared ask. Knowing Mr. Hillbilly, I'm sure the "H" stood for something else.

The Hillbillies lived like I imagined cavemen lived, only with electricity, which they used with guarded optimism. They had no need for a plumber. Slaves, however, were a necessity. They had to fetch water from a brook at the bottom of a steep hill. The water was used for drinking, cooking, and washing dishes, in that order of priority. I used to help carry buckets of water up the hill. It was the kind of work suited for convicts, but I helped in order to be rewarded with my two most favorite things: something sugary to eat and the sweet sound of a grown-up saying, "Lorna, you're such a good girl." It didn't seem to matter that my pail sloshed, splattered, and splashed most of the water right out of it and on me by the time I got up the hill.

The Hillbillies had a stinky, wooden outhouse for peeing and pooping. It had two grown-up sized rump holes and it was as black as a wet chalkboard down in those holes. I know. I looked once. There was a block of wood for little kids to step on to get up there to do their "business." I got a splinter on my rump once, sliding up there to do my "business." The multiple tasks of holding my breath, positioning my butt just right to avoid hanging too far over the black hole, and hold on for dear life proved overly difficult for a chubby little girl not known for her physical dexterity. I always pictured myself losing my grip, getting wedged into the hole in a V because of my round belly, and suffering a fate worse than death.

There were creatures down there waiting to nibble at my tender bare bottom, there must have been. I learned quickly to appreciate indoor plumbing.

*****

After I graduated from Cadyville Kindergarten, we moved to Connecticut. It seems like one day we were in Cadyville, and the next we weren't. I didn't know why we moved. That's because, being four years old, I wasn't entitled to such information, let alone being involved in the actual decisions grown-ups made. All I knew was that in Cadyville I had a daddy and in Connecticut I didn't. There wasn't even much fuss made over his disappearance, or if there was, it must have gone over my head. Once we moved, I forgot I ever had a daddy. At least for a while.

In Connecticut, for the first time in my life, I lived in a real house—one that wasn't supposed to move. It was really the bottom of a real house, or as I came to call it, the half-a-house. It was real close to other houses, but far, far away from Mémé and Pépé and the Hillbillies. There were low bushes lining all the yards in the neighborhood, but hardly any trees and definitely no forests or accompanying creepy creatures.

Two Ancient People lived in the top part of the house. They were Italian. I'd never seen Italian people before, and now here we were—surrounded by them because Mom said, "This is an Italian neighborhood." My blonde-and blue-eyedness stuck out more than my belly did in this neighborhood. Italians, I decided, were very friendly and made the best Italian food in the world, pizza being the best.

The half-a-house had everything the mobile home had, only more room for living and playing on the inside and less room for playing on the outside. Mom had her very own bedroom and so did Lisa. Tina and I still had to share, but we got side-by-side twin beds, not bunk beds, which reduced the danger of Tina breaking herself when she rolled out of the top bunk in her sleep. She was prone to such things.

We had plenty of room for playing on the inside of our half-a-house, so the limited outside yard wasn't so burdensome. Plus, there was a playground I could walk to if I crossed a street. Roads were called streets or avenues there. I had to get used to using metropolitan terminology so I would fit in better.

Mom enrolled us in a Catholic school. I did hard time there for three years: first grade through third grade. It was run by priests but all the teachers were nuns.

On our first day of school, Mom called from the kitchen, "Are you ready, girls?"

"Yes, Mommy," I replied as Tina and I ran as best we could from our bedroom to debut our new St. Morris Catholic School of the Perpetually Tortured uniforms designed to bring out the worst in any body type, at least for girls. The navy blue, wool jumpers were scratchy and cut just the right length to make chubby legs (like mine) look like stumps and skinny legs (like everyone else's) look like sticks. We also had to wear penny loafers and cuffed white ankle socks, further exaggerating leg stumps or leg sticks. The short sleeved white cotton blouses worn under the jumpers did the same thing for arms that the jumpers did for legs.

"You both look so nice," Mom said as she eyed our too-tight-around-the-middle jumpers.

"Do I have to wear this?" I whined. I dug at my backside. "It's scratchy and my shoes are ouchy."

"Yeah," said Tina. "I hate these clothes." She had a way of cutting to the heart of the matter.

All Mom did was smile. "Oh, you both look like such big girls in your nice uniforms. Mommy used to wear a uniform when she went to school in France a long time ago."

"But we didn't have to wear uniforms back home. I miss my old school." Tina had a natural talent for arguing, so I just quietly nodded in support and pulled at my underpants.

"I am sorry, girls. This is our home now, and your new school requires this uniform. You must wear it." She said it with her *that-is-enough* tone of voice. Then she collected Lisa, who was dressed like a normal person, but whose time would come, and we all walked the trail of many streets and avenues that led to our new school. My feet already hurt, and school hadn't even started.

I was the New Kid, so I had to stand in front of the class for the Catholic version of Show and Tell. It was mostly Show. Some kids were gawking and snickering, some were sitting like toy soldiers, one or two were picking their noses when Sister Mary Something wasn't looking. All of them were wearing navy blue and white uniforms.

"Quiet, Class!" Sister Mary Something shouted. I don't know where I ever got the idea that nuns were gentle and calm. "We have a new addition to our school," she kept shouting. "Welcome her like Good Children Of God. Her name is Miss Lorna." Maybe it was because I was five and short or because she was wearing a flowing black habit that wasn't at all slimming, but that nun looked gigantic to me. If she ever got into a fight with a grizzly bear, Sister Mary Something would have a few scratches and a creepy bear rug in her room.

After Sister Mary Something demanded that the class welcome me, I heard the usual lame attempts to rhyme *Lorna* with *torn-a, corn-a, warn-a,* or *sworn-a* from the gawkers and snickerers. The toy soldiers were mercifully silent, and the nose-pickers were too distracted to care.

In an attempt to refocus these Good Children Of God, Sister Mary Something interjected, "Ahem! Miss Lorna comes to us from a place called Cadyville. Say 'Hello' to her, Class."

"Hello, Miss Lor-na," they all chanted in that sing-song, insincere way.

I blushed so red I must have looked like the American flag, my uniform providing the white and blue. I looked down at my new penny loafers and suddenly noticed there wasn't a shiny penny in either slot. I was a girl who believed in omens, signs, and superstitions; that was not a good omen.

"Now, Miss Lorna, what do we do when people are kind enough to greet us?" Sister Mary Something was already testing me.

"Say 'Hello' back?" I offered shyly to my penniless shoes. Then I risked a glance upward at Sister's face to see what she had in store for me.

She nodded towards the class in that well-go-ahead-and-do-it kind of way. So I said, "Hell...o." My "hello" cracked in the middle due to nerves, so it sounded like I'd said a bad word at my new Catholic school in front of an irritated nun. The class, even the toy-soldier kids, burst out laughing when they saw the look of horror on Sister Mary Something's face.

Sister carried a big stick, both figuratively and literally. She whacked her literal big stick against her desk. I watched the kids jump. Their desks jumped, too. I jumped most of all.

"Quiet!" The room was already quiet so that was pure overkill on Sister's part. "Miss Lorna, take your seat." I could feel her hateful glare melting the wool into my back, making me itchier than ever. I rushed to the one empty desk in the middle of the middle row. At least I was in the middle. It was a familiar place for me, a place where I could fade into the background. I wondered how Tina was getting along in second grade.

*****

City living wasn't so bad. I got to walk to the playground and play with lots of neighborhood kids. Except when I befriended the old neighborhood drunk, my mother approved of my choice of acquaintances. She really liked my best friend, Skinny May, who lived in a whole house and had both a Mommy *and* a Daddy, just like Beaver Cleaver. The Good Humor Man in his ice cream truck came by our half-a-house every Saturday afternoon. I loved the sound of the bell and the yummy Creamsicles, when I was allowed to get one. Although Tina and Lisa often got something with chocolate, I decided I didn't like chocolate and would never eat it again. That was the first of many food-related attempts to draw attention to myself.

Except for the Ancient People living upstairs, our closest neighbors were the Dubious Italians. They weren't very friendly, and nothing delicious-smelling ever came from their kitchen. They had a boy close in age to one of us, but it was hard to tell which one of us because all I noticed about him was that he was really, really fat. If he fell on me, I was sure he'd have squished me dead. His older sister was kind of like Bee Hillbilly, only she wasn't pretty and she never looked after us. But she had a record player and played songs by the best band in the world, The Beatles. She kept her window open so I could listen and twirl around when she played "She loves you, yeah, yeah, yeah" over and over. Lisa twirled with me. Maybe they were only part Italian because it was nice of her to share her music.

We had family nearby, but we didn't see them too much. My aunt and uncle lived closer than Skinny May did. Mom said my aunt was my father's twin sister. I thought twins always appeared together, dressed the same just to confuse people, but I never saw my daddy at their house and my aunt didn't look at all like a man. The twin thing confused me, but I believed whatever Mom told me, so I just tried not to think too hard about it. Aunt and Uncle had three boys, who I guess were my cousins. I played with the middle boy the most. He liked danger and, for an altar boy, he was real good at fibbing. In fact, he was always cooking up some mischief and telling grown-ups that he didn't know anything about it. I didn't trust him, but he was my cousin and Mom said we had to get along with each other "to keep peace in the family." I don't think it worked very well because my aunt told Mom that I couldn't play with him anymore because I was a "bad influence" on him.

During the time we lived in the half-a-house, I noticed something was wrong with Tina. She was cranky and sick a lot; plus Mom was taking her to "physicians" and "hospitals," which would make anybody cranky and sick. I didn't know what was wrong, and Mom never explained. All I knew was that when they were gone, I was in charge of Lisa and me. I was under ten, and Lisa was always two years younger than me. Mom was never gone for more than a day, but a lot can happen in a day. Mostly, nothing did, except waiting and worrying on my part. I put on a good show for Lisa so she wouldn't worry, and I also made sure Mom never regretted leaving me in charge. The only thing that wasn't as she left it was the supply of food in the half-a-house. I was young, but I was observant and sensitive, too, and I soon learned that snacks were a comforting diversion when wondering what it would be like if Mom disappeared along with Daddy.

*****

In the same way that we disappeared from Cadyville and appeared in Connecticut, we disappeared from Connecticut and reappeared right back where I first started: in Chazy. Why? I didn't know. But like a boomerang, our family ended up back in a trailer parked next to Mémé and Pépé's house. My father didn't magically reappear, though, and I didn't expect him to come back. I had forgotten that real families, as opposed to TV families, even had fathers. But my other grandparents and their fruitfully multiplied family came back in my life in regular intervals. Summers always involved at least one or two "family reunions" with the disturbingly large crowds of people who said they were my aunts, uncles, and cousins. They hugged me as if they knew me. I hugged them back because I was kind of stuck.

My picnic phobia started around then.

In that move, we entered a New Moon mobile home, which was a squared-off, rectangular metal structure, not a rocket-ship shaped trailer. Belying its name, our fourth home was *not* mobile. It stayed put until, one-by-one, we all eventually vacated it to occupy separate homes.

I didn't know that was our last move as a family or that I would start fourth grade and actually graduate from that, my third, school. I kept my true best friend in Connecticut and didn't bother getting a true best friend in Chazy. I didn't want to leave a trail of broken hearts behind me. There were a lot of C places we hadn't lived in yet, and we were back in a home that *was* potentially mobile.

The four of us did a lot of negotiating in that two-bedroom, one-bathroom trailer. For the first time, Mom went to work at a job other than being a mother. My sisters and I were eleven, nine, and seven when we moved as a family for the last time. Mémé and Pépé were right next door again, but we were pretty much left up to our own devices after school and all day during summers. The potential for a territorial dispute or an estrogen-related calamity was ever-present, and the threat got worse with each advancing year, as my sisters weren't naturally inclined to be peace-makers. They were both headstrong and unrelentingly right about everything. Someone needed to dismantle the ticking time bombs, handle hostage negotiations, mediate between warring factions, and know when to call for emergency back-up. In other words, one of the three of us girls had to be dependably *good*.

As the middle child, I was effective at finding the middle ground. Keeping the peace was high on my priority list. Whether that was by nature or from experience, only a therapist could figure out. Maybe having lived in all of those C places rubbed off on me: I wanted to live in a *Calm* place.

I can't say that I was ever entirely successful.

CHAPTER 3: THURSDAY'S CHILD

I'm the middle child, but on the right again. It looks like Lisa needed some propping. Tina, too. I look robust and cheerful enough to hold up our whole gang.

From the age of five, I was afflicted with the belief that I was invisible in the way that other kids are afflicted with rowdy hair or teeth that insist on showing themselves even when their mouth is shut.

If I had a choice, I would have picked being *super-visible* rather than *invisible*. Super-visible kids with obvious *hey, look at me!* features can, theoretically, tame their hair and get their teeth under control; other kids who were nice to look at and had grace and confidence didn't need anything, not even an agent, to be popular. Their fan clubs ensured they got noticed. I didn't have a fan club, even though I was pretty and smart. My mom said so, and moms tell the truth. My hair was the color of the summer sun at noon and my eyes were sky-blue. When I smiled, which was a lot, my smile went all the way up my eyes. On the plus side, I had chubbiness going for me. People could easily see me coming and going. But none of that mattered because I felt like the most dispensable pup in the pack. I was the Middle Child, diagnosed by psychologists to have self-esteem issues, a criminal record, or both.

Knowing none of that, but sensing something amiss, a Little Voice inside Little Me said, *Lorna, you need to make sure mommy notices you.* If she didn't, I felt I might disappear completely.

*****

"Tell me about when I was born," I begged for the umpteenth time as bedtime approached. Mom never read to us. Reading was a school thing. Instead of reading, we said prayers to remind us that our souls needed saving if we should die while we were sleeping. That always calms a child before bedtime. "...If I should die before I wake, I pray the Lord my soul to take."

"Again?" She didn't have to sigh to convey the burden of my desperate request after a long day of single-mothering. She sighed.

Impervious to sighs, I nodded enthusiastically. To me, *my* story was way better than any prayer. I never said that out loud, of course, and I hoped God wasn't paying attention to the private thoughts of a little girl who hardly even mattered. We were Catholic, so I knew way more about Hell than Heaven. I didn't want to mess up my chances for eternity in Heaven because of a mere thought, but I knew that was a real possibility. I had seen *The Ten Commandments.*

Like a favorite book, I knew my story by heart. I could tell it without Mom's help, but I still wanted to hear it from *her.* Tina was seven and Lisa was three when my habitual inquiry as to my origins began. Even at five, I noticed they never asked about when they were born.

"All right, then," said Mom, and away we went, back to November 14, 1957. "It was cold, and I was making stew—"

"What day was it?" I knew that, and I also knew SHE knew the question was coming.

"Hmm. It must have been a Thursday. Yes, because I was making stew. The best stew I ever made."

I smiled. "And you never got any, right?"

"Right. Because you decided to be born. All right, time for prayers."

"That's all?" I frowned.

Her gentle but *no-nonsense* eyes insisted. I knelt beside my bed, slapped my hands together, bowed my head, and recited my prayers as piously as I could, reeling from resentment at that *Reader's Digest* condensed version of my birth story.

Prayers over, as Mom was tucking me into bed, I asked, "Why did you name me Lorna Lee?"

Another sigh. "Well, I thought Lorna was an unusual but pretty name. I only heard it twice. *Lorna Doone* from the book *and Lorna Luft*, Judy Garland's daughter."

"Who was Julie Garlan, Mommy? I forget." I hadn't forgotten, of course, but having been short-changed on my birth story, I wanted to get some mileage out of my name-story.

"Gar*land*," she said. "With a D. *Judy Garland*, dear. I remember her calling me "dear" as a term of, well, endearment. She hardly ever called me by my name except for the rare times she was upset with me. "She is a very famous actress who played Dorothy in the *Wizard of Oz*. Remember?" She nodded her head as if willing me to do the same.

I remembered and nodded. But I wasn't done yet. "And Lee? Why Lee?" I knew I was pushing it, but that was important information I needed to hear, just to make sure her story was the same each time.

"I love the actress Vivian Leigh and thought 'Leigh' would go well with 'Lorna.' But I did not know how to spell 'Leigh,' so I gave the only spelling I knew—L-E-E. I found out later that I had spelled it incorrectly." Mom spoke the most proper English of anyone I knew. That's because she came from France and had learned English from teachers, not people who already didn't speak proper English.

"So you made a boo-boo on my name?" I asked. "Did you make boo-boos on Tina's or Lisa's names?"

"No, dear. But I think 'Lorna Lee' is the perfect name for you."

Was she trying to make me feel better, or was she telling me that goofing up was part of my nature because it was part of my name? Knowing Mom, what she was trying to do was get me to stop asking questions and go to sleep.

It worked. My birth and name stories were enough to send me off to sleep knowing that my mother remembered that I was, in fact, her daughter.

This nightly ritual went on routinely until I was eight years old. Tina and Lisa never asked about their beginnings or their names, at least not that I know of. That perplexed me. Weren't they curious about how they came into the world or if Mom remembered them? Maybe they felt visible enough. I have often wondered how many children felt compelled to be authenticated on a regular basis. Based on my experience, it was one in three.

*****

At eight years old, I found a book of names and their meanings. Tina's proper name, I learned, is Christina, which means "Christ-like or anointed one." She was born on *Good Friday*. *Friday's Child,* I read, *is loving and giving.* That's how the poem went, and I took great stock in old-time poetry that made specific predictions about people's character without knowing a thing about them. Tina was destined for a sanctified and charmed life.

"Lisa," I further read, is a form of Elizabeth, which means "consecrated to God." She was born on a Monday—on George Washington's birthday and a national holiday at the time. He's the president everyone remembers because he was the first president and he had wooden teeth, which is very memorable and really weird. *Monday's Child is fair of face.* She was fated to be sacred and beautiful.

Superstitious by nature and melodramatic by necessity, I knew in my heart that our names and dates of birth were no accident. Plus, I had heard too many adults say, "The Lord works in mysterious ways." Both of my sisters had arrived on vacation days so they could be honored, as was good and proper. My sisters were untouchable instruments of the Lord Himself; they were sent to earth for some Divine Purpose and to maybe become movie stars or great humanitarians while performing their miracles.

God probably told Mom what to name them and when to have them by sending an angel to speak to her in a dream. Catechism classes and blockbuster biblical movies starring Charlton Heston were all the religious training I needed to be assured The Divine had a Hand to play in the Fate of My Family.

But what plans did God have for me? What did He whisper into my mother's ear to make her name me Lorna Lee? Certain that her decision was guided by more than the name of an obscure and tragic fictional heroine or the daughter of a self-destructive, although extremely talented, actress, I expectantly flipped through the Book of Names to the L's.

Lorna, I discovered, means "alone" and is the Old English word for "lost." Lee (or Leigh) is the Old English word for "meadow."

What?

Besides that, I was born on a Thursday right after Veteran's Day and well before Thanksgiving. Nobody got a vacation day for my birthday.

And the poem said, *Thursday's Child has far to go.*

It figured.

No wonder I felt invisible! While my sisters were noble souls ordained for some divine mission or public acclaim, I was destined by my very name to be wandering aimlessly in a field somewhere...lost and alone. For a very long time.

I soon began campaigning to change my name to *Angelique,* which means "like an angel." With a first name like that, I wouldn't even need a middle name. Why my mother hadn't thought of that, I'll never know. My celestial sisters treated my name-change crusade with a level of disrespect generally reserved for substitute teachers. Mom told me to stop being so silly.

I decided I would wait until I was an adult and have my name legally changed to Angelique. Or maybe that would be my stage name when I became an actress or a nun, my two dream careers. It's hard not to notice a nun or an actress, especially when her name is Angelique.

*****

I was *The Anointed One's* younger sister. Tina was very special, and not just because she was the first born. She almost *died,* and that's a hard act to follow. She was almost dying for six years, so it was kind of hard to miss. I, being reliably healthy on the other hand, was easy to overlook. After she got her operation and recovered, her talent was *not* dying. She even got her very own black and white TV set because she wasn't dead. I wasn't dead, either, but I didn't get my own TV.

I was *The One Consecrated To God's* big sister. Lisa was special because she was the youngest, the baby. Her talent was being artistic, and her artisticness emerged before she was out of diapers. Dogs she drew looked like dogs, not blobs. People she drew had shapes—they weren't sticks with grossly large heads and pokey hair. Her artistic genius was excessively encouraged. And she also had illness on her side. Lucky Lisa had chronic bronchitis. Her fevers and window-rattling coughs kept her in neck-and-neck competition with Tina's mysterious disease. Mom was so busy fretting over Sick and Sicker, I could've joined the circus and not been noticed until my first postcard from *The Road* arrived.

Compared to my sisters' wing of the *Dr. Kildare* Children's Ward, I was as healthy as the Blue-Ribbon Pig at the county fair. Mom never had to worry about me not breathing. I never even got the chickenpox.

I was cursed.

When I was seven, however, I was blessed with not one, but two episodes of illness. I got my first migraine while seeing the first-ever indoor picture show my sisters and I got to watch. *The Ten Commandments* was a loud, powerful movie. Like the Red Sea, the inside of my head started parting and splitting and I got an oogey feeling in my tummy. I decided the movie was aimed at sinners. Since God could be very, very mean to sinners, I must be a sinner because what was happening in my head was pure meanness.

I think the movie lasted ten hours—one hour for each Commandment.

"Wasn't that a *great* movie?" Tina asked. She was on a high from her first indoor cinematic experience. With all the pestilence and disease befalling the heathens, she must have felt, by comparison, not so ill-fated.

"Yes, it was," Mom replied happily as she walked her three blonde cherubs out of the movie theatre. "Yes, it was. How about some strawberry shortcake when we get home?"

"Yummy! Oh goody gum-drops!" Lisa skipped ahead a little more quickly as she squealed in delight.

The stabbing sound of her joy through my throbbing head made me want to puke on the sidewalk.

Mom noticed my unusually grave mood and ghostly pallor, though my sluggish gait looked normal because I was a husky child who didn't move quickly unless food was involved.

"Lorna, are you all right?" Mom asked. "We are going to have strawberry shortcake—your favorite."

Who was she kidding? Anything non-chocolate and sweet was my favorite.

But the mere mention of food nearly caused me to collapse and wish for God to strike me down dead. This was a reaction to food with which I was quite unfamiliar. "Mommy," I managed to whisper, "I don't feel very good."

"Well," she replied, "the fresh air on the walk home might help."

It didn't.

Directly upon arriving home, I went to bed and stayed there. I had visions of my little family gathered around my bed, weeping, praying for my salvation, and tending to my every need. Instead, my little family gathered around the kitchen table without me and enjoyed their strawberry shortcake. My first migraine went relatively unnoticed, like a blister on my toe.

Later that year, when I was graced with the mumps, I was sure the time was ripe for a bedside vigil. But Tina's mystery illness trumped my lumpy one. My mother had to take Tina to a special, far-away physician. Five-year-old Lisa took care of me while Mom was away for the day. She had the job of providing me with ice packs from the freezer. To get them, she had to climb the step-stool Mom had set in front of the refrigerator so she could reach the freezer, which was on the top. Although I was the one suffering, Lisa was the real hero in that situation.

It figures.

It wasn't long before I developed what might be called a "complex." My belief that I was *invisible* spiraled into full-blown despair due to the obvious fact that I was just plain insignificant—a dust bunny under the canopy bed of life. I took to patting my round belly just to make sure I was *there*.

*****

"Mommy, is there *anything* special about me?"

Mom was, as usual, busy. She was in the middle of making dinner. Meatloaf. I was about eight years old.

"Lorna, not now." She wasn't being callous, just matter-of-fact. Meatloaf assembly required her undivided attention.

"Just *one* thing?"

"Well, you *are* persistent," she said. Then she cracked some eggs and sank her hands in the red meat mush.

"What does 'per-sis-dent' mean?"

"Persis*tent*. You do not give up easily when you want to know something."

"Does that make me *special* or *not nice*?" I asked. I looked at my shoes as if they might have the answer. Then I peeked up at Mom.

The meatloaf mashing stopped. She looked down at me. "It makes you very special, dear."

I wanted to ask *how* persistence made me special, but she continued talking in a brilliant preemptive strike.

"You are very smart and have a way of making people laugh. And you care about other people's feelings. But the most special thing about you, Lorna, is I do not ever have to worry about you. I am so grateful that you are such a good girl and you are so healthy."

Then she wiped off her hamburger hands and gave me a big hug. That hug made me feel very real, very *not invisible.*

My complex became a mission at that very moment. More accurately, I became a girl with a complex on a mission. My mission was to be *One Less Worry* for my mother. To be a Perfectly Healthy Good Girl.

Only I didn't know how and I didn't know if I could.

Thursday's Child really did have far to go.

CHAPTER 4: STORIES AND LIES

I was as sturdy as my bike. Good thing, too.

In hindsight, I probably set the bar a little too high for myself. Being a Perfectly Good Girl was Grueling. My intentions were top-shelf, but my common sense was bargain-basement. Plus, I was a natural-born klutz.

It's a good thing I had lots of "baby" fat to cushion the inevitable falls, crashes, and mishaps that made my childhood interesting. Being chubby wasn't embarrassing when I was young; it was a lifesaver. But for every blunder, I had to create a new story to maintain my Good Girl image. I had to for my mom's sake. She had enough to worry about without wondering if I would survive the day.

I began botching up even simple tasks early in life. Most of my mishaps began when we were living in Connecticut when I was between five and nine years old.

The blunders didn't stop when we moved, so it's not like I was cursed in Connecticut. I just had less supervision and thus more opportunities to let my clumsiness shine in those Connecticut days. The extra pressure from the nuns at St. Morris Catholic School for the Incessantly Damned probably added stress to be perfect, just about guaranteeing I would falter. After I grew up and went to Heathen School, I simply had fewer excuses for goofing up. But that didn't stop me.

The best I could do was aim for perfection and act like I was as good a girl as I pretended to be. At least I was great at acting.

*****

Sometimes Mom needed bread or bologna, or maybe I needed it. If Tina was sick, Mom had to stay home with her. Lisa wasn't in school yet, so she didn't know her way around the neighborhood and was fuzzy regarding the concept of currency. So Mom had only me to send to the market for absolute sandwich essentials. I was six or seven, but I was a Smart Girl. Adults told me so all the time. Which only made my blunders worse.

For reasons known only to my Guardian Angel, I could find my way to the corner market. It was the return trip that confused me. With the focus of a dog watching its master eat an ice cream cone, I collected the absolute sandwich essentials on the list Mom gave me. I held out the money Mom gave me for the grocer to take. He gave me back what he didn't want, plus a big paper bag with the food in it. I always thought that was such a good deal. I entered the market with just money and left with food *and* money *and* the paper bag. Maybe it was that miracle of commerce that disoriented me, or maybe it was just my right/left-disability (to this day, "left" and "right" send my brain into fits of misfiring neurons). Whatever it was, I always felt like I had stepped out of the market and into an alternate universe—like Dorothy not being in Kansas anymore. Nothing looked the same. I was all turned around. *Which way was home?* I went to the store with the firm faith that I could find my way back home again. When Tina was well, I tagged along with her lots of times. I should have known the way back home by heart. And when she was there, I always did. But when I was alone, my internal navigational system couldn't find the signal, and I was left with a useless blinking question mark where my brain should have been.

The first time Mom had to drag Tina and Lisa out to find me. The second time I made it home without a search-and-rescue team, but with the help of an old, stubble-faced man who smelled of cigarettes and beer. He held my hand, winked profusely at me, and called me Blondie, even though I told him my full name. My full address, too. He kissed me on the cheek in front of my house. That caused Mom to sternly lecture me about trusting strange drunk men and giving out our address. To this day, I'm sure my Guardian Angel must have been up to some mighty naughty shenanigans in Heaven to be assigned to me. Mom didn't let me go to the market alone a third time. Even though I wanted to be her trustworthy helper, I told her I didn't feel like shopping was the best use of my natural talents.

*****

Physical prowess was not my strong suit when I was young. In those days, kids were expected to go outside and do things, like play on the playground or in the streets, or ride bikes or do all the other things that kept children away from adults. But even at a young age, I knew I could be a danger to myself and others if I attempted anything resembling physical activity.

I needed to learn to ride a bicycle, for example. I didn't want to, but I had to. Kids my age all knew how to ride the clunky one-speed bikes made out of iron that we all had. Those were the only kind of bicycle there was back then. Not being a natural athlete, learning to stay on the thing took me enormous time and effort. Mom knew that I was not her most physically agile child, so she made me practice on the lawn. If I fell, grass stains would be her biggest worry. Have you ever tried to steer and pedal a bike that weighs as much as a cannon on grass and dirt when you couldn't keep your balance? It's discouraging work. I asked Mom if I could practice falling off the bike on weekends in the parking lot of the Catholic school we attended. Since there wouldn't be any traffic there and it was holy ground, maybe a Bicycle Miracle would occur. I could tell by Mom's pursed lips that she had her doubts, but she finally gave her consent.

The day when I was able to keep my balance and really *ride* for the first time is forever carved in my mind…and in the bushes lining the parking lot of St. Morris Catholic School for the Eternally Miserable. I was so excited that I had finally managed to pedal for a moderate distance without the inevitable *wobble-tip-fall,* that visions were arising in my head of pedaling around the neighborhood with the wind gentling tossing my blonde hair to and fro. I was pedaling around the parking lot, reveling in my new ability and dreaming of the places I could go with my "wheels" and flowing blonde hair. That's when the Bicycle Miracle happened. Some might call it the Bicycle Curse, but those people probably call all catastrophes curses.

I was so distracted by my visions of my future biking destinations that I forgot how to *stop* that hurtling iron heap. Even though I'd stopped pedaling, it was still picking up speed. I must have been going downhill. This looked like a problem because I was headed straight for a thick hedgerow at the end of the parking lot. I kept trying to stop the bike, but I just couldn't remember how. I knew there had to be brakes, but until that point I never had to use them. *Falling* (after a lot of wobbling) had always been my primary stopping technique. Putting my feet down—my usual technique for stabilizing myself—surely was not the proper technique for halting a run-away cannon. But I didn't have a lot of time to reason through that conundrum before I slammed at full speed into the thick hedgerow, leaving a Lorna-sized hole in the shrubbery. I was scratched up from head to toe. Little green twigs stuck out of every crack and crevice of my bike and me.

I call this a Bicycle Miracle because *I survived.* Less hearty children would have perished in a head-on collision with those tall, strong hedges. But, miracle or not, I still didn't feel very victorious going home with green twigs everywhere from my hair to my underwear.

Mom was aghast when she saw me come inside. "Lorna," she asked, "what happened to you?"

"I think there's something wrong with that bike!" I told her. "I figured out how to ride it, but there aren't any brakes. I couldn't stop it, so I bumped into some bushes near the parking lot." It was all true, merely a pastelized version of reality.

"No brakes? They were working when Tina rode it."

"Well, they didn't work just now! I hate that bike. It's too big for me." I started to cry, hoping Mom would forget about the brakes and focus on her little girl, who looked like she had barely survived wrestling with a mutant Venus Flytrap. It worked.

Thanks to the sorry state of forensic science back then, no one was able to trace the girl-sized hole in the shrubs lining the parking lot of St. Morris Catholic School for the Eternally Suffering back to me. No one could thus either confirm or deny my story about the failed brakes.

*****

I wasn't aware that I was a "beefy girl." Children in the 1960s didn't feel the heavy cultural pressure to be thin that children feel today, so I licked my dinner plate clean and ate sweets with guiltless joy. Thin kids looked deprived and acted defensive, as if they were in constant danger of breaking, whereas my weightiness made me feel safe and sturdy. But I was never first to be picked for team sports in gym class.

The school playground was a mixed adventure for me. Swings and slides were a breeze because momentum was on my side once I got over that nasty little issue of inertia, which I didn't yet understand but definitely felt. Once I got going, though, there was no stopping me. Monkey bars or jungle-gyms that required climbing and hanging, on the other hand, were simply a bad idea for any plus-sized child. Since I was a Smart Girl for whom personal safety was always a high priority—right up there with saving my soul from hell and never being late for meals—I avoided these playground danger zones.

When I was about eight years old, however, I uncharacteristically became involved in a girl-gang monkey bars competition on the playground of St. Morris Catholic School for the Immaculately Damaged. That was unusual for me for three reasons:

1. The monkey bars were foreign and dangerous territory.

2. I was never one to gamble, especially with my life.

3. Other than my sisters, I usually played exclusively with my best friend, Skinny May.

Yet there I was, smack dab in the middle of a contest with three skinny girls. One of them was Skinny May. She's probably the one who got me into the competition.

The wager was this: the girl who could hang the longest by her knees from the top of the bars would win. *Win what?* I'm not sure, but first prize should have been the right to watch the others hang upside down until at least their heads got fat. I knew that betting was *at least* a venial sin, but, if we were going to Purgatory, we'd all be going together. The thought of having company while I waited, burning, to get into Heaven, was oddly comforting.

There were four of us in that contest, and I was the meatiest of the bunch, which gave me the opportunity to go last in the competition. One of the other girls had a genuine Mickey Mouse watch with a wispy tail as a second hand, so she was the official Time Keeper, even for herself.

"Wow! Two minutes and thirty-seven seconds," the Skinny Official Time Keeper announced. "Lorna, I bet you'll never beat that." She had just finished and was, therefore, the one to beat. No one thought to question her upside-down time-keeping accuracy.

I had just watched as the others, one by one, nimbly climbed to the top of the monkey bars and, like future Olympic gymnasts, flipped into position and just hung by their knees. They could have bided their time doing Cat's Cradle if they'd had the forethought to take some string up there with them. Each girl's time was a few seconds longer than the previous girl's. Each undernourished contestant easily flipped back upright and scaled down to safety. Their faces were red from being upside-down, but they didn't look flushed. They glowed. Not one of them looked like they were even breathing hard. Their boney ribcages were puffed up with pride not oxygen.

I was audibly panting and looking rosy just in nervous anticipation of my turn. *How*, I was wondering, *will I squeeze myself through the bars and wedge myself upside down in the middle of this sinister-looking contraption? Why couldn't this be a slide competition?*

Pulling my tight T-shirt over my shorts in a futile attempt to cover my belly and marshal some dignity, I began my ascent. All I could think of was these three skinny girls watching my chubby rump and stuck-together thighs lumbering up the very same bars they had wafted over. They were greyhounds; I was a basset hound.

"I can do this. I can do this." I whispered to myself, wasting precious breath. Then I began to breathe conspicuously. Witnesses might have said I was hyperventilating. Then my hands began to sweat. I sensed trouble. Pausing at the top, I looked down at three small upturned faces. Way down.

"Well? What's the matter?" Skinny Sally had her hands on what should have been her hips.

"I don't think this is such a good idea," I ventured.

The Skinny Official Time Keeper heaved a sigh I could feel all the way up to the top of the bars. "Listen," she said. "This is a contest and you're the last to go. You have to do it like everybody else did." She would've made a very good Game Show Host or Military Drill Sergeant.

"Okay, okay," I said, against my better judgment. I balanced my white Keds-clad feet on one of the bars, rested my belly on another for balance, and wiped my hands on the front of my T-shirt to dry them off. Then I assessed the widest point of entry to that ominously high apparatus. It was then that I noticed the monkey bars of St. Morris Catholic School for the Eternally Tormented were anchored in cement. *Cement?* I always thought the nuns just pretended not to like us. Anchoring playground equipment in cement proved to me they weren't bluffing.

"Come on, Lorna, we don't have all day," Skinny May called up to me. We actually did have all day.

I took a deep, shaky breath, and then blew it all out so I could squeeze between the two horizontal bars that formed an X at the summit of the monkey bar torture chamber. Then I grasped one horizontal bar with both hands and hung on until I could shove my chubby legs through the spaces between the bars to reach the one from which the back of my knees would eventually and hopefully hang. Hang on for dear life. When I felt the monkey bars digging into my tender behind-my-knees flesh, I let go of my hand grip. *I am in the middle of the monkey bars hanging upside down by my knees!* Pride rushed into me as quickly as the blood went rushing into my head. *I did it.*

"Start the clock!" I yelled with conviction born of upside-down self-satisfaction. Who cared about the cement below my head? I was in the competition and I could win it.

Before long, however, I felt the sweat pooling behind my knees. Didn't the skinny girls sweat? I was pondering that weighty question when my knee-grip on the bars, my winning place in the competition, and, conceivably, my life slipped away from me.

In my mind, I drifted—no, wafted—to the ground like a trapeze artist making her final decent, the awe-struck audience silent in amazement at my graceful litheness. In reality, I plummeted like an anchor. I landed flat on my back.

Skinnies 1, 2, and 3 just stared at me through the bars for what seemed like a long time. I stared back, but I couldn't breathe. I thought I had broken the part of my body responsible for keeping me alive. Had the Skeletal Triplets been braver, they might have poked me with a stick to check for reflexes. I expected at least that much from Skinny May, my best friend. But what did they do? They all deserted the crime scene, skedaddling like the greyhounds they were, before the police—or worse, the nuns—inevitably found my dead body.

So there I was, alone under the playground equipment, contemplating my death. I knew Mom would not take the news well. I was her only healthy child and I was dying in a freak monkey-bar accident.

Imagine the obituary.

Then my breath came back. *Haugh.* It sounded stunningly loud and drawn out, like in the movies. It was dramatic. Too bad the Emaciated Traitors weren't there to witness the Monkey Bar Miracle. (It was miraculous for the same reason the Bicycle Miracle was miraculous: I lived to tell about it.)

"I'm breathing," I whispered up to the monkey bars.

"I'm alive," I told the cement.

"I'm in big trouble," I groaned to no one in particular.

I was probably seriously wounded. I had some explaining to do. And the truth seemed like a really bad idea. Mom would ban me from the playground without a bodyguard, and bodyguards were hard to come by for common people like us who were not in the Witness Protection Program. But if I had died, my life would have been a lot simpler. I would still be a Good Little Girl Heartbreakingly Taken Before Her Time in a monkey bar-related tragedy clouded with mystery—like Marilyn Monroe, only way younger, without the sexy body, and with the corpse fully clothed on cement under the monkey bars. Dead, I was a beloved legend kept alive by a scandalous death. Alive, I was a liability. Someone who must be "handled."

Since no one came over to examine the body, I had time to contemplate my situation without having to make small talk. I tried moving. Everything hurt, but I was eventually able to get up and hobble home.

My left knee was the single most bruised part of my body. It was swelling and looked as if it was occupied by aliens. *How would I explain this?*

But no one noticed that anything was wrong with me until the next day. That was good because I had time to concoct a plausible story about my bruises and limping that didn't involve the truth. I was, however, disappointed that my bowling ball-sized left knee went unnoticed. I should have known: I was normal, no-problem Lorna. Trouble surrounded my sisters, not me. Being good really made a person invisible. At least it did in my family.

Mom finally noticed my left knee was the size of an adult head and the color of a rotten eggplant. This happened while I was getting dressed for school the next day. "Dear Lord, Lorna! What happened to your knee?" She never used holy words on week days. I was very satisfied.

"I fell off my bike." I couldn't lie to her face, so I spoke into my own belly. My face reddened as I imagined another few years in Purgatory. Maybe even Hell...I wasn't clear on the sliding scale of fibs and lies and their relative damages to my eternal soul.

"When? Why did you not tell me?"

"Yesterday. After school." I was back in comfortable truth-territory, so now I was looking right into her serious eyes. "I was afraid you wouldn't let me ride my bike anymore." I chose the bike lie because I knew she wouldn't take away my bike. That was unthinkable.

With motherly kindness, she said, "Oh, Lorna. This looks very serious. I must take you to a doctor." Then, more sternly, "You should have told me right away."

Tears welled up in my eyes—tears of relief, pain, guilt.

"How much does it hurt?" she asked.

"A lot."

The tears spilled over. She wiped them away. I think that made both of us feel a little bit better.

The physician checked me over. I had scrapes on my arms, hands, and legs. The bruises on the back of my knees and the nasty bump on the back of my head contradicted my bike-accident story.

"How did you manage to get these injuries?" He fondled the backs of my knees and the tender knot protruding from the back of my skull. "You said you fell sideways, right?" Leave it to a physician to be logical. I had almost died under the monkey bars. That has a way of traumatizing a kid. How was I supposed to think of all the angles of my story? Shrugging my sore shoulders, I said, speaking to my belly, "I dunno. I was peddling; then, I was on the ground. It happened fast." Then I started to cry, which turned him from skeptical to sympathetic. I liked him a lot better after that.

He said I had a sprained knee.

*****

Over two decades later, when I was in my thirties, I told Mom the truth about my sprained knee and some of my other mishaps. I think she had figured out the truth or something close enough to the truth, so my confession was more of a confirmation. She also knew my intentions were pure and I have a very well-developed imagination. What she didn't know then—and neither did I—was that being her perfect child meant also being a storyteller and an actress to preserve the illusion.

Aching for Mom to lavish attention on me for being her one dependable Good Girl, I always told my stories so Mom wouldn't have to worry about me like she did about my sisters. If I had had more common sense and been less of a klutz, I wouldn't have messed up so much and had to cover up my messes with my stories.

But now I wonder...are stories just fancy lies? Or perhaps lies are simplified stories. If I was a storyteller, I was on safe, even acceptable, ground; if I was a liar, I was headed for Hell. And that was no place for Mom's Perfectly Good Girl.

CHAPTER 5: MISSION IMPOSSIBLE

I'm squinting at the brightness of my halo. Yes. That must be it.

Was I (deep-down) a rotten lying Hell-bound kid, or a perfectly good facsimile of a Perfectly Good Girl? The more I thought about the answer to this question, the more confused and worried I got. So I decided to stop thinking about it. I was blessed with a combination of brains and the pudgy-blonde-cherub-look so familiar in all those paintings with God in them. That meant I could pull off my Perfect Child act because I wanted to, needed to, *and* knew how to do it. At least that's what I told myself. I tended to listen to myself because hardly anyone else did. Which is a dumb reason to listen to yourself. But I was young and didn't know any better.

Since my mom worried about my sisters because they tended to get sick and didn't like each other much, I was her only hope for a trouble-free child. I could have aspired to be a merely Good Child, but I had to up the ante and aim for perfection.

If I'm going to do something, I'm going to do it all the way.

It is that mindset that explains so much about the successes and failures in my life. It also explains why I had more boyfriends than my sisters did...but I'm getting ahead of myself.

*****

Here's what I knew. Good Children knew and obeyed the rules most of the time. Perfect Children, like I aimed to be, obeyed the rules *all of the time*. And with good cheer. Perfect Children were as rare as pirates' treasure maps that actually lead to treasure. Other children—good and bad—generally found Perfect Children insufferable...or worse. While I longed to be loved by everyone, being cherished by adults—especially Mom—was more important to me than any dirty looks I got on the playground.

In Catechism, I learned about Joan of Arc and maybe one or two other women who suffered for their goodness. If they could do it, I could, too. I decided that I wanted to be a nun when I grew up. Nuns had to be perfect. I figured their mothers were proud of them, and who in their right mind could not love a nun? They were married to Jesus and were quiet almost all of the time unless they were around children. Plus they wore those baggy, long-skirted, black outfits that hid a multitude of figure flaws. It seemed like the job was made for me.

I took my Perfection Mission seriously and paid close attention to all adults and followed every rule I knew of. I was polite, quiet, obedient, helpful, cheerful, as tidy as a messy kid could be, smart, and as trustworthy as a kid with no common sense could be. I was, basically, every adult's dream and every other child's nightmare. Even allowing for my occasional lapses in tidiness and common sense, I tried to make up for my mistakes by being extra contrite.

Adults seemed mixed on their feelings about Perfect Children. Some cherished me, holding me up as an idol to be worshiped—or cloned, if possible. Teachers at heathen (that is, public) schools were most likely to treasure Perfect Children.

"Lorna," said Mr. Elvis Hair, my sixth grade teacher, "I bet *you* know the answer to this math problem." He gestured for me to come to the front of the class to solve the equation on the chalkboard. My reputation as a not-dumb blonde was legendary at school.

I blushed, my usual reaction to any attention drawn to me. I knew the answer, but I kept my eyes fixed on my math workbook until I heard my name. Mr. Elvis Hair looked like my mother's favorite sexy singer, Englebert Humperdinck. He was way too swarthy for a teacher. I eagerly anticipated parent-teacher nights for more than a glowing report on my grades. Mr. Elvis Hair would make a good match for Mom.

"Oh, come on, Lorna," he repeated. "Get up here and show the class how to solve this problem." Teachers always had more confidence in me than I could ever conjure in myself.

I wiggled out of the school desk meant for children svelter than me and, with head bowed, galumphed to the front of the class and solved the problem effortlessly and with perfect penmanship—a tricky thing to do with chalk.

Mr. Elvis Hair could barely contain his enthusiasm. He nearly applauded. I secretly hoped he wanted a daughter just like me. "Perfect, Lorna! Great job! Class, see how easy this is?"

But when he added that last bit, I felt the cold chill of my classmates' ire.

"You may go back to your seat, now." Mr. Elvis Hair said.

Although I wanted to stay in the warm glow of his admiration—and I needed his protection—I had no choice. I cautiously made my way back to my seat. No one dared shoot a spit ball in Mr. Elvis Hair' s class, but Kirk—a boy with dark horn-rimmed glasses and geeky plaid shirts that belied his ineptitude in math (and every other subject)— "just happened" to stretch his foot out as I was passing by his desk. Good thing I was looking down to avoid scary-sixth-grader eye contact. I avoided what would have been a graceless swan-dive onto the linoleum floor.

A battle of titanic proportions waged inside me. Perfect Lorna could see how easily grown-ups were seduced by correct answers and the ability to follow instructions. But Smart and Savvy Lorna didn't want to be the first victim of an inside hit at my otherwise boring school.

One night, I purposely answered two math homework questions wrong. I was desperate, but not reckless.

It was Mr. Elvis Hair's practice to hand out the papers with the highest grades first and let the losers sweat it out to the very end to get their pathetic, failing results. That was known back then as "motivation."

The day after I made those two mistakes in my homework, Mr. Elvis Hair made his way toward my desk first, as usual. But he didn't have his *this-is-my-favorite-student-of-all-time* look on his face. His thick, manly eyebrows were scrunched together. His face cried, *Lorna, I'm worried about you, should you see a doctor*? Even with two mistakes, I got the highest grade in the class. But there were red marks on my paper, too. Big ones around the wrong answers. And a note in the margin. The kids around me could see the evidence that I wasn't perfect after all.

"Hey," Cindy whispered to Dee loud enough so I could hear, "Lorna got something wrong!"

"Really? What?"

"I can't tell. But Mr. Elvis Hair gave her *what-for* for it."

Dee sat a little taller and grinned. Cindy, too. They seemed pleased.

My *what-for* note read, *Lorna, what's the matter? You know these answers. Please redo and I will give you a 100.*

During recess, my best-friend-for-the-month, Sherry, sidled up to me. "Lorna, I heard Mr. Elvis Hair got mad at you," she said with lace-thin concern. She was obviously digging for dirt.

"Oh," I murmured, "I just got a few homework answers wrong. That's all."

"But I heard he marked up your paper and asked for a conference and all."

I could tell she was aching for some really bad news about me. There wasn't a whole lot of intrigue in sixth grade, so anything that happened had real public interest appeal. If it was true, it would be even better.

"No," I told her. "Nothing like that."

"He didn't tell you to stay after school?" I could see her chest flatten, and it was already pretty flat to begin with.

"Nope. But I have to redo my homework." I thought that might reinflate her. It did.

"Oh." She brightened. "He's such a meanie." Then she ran off to a group of girls conspicuously standing nonchalantly next to the soccer field. I could tell she was spreading some kind of news about my fall from academic grace by the way they kept looking back at me.

Later in my academic career, my intelligence would become a source of popularity. It took a long time, however, for my classmates to figure out that having a smart friend might come in handy. Teachers, however, caught on quickly and adopted me as their pet year after year.

*****

Some grown-ups—friends, parents and relatives, mostly, but maybe strangers, too—treated me with an odd concoction of appreciation and disbelief. But I wasn't aware of strangers' opinions of me because I wasn't supposed to talk with strangers unless they seemed sad or were trying to help me when I got lost. Then I figured it was just polite to speak with those nice people. There was an unspoken "but" after every "That Lorna is such a good girl...." *Surely*, they must have thought, *surely she is too good to be true.* I could see it in their ambiguous smiles and shifting eyes. It was the same look that grown-ups get when they're cornered at a family gathering by a relative whose new job involves sales. Their suspicious reactions to my goodness were unsettling for everybody.

Except for me, Perfect Children didn't exist in my world. That makes me sound snobby, but just ask my mom. She'll tell you I was as close to a Perfect Child as she knew. And she was raised in a convent, so she wasn't prone to lying, and she learned to have very high standards. Not only did I not run across any other Perfect Children, but I didn't run across any Evil Children, either. Evil Children were out for blood and took their orders from the Devil. Or a more evil older sibling. Most children in my little world were either Mostly Good or Mostly Bad Children.

Mostly Good Children knew the rules and tried their best to follow them. But they invariably flubbed up and felt awful about themselves. They said "I'm sorry" a lot and spent a great deal of time wishing they were someone else while they were being punished.

Mostly Bad Children came in different flavors: those who didn't bother to learn the rules, which made them seem lazy and ignorant; and those who knew the rules but didn't follow them because they thought the rules were stupid, which made them seem really bratty. There were also children who made fun of Mostly Good/Perfect Children, which made those making fun seem mean and nasty. But Mostly Bad Children generally seemed to have more fun, regardless of how grown-ups felt about them or what punishments they received. If they got caught. I watched these children closely because I was both their victim and their secret admirer.

Perfect Children had to know all the rules, follow them all the time, and be a shining example for all the other children, who hated them. Perfect Children, if they make it through childhood, are often found in:

1. Therapy, as either the client or the therapist

2. Prison, as the guard or the inmate

3. Their homes or offices, writing about their stressful childhoods.

*****

So I tried to be a Perfect Child. But my mission in life turned out to be Mission Impossible. Trying gets a child, even a nearly Perfect Child, only so far.

One thing that really tripped me up was body function noises. Perfect Children simply weren't supposed to make those noises. Other children did, and the Bad Children were even proud of them. It's hard—possibly fatal—to stop a burp, hiccup or fart once it has commenced. Sneezes, when handled with discretion, were allowable because, like detonating the atomic bomb, they were unstoppable. But it seems to me that adults assumed that children had some magic power to stop a burp, hiccup or fart in mid-eruption. Choosing to stop separated the Perfects from the rest of the pack, but I never felt that choice was involved. When my body needed to expel something *pronto*, I had to let it go. Not letting it go would violate a natural law. Even Galileo, Einstein, and Mr. Spock knew better than to mess with natural laws.

During the tortuous Catholic celebration leading up to Easter, I attended the interminable Stations of the Cross. This very solemn ritual was held on Friday of Holy Week. It was called Holy Week because Good Friday lasted about a week. If that's not a miracle, I don't know what is. On the Good Friday in question, instead of feeling pious or sad for Jesus for having to carry his own cross, I felt the need to go to the bathroom. I'd had an egg salad sandwich for lunch before going to church. There should be a rule against egg salad before church. Slipping out of the pew to find a bathroom never crossed my mind. *Did churches even have bathrooms?* It seemed unholy to pee or poop in church.

I felt rumbling in my belly, then lower. Squirming to prevent an explosion only got me looks of disapproval from Mémé and Mom. Soon Pépé and my sisters were taking an interest in the developments. Holding in the amassing gas was agonizing, but letting it out was inconceivable. I'd rather be taken out on a stretcher with a burst intestine than fart in church.

But of course physiology won out over dignity, and out came a long, loud, *send-me-to-Hell-for-sure* fart. During a moment of silent prayer. Any physical relief I felt was overshadowed by my unspeakable embarrassment and the foul odor that was surging up like a tiny mushroom cloud. There was no hiding who'd done it. I blushed a divine shade of cardinal red from scalp to sole; Judgment Day was upon me, and it wasn't looking (or smelling) very good. While everyone else in the church did their best to overlook my noxious, broken-muffler, butt noise, my family felt obliged to react.

"Lorna!" Mom and Mémé whispered in unified mortification.

"Lorna!" Pépé and my sisters whispered in wonder and with a touch of respect.

To seal my wickedness, laughter bubbled up uncontrollably in me. It was just like the smelly fart. It was as if Beelzebub himself were possessing me. I was his foul instrument, and there was no stopping my blasphemous laughter. I bowed my head so no one could tell if my heaving shoulders were evidence of sobs for Jesus' suffering or devil-possessed fart-giggles. I tried to look reverent, but my reputation was forevermore soiled.

My underpants were, too.

My Perfect Child status took a major hit that day. Any aspirations I had of becoming a nun evaporated quicker than the stink of that egg salad-sandwich fart, which hung around for a very long time. My mission was in serious jeopardy. *Could I do anything to restore my reputation? Or was it ruined for good?*

For once, I didn't have to make up any sins during confession the next day and then add, "I lied once," to satisfy the priest. On that Saturday, I had a real sin to confess.

"Bless me Father, for I have sinned once since my last confession."

"Only once, dear child? Father admires your devotion to our Lord's commandments."

"But, Father. It was a bad sin. A very bad one."

"Tell Father, Child. The Lord forgives all sins." I could almost hear him smirking. He didn't think a little kid could really commit a whopper of a sin. Well, I'd show him!

"Umm, He forgives all sins? Even if you fart during the Stations of the Cross and it's a really stinky egg salad-sandwich farty smell?"

"Ahem! Is that the sin to which you are confessing, Child?" The smirky sound was gone. He had been the priest doing the Stations of the Cross. Maybe he'd heard and smelled the fart.

"Yes, Sir."

Silence. *Was this my penance? To sit in silence with a priest after my confession hung in the air longer than the fart did?*

"Say three Hail Marys and five Our Fathers," he finally said. "Oh, and light a candle in honor of Jesus. Your sin is forgiven. Go in peace and sin no more."

"Yes, Father."

As I left, I wondered if the candles on the altar were scented. Today, I wonder if his long silence hid silent laughter.

*****

I was beginning to see that my mission to become a Perfect Child was kind of like tacking Jell-O to a wall—the more I tried, the faster it just slid away. In impeccably anti-Perfect Child fashion, I became frustrated.

The Perfect Thing to do would have been to grin and bear my frustration. Being only human and not a nun, however, I let the stress build up. It was only a matter of time until I would either *ker-splat* or *ka-boom* from all the internal pressure. Most of the time, I swallowed up my feelings with a chaser of something sweet, but there were times when I just had to let things out of my system.

Trouble always followed.

Enter cuss words. Some adults and Bad Children can swear with aplomb. I always stayed away from those children and those words. I was determined to live a wholesome, G-rated life.

I knew some words were Bad just by the way they were always spoken. Their precise meaning was lost on me and I was fine with that. About the dirtiest words that came from my mouth, therefore, were *darn it, gosh,* and (if the circumstances were truly ugly) *poopy-head.* Except for Uncle Hillbilly, who was easy to avoid because he was a shut-in drunk, I heard the widest variety of cuss words on the school bus. I believe those yellow conveyances are actually the portals through which Satan travels between Earth and the Underworld. They're devilish modes of transportation. Innocence is lost and crime bosses are trained on school buses. The first time I heard the F-word was on my school bus. I knew it was Bad just by the way it hung in the air—like my fart in church, only way worse because it kept getting repeated.

When I was thirteen years old and hormones were undoubtedly possessing me, I became uncharacteristically furious with my older sister. The anger (or aging hormones) have erased the details of what circumstance ignited the fire within me, but I remember what happened after Tina stormed out of the trailer in her typical *I'm-having-the-*

last-word style. Well, that time I was determined that *I* was going to have the last word, and the word was going to be a doozy. I didn't even care that my last word would be spoken to an empty room.

I took a deep breath and formulated the Grand-Pooh-Bah of all cuss words in my mind. F...Fu...F...Fu...F... And that' s as far as I got. I was convinced I had developed a sudden, unexpected stutter. The F-word was stuck in my mouth. I took another deep breath, and then gave it all I had.

"F—k you, Tina!"

Success!

There! I had said it! I had pronounced the evilest of all Bad Words. And no one had heard me, not even my sister. Well, I suppose God heard. Saying the word was disturbingly disappointing. I expected liberation...or at least pleasure. Instead, I wanted to take it back. I felt as dirty as the word itself. That was the day I lost my linguistic virginity, and there was no going back. If I had teetered from grace by farting during the Stations of the Cross, saying the F-word had just catapulted me into Hell. I was a goner before I ever got to be an up-and-comer. *Did Joan of Arc ever say the F-word? Did any nun worthy of her habit drop the F-bomb?*

So I swore off of swearing. My hope was that I'd stepped off the path toward corruption before the Devil and I got formally engaged.

Then something dawned on me. I was thirteen years old. I had *options.* Mom had fewer worries about my sisters. My mission needed rethinking.

There must be a way to be Perfect *and* live a little. As Mom always said, "Lorna, you are such a smart girl."

*****

During the summer before my fourteenth birthday, I was on fire. Things were shifting around faster than a fat lady doing the Watusi. By "things," consider this list:

1. My baby belly fat redistributed itself upward. I developed impressive symmetrical breasts—all the boys' eyes said so. My body changed in other ways, too. I slimmed down that summer without even trying. Since I lived in the country and my nearest friend-for the-summer was four miles away, I walked a minimum of eight miles a day (to and from her house, she never came to my house). My belly disappeared and my once stocky legs became svelte and shapely.

2. I got my period, which, at first, was horrible. Initially, I thought I was dying from some mysterious disease. No one in my all-female family ever spoke of feminine issues, and schools didn't teach us about such private matters in health class until eighth grade. Maybe the teachers thought if they waited to tell us, we would wait to menstruate. I finally figured out I wasn't dying when I lived to see the bleeding end after about four days.

3. I read the *Summer of '42*. That novel was the equivalent of a sex-education textbook. Until I read it, I thought babies were made when a male and female lay down on the same bed and fell asleep together. Why else did people call sex "sleeping together"? I was shocked (and a bit grossed out) by how sex really happened, but it sure made more sense than just lying down together and nodding off.

4. Because boys noticed me, I started noticing them. The attention I craved from adults was replaced by attention from boys. That took some getting used to because boys were alien to me. The only male I ever knew well was my step-grandfather, Pépé. He was nice enough, but he puttered around the yard in baggy pants, smoked a pipe, loved fart jokes and professional wrestling, wore thick eye glasses, had really big ears, and was pretty much bald. I was hoping that males varied in their interests and appearance. Lucky for me, they did.

5. I gave up trying to please God. There was just no pleasing that deity. I felt good about this decision, but I felt guilty, too. I hoped that my guilt made the Powers in Heaven feel a little better about another one that got away. *She may have left the fold, but she'll always have the gift of guilt we gave her.* But I had earthy interests to pursue and striving for perfection was really getting in the way now. Although I maintained the persona of the Perfect Girl because my reputation was important to me, I gave up the Nun Dream. My healthy interest in the opposite sex and my curiosity about my own budding sexuality, especially as it related to getting attention from boys, was decidedly not a habit befitting a nun.

6. Since I lived in a trailer next to my grandparents' house, which was situated in the middle of a cornfield, I didn't get much of a chance to try out my new-found, earthy femininity until school started in September. My reputation as a straight-A student was as shiny

as those golden stars teachers always stuck on the top of my homework and I wouldn't let it get tarnished. Yes—I only craved attention from adults until I got interested in boys my age— now I wanted attention from the boys, too.

7. Although the boys in the seventh grade noticed my new and interesting curves, they were too shy to do anything but ogle and snicker. My first boyfriend was a tenth-grader, but that came only after I turned fourteen in November. Our relationship was romantic and stupid at the same time. All we did was kiss, but he said he wanted to marry me. So did his younger brother. I didn't take either offer seriously. He played baseball and left school early to join the Navy.

8. My second boyfriend played soccer. We were both in tenth grade and dated for six years. I was sure we were going to get married. He promised. That's how he got me to do the things Miriam and Hermie did in the *Summer of '42*.

9. All Mom knew was that I had lots of social engagements and my grades continued to be sky-high. I was still her worry-free girl. No worries for her, that is. On the surface, I still was the Perfect Child.

But I had worries of my own. On one level, my reputation was untarnished. On another level, I felt a storm brewing because I had to keep all my doubts and worries inside me, safely away from Mom and any other person who might notice me. I still desperately craved visibility.

I probably shouldn't have kept so much storminess bottled up inside me.

CHAPTER 6: IT WAS ALL IN THE GENES. AND IN THE JEANS

Back then I was a "social drinker." But I liked to stay hidden in the background. That's me, behind the bottle of Cold Duck. How prophetic.

I didn't know it then, but I came from a family that liked to booze it up. Something about my family was very different from Beaver Cleaver's family. Different from the Waltons, too. None of them served little kids wine at Sunday meals or cured a cold with frequent shots of brandy. I don't remember Mr. Cleaver sharing a cold Topper beer with the Beav like Pépé regularly did with me. And that was just the obvious drinking. My mom spiked her fruity Jell-O salads with brandy to "preserve the freshness of the fruit." Liquor was just as much a part of my food pyramid as bologna and potato chips were.

Alcohol watered the roots of both sides of my family tree. Alcoholics didn't exist back in the old days, of course; people who drank alcohol were called either drunks or drinkers. "Drunks" were despicable people who were the subject of loud whispering and sideways looks from polite people—the ones who could hold their liquor. "Drinkers," on the other hand, were respected members of society, whether they slurred their words or not when they had a "few too many." My dad, who I was told couldn't keep any job long enough to have a real career before he vanished, was a "drunk." His dad, my grandpa, was a church-going, family-oriented dentist. No matter how drunk he got, he was merely a "drinker."

My mother's mother (Mémé) was Finnish, a people (I came to know) who are famous for three character traits: drinking, despair, and dancing. These traits must be related in some way, though I'm not sure how. My mom's real father (not Pépé) was French. Need I say more? Even though Pépé wasn't a blood relative, he had a lot of influence over me. He was half American Indian and half hillbilly. I never stood a chance at resisting the temptations of alcohol, but somehow both my sisters did. I guess I was just lucky.

Maybe if someone in the family had told me that lots of my relatives had had close encounters of the disastrous kind with booze, I might have passed on all those straight-up glasses of Cold Duck wine on Sundays. Maybe I could have asked Mémé for Vick's Vapo-Rub rather than juice glasses of brandy when I had the sniffles. Perhaps I would have turned down Pépé's offer to take the first glug of Topper beer each time he cracked one open, something he did a lot. But then, again, maybe I wouldn't have.

Like a number of my ancestors (about whom I knew nothing at the time), I took to alcohol like a weed to fertilizer. But no one knew because I got so good at acting like the Perfect Girl, and I was pretty sure Perfect Girls weren't supposed to get buzzed. My family knew I eagerly drank the wine, brandy, or beer they offered me. What they didn't know was how much I enjoyed the woozy feeling I got after drinking.

I was about ten when I got my first real alcohol cravings. Before then, I just readily accepted whatever was offered by the trusted adult doing the pouring. I wasn't greedy for more. But some alcohol-lust inside of me was triggered when I entered the double-digits. I developed a serious hankering for booze, anticipating its burn and relishing its afterglow. Opportunities to satisfy my alcohol-tooth came mostly on weekends. Unless I was blessed with a cold. Mémé and I were in complete agreement that brandy was the best cure for a cold ever invented.

My first real boyfriend and my first real need for alcohol collided in my tenth-grade English class. My teacher was reading a poem aloud. She stopped after a line that ended, "long blonde beauty" and asked my future first serious boyfriend what that line reminded him of.

"Lorna," he said.

That got my attention. I immediately got a crush on him, which was my modus operandi for the rest of my life. If someone noticed me, I took great interest in pleasing him or her. In an instant, that boy turned from someone I hardly noticed into someone I couldn't stop thinking about. I was sixteen when we started dating. I was still innocent in the ways of boys and sex. He was also sixteen, but his hormones were way ahead of mine. So was his sexual experience. To please him, I had to loosen up. To loosen up, I had to get drunk. Thus I began to drink to keep my boyfriend happy and me woozy enough to tolerate him boinking me regularly. He needed me to drink a lot.

I drank prodigious amounts of alcohol before I went out in public so I wouldn't have to embarrass myself by sneaking behind a bush to slug from a bottle that was cleverly hidden there. Perhaps I did go behind the bushes sometimes. It's hard to remember specific details about my whereabouts and behaviors when there was more alcohol than oxygen in my bloodstream.

My unofficial career as a bona fide alcoholic began in the 1970s, but I never thought I had a drinking problem. Stuck in that old-fashioned mentality, I believed that anyone who drank too much was a drunken derelict, and I refused to define myself as a derelict. I was a popular straight-A student. I was involved in lots of high school activities. Plus I didn't have that derelict look. I always appeared neat and tidy. So what if I didn't remember everything that happened the night before? People forgot things all the time in the 1970s.

Sometimes I lost track of how much I was drinking and, thus, lost track of myself. I always ended up home, though, and so my family never suspected anything in me was fundamentally flawed. One morning when I threw up in the kitchen, for example, I blamed it on food poisoning. They didn't question me then because of my reputation for being such a good and honest girl. Or maybe because they were distracted by the puddle of puke. I soon discovered that, because I was so accomplished at playing the role of the Good Girl, I could bamboozle even the people who knew me best. I wasn't a Perfect Girl (I'd just barfed all over the kitchen), but I was still Good. That was good enough. I knew I could get away with just about anything. All I had to do was keep up the appearance of being Lorna the Good Girl.

Living a dual life might seem easy for Superman or Batman, but it wasn't easy for me. By day, I had to be the shining academic star, the even tempered, helpful person

Mom and other adults had come to expect. On weekend nights, however, after my boyfriend got me liquored up, I was his "sexy thing." Pretty soon I had to start sneaking drinks just to relieve the pressure I was feeling because I was hiding my drinking and living a dual life. It makes perfect sense to someone who is spinning out of control but trying to appear in complete control. Just ask any perfectionist or psychopath.

The one pressure that had me guzzling, not sipping, the booze was sex. It came down to two fairly simply scientific equations:

1. Boyfriend (intending to get into my jeans) + Good Girl (wanting to stay in my jeans) = Celibate/Sad Boyfriend

2. Boyfriend (same intent) + Alcohol + Guilty Good Girl = Good Girl with Reduced Inhibitions = Happy/Satisfied Boyfriend

Since the sum total of my sex education up to now was Hermie's exploits in *The Summer of '42*, I was what most people would call naïve about sex. Although the era of so-called free love had come and, I guess, was still coming, I totally missed it because my family was repressed when it came to matters involving peoples' private parts. My mom never spoke about anything resembling sexuality and, since she didn't have a husband, I never saw her as a woman doing womanly things that might lead to stuff involving private parts.

When I was about twelve, Mémé, in a surprising tea-time discussion, dove head-first into a pithy discussion about sex. English was her third and worse language, but I understood her perfectly well.

"Anyway," she said, "sex no good. Men want sex. Anyway. You must do sex if he say so, anyway, but only if he you husband. Anyway, just for babies. Sex not for you.

Sex for man, anyway, not for you." Mémé used "anyway" like most people use "um" or "ah"—as a vocal comma or verbal tic, a place to pause and collect her thoughts. That day when she delivered her Sex is Evil lesson, she had a piercing look in her eyes. I thought she looked like a hawk watching a field mouse. I was scared. Then she offered me a cookie, which helped to take the edge off my rattled nerves, but my "va-jay-jay" was pinched up tighter than size 9 wide feet in a pair of cute size 7 narrow heels.

The only way I could get myself out of my jeans and let my boyfriend show me how much we loved each other was to get good and hammered. I was told I was a very hot date. Too bad I was never there to enjoy it.

Even when my family started wondering why their booze tasted watered down, they never suspected me. I was Lorna, their Good Girl. My reputation was 100 proof. Like a tightrope walker in a three-ring circus, all I had to do was put on the show and never let my audience know how I felt inside. The show was for them. I just kept saying to myself, *You can pull this off, Lorna. Smile and fake it if you have to. The show must go on! You can't disappoint anyone.* I pulled it off. I was convinced that I was destined for a career in acting.

*****

When I wasn't drinking, I was craving. And not just for booze. Nowadays, I would be diagnosed with Obsessive Compulsive Disorder (OCD). Back in the 1970s, I just had what they might call quirky habits. Okay. Maybe I was weird. You be the judge. Here's some evidence:

1. I needed to be perfect. My homework was fit to be framed. I knew all the answers in class and I knew my teachers knew it. While I loved doing English homework so I could master perfect

penmanship, math homework was my favorite because I could present my calculations precisely, with each number perfectly aligned and the answers always triple checked for accuracy. I was polite, friendly, and quick-witted. I got laughs from people who might otherwise snub an insufferable perfectionist. Being perfect is hard work if you're perfect; if you're not, you take a heaping dollop of the escape mechanism of your choice to ease the burden. At least that's what I did.

2. I was the girlfriend of a popular athlete, so I needed to be the best, most attractive girlfriend I could be. I lost weight and kept my curves in all the right places. Genetics, while it was my foe in some ways, was my friend when it came to my looks. I was born with blue eyes that stayed clear blue and with blonde hair that stayed light blonde with no help from hydrogen peroxide. Both my grandmothers were amply endowed in the bosom department. While I inherited some things from my ancestors that I'd rather not have dealt with (migraine headaches, booze-lust), I was happy to accept stunningly large, symmetrical breasts. The rest of me wasn't bad either, once the baby fat melted off. I managed that by going on mini-hunger strikes (three-days a week of just water during my sophomore year in high school). Mom wasn't quite sure what to do with me, especially since I needed a whole new, smaller, wardrobe. That's what she noticed. Boys noticed my new shape. I was sexy jail-bait, loving the attention from the boys but not the consequences. Drinking made it easier to

be easy with my boyfriend and flirty with everyone else.

3. Part of my birthright was my craving for carbohydrates. Not knowing that alcohol metabolizes into simple sugar, I was a sitting duck for anything starchy or sugary. When I wasn't drinking or starving myself, I was eating anything I could get my hands on that was sweet or would quickly convert to sugar. Mom could have saved a lot on her grocery bill if she would have just bought a gallon of cheap vodka a week for her good middle child.

Lorna's Starve-Yourself-and-Get-Skunk-Drunk Diet Plan wasn't a practical long-term solution if I wanted to live to be old, which I defined at that time as "past thirty." I needed a new plan that still involved booze but kept food in the picture to give my body (with the possible exception of my liver) a fighting chance. So I introduced a foreign concept into my heretofore sedentary life: exercise. I kept my sexy figure by walking, mowing the lawn, riding my bike, and dancing. If I defined these activities as "helping me to look good" rather than "work," they were much more pleasant.

The one exception was dancing. Dancing was in my blood. I loved it. The only time I didn't mind working up a sweat was on the dance floor. My sisters and I were legendary in our little rural town for our uncanny rhythm. We should have been *Solid Gold Dancers*. Dancing to a loud rock band—even a really bad one, which was the only kind available in our area—was freedom for me. I could let go of my inhibitions in public without my alcohol crutch.

Wearing hip-hugger jeans and a tube top (that was the fashion back then) and shaking my sober booty with my sisters, I was a swanky, sexy, blonde goddess. Not even my boyfriend would dare to dance when my sisters and I were doing our spontaneously choreographed routines on the dance floor. We just followed the drums or the bass guitar and let our hips do the talking.

The drinking came later in the evening, when my boyfriend was ready to leave and get horizontal. I loved those dances and didn't want to leave, but he wanted to do something other than watch me dance. I never wanted to risk disappointing him because he was supposed to be my husband someday, and I wanted to be the best someday wife he ever had. While I was dancing, I got a glimpse of Liberated Lorna with all her senses fully engaged. But the pull to be a perfect girlfriend yanked me away from my sisters, the music, and the magic of being me. With every swig of vodka, my weapon of choice, I let myself melt into the whirly-swirly world of not-really-me.

With all the drinking and sex, it's easy to forget I was trying to be everyone's version of perfection. Many young women engage in these behaviors and end up convicted of vehicular manslaughter due to driving while schnockered or with post-partum depression (from having a baby and having to balance drinking with childcare).

I was one of the lucky ones. My high school years were productive, not reproductive. That was probably due to my Supposed Future Husband's responsible but begrudging use of condoms. Or perhaps my blood-alcohol level confused the dickens out of my reproductive cycle. My eggs were probably lying down, passed out in my ovaries. I didn't have my own car, so I rarely drove. Consequently, I'm sure I saved a lot of lives and, to this day, my driving skills are adequate, but only when going forward. I am reverse-gear challenged and believe that this is directly correlated with my lack of youthful driving shenanigans. It has nothing to do with my gender and natural blondeness.

To keep up my Perfect Lorna act, I did my chores, was polite to my elders, socialized with my girlfriends, and got straight-A's in school. I also participated in numerous and inexplicable school clubs:

1. The Ski Club. I didn't actually ski because I'd learned the hard way not to strap anything to my feet and expect it to turn out well. Born without even a smattering of what some people call "physical intelligence," I must have joined because either they needed at least one more person or the club trip to the mountain would be cancelled, a cute boy was in the club and I wanted to be near him, or I was trying to avoid some cleaning extravaganza Mom had planned for that Saturday. It's probably noteworthy that the one ski trip planned for the year got cancelled due to a snow storm.

2. The Bowling Club. Does bowling even qualify as a sport? If it does, I shouldn't have been in that club on the grounds that I was never into sports. What self-respecting sport is played in an alley and practically requires beer drinking by the so-called athletes who play it? If bowling is not a regulation sport like football, hockey, or badminton, I still shouldn't have been in that club because there was a competitive element to it (like chess club, only without the prestige and the silence), and I'm not competitive by nature. At least I'm not competitive with other people. And what's more competitive than people in goofy shoes trying to look athletic as they wing a twenty-pound ball at ten innocent, tippy, bottle-shaped gizmos at the end of a high-glossed wooden alley-way? I joined the bowling

club for two reasons: to avoid religious instruction that was offered as part of an optional curriculum during the last period in the school day and because the bowling alley was in the same building as a bar that had awesome soda and snack vending machines. (Competition revealed itself on the bus ride back. Who had the best snacks and/or belly aches?)

3. The Library Club. Okay, that one made some sense given my "intelligence intelligence." The librarian loved me because I was one of the elite—the one percent—of the student body who both understood and respected the Dewey Decimal System.

4. The Chess Club. Since I had a crush on several of the boys in that club, it seemed like a good idea to join. I knew nothing about the game except that it took place on a checkerboard, and I could play checkers if my opponent didn't get all greedy and tricky on me. But chess was a different story. Each game piece has different rules, and all that chin rubbing while seemingly mesmerized by a checker board seemed creepy to me. Maybe I thought it was the Chest Club and I could be the queen, especially since mostly guys joined the chess/chest club.

Since I was dating a soccer-turned-basketball player, joining the varsity cheerleading squad was unofficially mandatory. Some other girls who were dating basketball players "encouraged" me to try out for the basketball cheerleading squad in my junior year of high school. If you were dating a player, you were "supposed" to be a cheerleader. My problem, which became their problem, was that I didn't fit into that clique as well as they would have liked. I was shy; they were flashy. I talked to anyone who talked to me—even the nerdy kids; they only associated with each other. I thought it was unkind to make fun of other people; they thought it was fun to be unkind to other people. I was a klutz; they weren't acrobats, but their limbs obeyed their brains much better than mine did. Given that I am directionally challenged ("left" and "right" befuddle me) and couldn't manage a cartwheel or a split, I believe that my bouncing breasts made it on the squad and I just came along to keep them company. They were quite popular with the team and the fans. So were my long blonde hair, blue eyes, smile, and enthusiasm. I was an excellent speller ("Give me an S!"). That may have helped, too.

I was also a member of the National Honor Society; junior, then senior editor, of the yearbook; and the valedictorian of my graduating class.

That was by day.

By night, I was masquerading as the little-known super hero, Super Sloshed. You don't hear much about this character because she rarely uses her powers to help others, as she's either incapacitated, incarcerated, or in rehab. When I was on my way to Black-Out Land, I was funny, flirty, and could be talked into just about anything. Just about.... I don't remember most of what happened because I was drunk. I know, however, that I was never injured, pregnant, or involved in a bank heist. How do I know? No sirens. Maybe my hair and mascara got a bit messy and my bra wasn't always properly in place, but these minor errors could be fixed without police involvement before I got home.

No one—not my teachers, club advisors, friends, nor my mother, sisters, Mémé or Pépé—suspected anything. They all believed that Perfect Lorna was innocently dating a nice young man. The "nice young man" knew about my drinking, of course, but he never knew *how much* I needed it to get myself to be the Lorna he wanted me to be.

*****

Someone must have asked me what I wanted to be when I grew up. I had thought about career goals since I was a small child. My career choice usually wavered around a nebulous ambition—"I want to help people." Between the ages of five and seven, I was sure I wanted to be a nun. After I spent some time at St. Morris Catholic School for the Eternally Cursed, however, where the nuns used rulers as weapons rather than as tools for drawing straight lines, I decided there must be a better way to help people. Maybe it was Tina's mystery disease and her brush with death or my little-girl crush on *Dr. Kildare*, but at age eight, I switched my career aspiration to nursing. Nurses helped people feel better and get better. That was the job for me. I held on to that dream for years. But I let that dream go when I realized that nurses had to stick needles in people. How on earth did that make people feel any better? It made me feel queasy. During my teen years, I fantasized about becoming a famous actress. I could make emotions bubble up into my eyes or I could hide them deep inside me. It was as easy as flipping a switch. Tina said it was hormones, but I knew I had a Natural Talent. Rehearsing made-up scenes of a dramatic encounter with a would-be lover, I could spend hours in front of a mirror in the one bathroom in our trailer. My sisters didn't appreciate my dedication to my craft.

Then it came time to apply for college. I had to pick a major. Acting was a dream, but not a viable job. Nursing was out. So were the occult (another interest of mine) and professional reading. The only other idea I had was my interest in what made people tick. Every magazine personality test I found, I took. I was curious about people. Could I turn that into a career?

I turned to Mr. Too-Much-Coffee, my guidance counselor, a man who was supposed to both guide and counsel me. But he wasn't what you'd call a *go-getter*. What he mostly did was substitute teaching and coffee drinking. When I asked for guidance, he gave me the Dictionary of Occupational Titles (the DOT) and left to get another cup of coffee. Since I was my class valedictorian, I thought Mr. Too-Much-Coffee might take a little interest in me and my future. Maybe if I had been a star athlete, he would have, but that was before Title IX and we didn't have athletic programs for girls. I wouldn't have stood out as that kind of shining star, anyway. As I thumbed through the DOT, I discovered psychology. I thought I'd hit pay dirt. Then I read that I needed to get at least a master's degree to do anything in the field of psychology. The end of the section referred me to related fields. One of them was sociology, a discipline I never heard of before. Being the curious sort, I turned to that section. Sociology sounded interesting enough, and there were jobs a person could get with just a bachelorette degree. Or was that bachelor's degree? I wasn't sure about the details, but I had at least picked my college major. I left Mr. Too-Much-Coffee's office having done my own guidance and counseling. That gave me confidence that I would make a good sociologist. Whatever that was.

Then I had to decide where to go to college. I wish I had known that universities were looking for top graduates in high school and that they would pay my college tuition. But no one told me. No one encouraged me to apply to the "name universities"—neither Mr. Too-Much-Coffee nor any teacher who professed any love for me (on a purely professional level) on a daily basis. I didn't know about the wide world of academic possibilities that was open to me in 1975, and I certainly didn't feel confident enough to explore that world without encouragement. Plus, I wanted to stay near Supposed Future Husband, the guy I got drunk for so he could have sex and I could have someone to love me. So I went to my local state university.

*****

Freshman year of college, I stayed home and commuted to school. The year before, Tina had gone off to another campus of the state university, one that was as far away from home as possible, though still in New York. When she came home for breaks and over the summer, the trailer seemed to shrink. The four of us had once fit into the trailer comfortably enough, but now that we were all grown up, it felt more like a doll house. To make the tight quarters tighter, I adopted a full-sized Old English sheepdog named Humphrey, who (being a victim of a divorce) needed a loving stable home.

Something had to give before the trailer exploded.

During my second semester of college, when I was eighteen, Humphrey and I moved into a sketchy but affordable apartment building fifteen miles from home. Since I didn't have a car, I got my exercise walking to campus from downtown and back. My apartment was on the third floor of a four-story building, so I got vertical exercise, too.

There were positive aspects to living in that apartment and challenges to living there. On the plus side:

1. For the first time in my life, I had privacy. That meant Supposed Future Husband and I could "do it" in more comfortable settings than, say, an open field. We didn't have to worry about his parents coming home unexpectedly.

2. I could drink openly and whenever I wanted to.

3. I could rehearse dramatic love scenes in front of my own bathroom mirror for as long as I wanted and without anyone but Humphrey interrupting me.

4. I could drink openly and whenever I wanted to.

5. I was the only tenant who was allowed to have a dog—and he was a big one. Humphrey was the opposite of threatening, but he had a big, happy bark that was, apparently, easily misinterpreted by would be robbers. Why was I the only tenant allowed to have a pet? Blonde, blue eyes, sexy figured tenant + landlord with hope in his heart and heat in his pants = latitude on rules. That is as far as it ever got, but that was enough.

6. I could drink openly and whenever I wanted to.

The challenges were:

7. The place was a dump. When I moved in, the "kitchen" was a hot plate on a narrow counter. The refrigerator was directly in front of the toilet in the bathroom, and the bathroom sink doubled as a kitchen sink. I must admit the bathroom was roomy. It was also painted blood-red.

8. I worked out a deal with the landlord to have a reduced rent if I kept the hallways and stairs clean (vacuumed, swept, mopped, free of beer cans, bodies, and other inanimate objects). While the rent was affordable, I had to do what I had always avoided while home—cleaning—to make it affordable.

9. No matter what the weather, I had to walk Humphrey at least twice a day to do his "business." I also had to walk back and forth to campus. I put a lot of miles on my tootsies in rain, snow, blazing sun, frigid cold, and everything but sandstorms.

Thus began my life as a responsible adult. I had my own apartment, my own dog, my own Supposed Future Husband, and my own drinking problem. Just like in high school, I separated Learning Lorna from Lorna the Lush. Unlike in high school, I was drinking more and hiding it more from everyone, including Supposed Future Husband. My acting abilities improved as my liver worked overtime.

I graduated *magna cum laude* from college, but I wasn't a happy, if drunken, camper. Even with all that walking, I managed to gain a significant amount of weight during my college years. I wasn't flabby, just bulky. Because I was above average height, I could carry my weight well enough to have people (including me) think I was simply "big boned." At least that's what I told myself.

As my relationship with Supposed Future Husband continued, I found ways to avoid having all that sex I never wanted to have. But just as I was beginning to really enjoy this new phase in our relationship, he broke up with me for some hotsy-totsy NYC momma he met in the human sexuality class I'd suggested he take. (I thought he would learn something about how male and female sex drives differ.) He dumped me right before graduation. Six years of drinking and sex wasted.

I was heart-broken. I did what any broken child would do: I went crying to my mother.

She was never one to mince words or sugarcoat anything, so as I sat there, sobbing on her couch, my face puffy, red, and blotchy, she said, "Well, no wonder he left you. Lorna, look at yourself. You are fat and you are dressed like a farmer."

Okay. So I wasn't dressed for the prom. I was wearing bib overall jeans, a man's plaid shirt, and work boots colloquially known as "shit-kickers." But did she have to be so brutally blunt when I was so obviously vulnerable? I stopped sobbing to briefly process what she'd said, then ratcheted up my sobbing to wailing.

"Lorna," she said, "I am sorry if I hurt you by saying that. I was just trying to say that you have let yourself go, and you can be so pretty when you want to be." She was trying to calm me down.

"I know," I gasped. "I'm sorry. You're right."

"How about a little bit of brandy?" she offered. "It might help you calm down."

I forced a weak smile. "Okay. But just a little."

I'd come home to be comforted, but instead I was confronted. All I ever wanted was for Mom to notice me. Well, she noticed me, all right, she noticed me in all my imperfection. I wouldn't let that ever happen again—for my sake or hers. Perfect Lorna was coming back…with a vengeance.

"Thanks, Mom. The drink helped. I feel a little better. May I have another one?"

"Sure, Dear."

It's hard to believe I never took a course in acting. Some people are just born talented. If only I had known the power of that talent, I could have used it for good, not brandy.

CHAPTER 7: I WILL SURVIVE

This was the man who walked into my life when my Supposed Future Husband walked out on me. Yes, I survived just fine.

I couldn't believe my luck. Gloria Gaynor's song, "I Will Survive," was the number one hit in 1979, the year that Supposed Future Husband (who, just to keep the record straight, I never married) ditched me for the dark-haired, brown-eyed Anti-Me, or as I liked to call her: Sheba, Exotic Hussy. I sang Gloria's anthem day and night like my life depended on it. Well, my life did depend on it. Gloria went from broken wimp to kick-butt woman in about three minutes just by singing that song. At first she was afraid. She was petrified. *I hear you, Gloria.* Then about two minutes later she's booting his sorry shorts out and she's saving all her lovin' for someone who deserves her. I needed that kind of instant courage. My dog was my only true-blue companion, my family was always there for me, and alcohol was the crutch that kept me hobbling through those long, lonely days and nights.

After I received my mom's unique reality check, I took a serious inventory of my situation. After several years of dating the same guy, I had indeed let myself go. It happens. Excessive drinking, passing out, and lifeless sex apparently don't do much for a girl's charm. I tried to hide my expanding assets as well as I could with farmer attire, which was the acceptable dress code for those times and my locale. But just as black paint can't transform a hot-air balloon into a stealth bomber, bib overall jeans didn't cover all that there was to cover.

Sheba, Exotic Hussy wasn't classically pretty. She was classically urban Chicana. Her dark features and Diana Ross Afro accentuated her short but definitively voluptuous hussy-self. Plus she had location going for her. She hailed from the one place Supposed Future Husband wanted to live: New York City. When he talked about The Big Apple, he had that starry-eyed look that Mickey Rooney used to get in those 1940s Broadway-bound movies. But flashy, imposing people and places easily overwhelmed me. Who could live in a city that never slept, anyway? With all those insomniacs roaming the streets, it's no wonder crime rates were so high.

Maybe, it was dawning on me, Supposed Future Husband and I weren't meant to be married. He'd already had the foresight to notice our differing preferences in sex (he wanted some whereas I didn't) and location (he wanted bright lights and bustling smoggy atmosphere, whereas I wanted to live in a quiet cave) and decided to do something about it. I just wished he hadn't had his Plan B in place when he cut me loose, especially when all I had was my Plan A.

First I tried to lure him back with a bold attempt at seduction. I found some non-farmer clothes and made a nice meal for him. He'd always loved Humphrey, so I brushed him to look his dog-show best. After the meal, which included reminiscing about the good old days when he still liked me, I put on some swanky music, lit some candles, and invited him for one last taste of me. Perhaps it was wrong to tempt him into pity-sex, but that was the only kind I had to offer. After he'd satisfied himself, he thanked me for a nice "good-bye evening." He left me with a little going-away present: crabs. Not the kind one finds at posh restaurants, but pubic lice. I had no idea why I had such a remarkably itchy crotch until, in an extraordinary effort of flexibility, I was able to take a look and see little black critters busily scurrying where none had been before. Mortified and determined not to tell a soul—not even my physician—I went to Planned Parenthood. They had a reputation for dealing with women who had secrets.

I decided two things after my successful visit to their office:

1. If I ever needed an abortion, I was happy they had a file on me. Everyone there was professional (they didn't laugh or judge) and helpful. They gave me stinky shampoo that killed the crabs, the remnants of my self-esteem, and any hope for a sex life for quite a while.

2. If I ever saw Ex-Supposed Future Husband again, I would tell him and Sheba, Exotic and Infected Hussy to keep their pubie-cooties to themselves.

"I Will Survive" was on a continuous play-loop in my head and I was singing the song with a lot more oomph than before. At first, I *was* afraid. I was scared silly. But then, after the Disgusting Crab Caper, I found the courage to be a girl without a boy, as long as I could be a girl with a kick-ass song, a crab-free crotch, and enough vodka to get me to that place of not caring about boys or if my neighbors wanted to kill me and Gloria.

Because Ex-Supposed Future Husband had left me for someone who was so different from me, I decided I really needed to change my image. I began with the obvious and easy things I could afford. I cut my long blonde hair. It was, along with my blue eyes and ample chest, one of my best attention-getters. My hair was what had originally attracted him. Six years later, I remembered this. Now I wanted that "long blonde beauty" gone. It was a silly act of defiance because I loved my hair and it *was* beautiful, but I was too chicken to get a tattoo that said *Notice Me*. So the hair that hung down to the middle of my back vanished.

And I myself was slowly vanishing, too. I didn't require much food. I ate to be social and to do something with my mouth when I couldn't drink. Being single meant I didn't have to eat just because someone else wanted me to keep them company while they were eating. That discovery was a lifesaver to me because I was poor. Now what little money I had for food went to Humphrey and alcohol. I stopped eating proper meals. I ate simpler foods: lettuce sandwiches (iceberg lettuce, Miracle Whip, two slices of white bread), popcorn, and Granny Smith apples. I didn't need a nutritional consultant to tell me that that diet seemed to cover most essential food groups. Although I wouldn't recommend trying this if you want to shimmy into your prom dress or bathing suit, I lost a lot of weight.

In a less obvious act of self-mutilation (or image make-over), I also got my ears pierced. Until now, I had been morally against putting holes in my body where none existed. Well, I was against it mostly on the grounds of squeamishness, but I was firm in my conviction. But one day as I was walking Humphrey past a jewelry shop we had passed hundreds of times, I saw the reflection of my bobbed blonde head in store window. I was beginning to lose a little weight and my reflection looked so *plain*. Either I had to do something to spruce myself up or I had to seriously reconsider my original career choice of becoming a nun. I had a sudden vision of me dripping in diamond earrings, which I took as a sign to steer clear of the convent life. I went inside the store. The "little pinch" the saleswoman said I would feel as she pierced my ears (for those diamond earrings) was more like a shot through my earlobe with a nail-gun. Which is kind of what she used. She said there probably wouldn't be any blood. There was blood. Then she told me things about alcohol (rubbing, not drinking), turning the stud (metal, not male), and what to do if it got red and swollen (my ears, not my "va-jay-jay"). I was kind of in a daze, having been nail-gunned for the first time, but the gold studs I picked looked nice and my ears didn't fall off. It was a successful experience in self-mutilation.

My golden hair was gone and I was on my way to a new Lorna. Well, kind of new. But "new" didn't necessarily mean "better."

*****

I wasn't drinking nearly enough to keep myself occupied or properly anaesthetized, so I began drinking more. Because I was alone, most of my drinking was solo. I still didn't see anything unusual about my love affair with cheap vodka. What else did I have to do with the long nights and weekends? I wasn't hurting anyone when I was drinking. Indeed, when I was drinking, I wasn't hurting at all.

Although the vodka I was drinking was cheap, it still cost money, as did what little food I was eating, plus my utility bills, discounted rent, and Humphrey expenses. But I didn't let that worry me. Whether it was my pickled brain or my natural-born predisposition, I was never a planner. That meant I didn't think too far ahead in terms of jobs or major life decisions. I didn't realize it then, but I was operating on an implicit faith that everything would turn out just fine, so I didn't have to waste any time or energy trying to plot and plan. This strategy worked much better for major life events like jobs than it did for minor ones like dinner parties.

My Social Security benefits were about to run out because, having graduated from college, I was too old to be considered a dependent child of a vanished father. But I didn't have to worry about money because my favorite professor offered me a summer job as a research assistant on her grant. I didn't have a plan for how I would earn my own money or what I would do that long summer, the first summer I was single in six years. But not planning worked out just fine. I didn't realize that my professor had a grant or that she had targeted me as "one of her best and brightest" students. I aced every sociology class I took, but I was still surprised that she hand-picked me to work with her elite team. I just chalked it down to dumb luck. Like everyone else in my life except my dog, my new boss had no idea the whiz-kid she hired drank vodka straight out of a bottle to avoid the annoyance of continually pouring the stuff into a glass.

In the mornings, our team of six research assistants entered data onto keypunch cards. In the afternoons, we proofread our morning's work. Those were mind-numbing days. Like privates at boot camp, we all needed something to help ease our mutual pain, and nothing spelled "relief" like Happy Hour. Our favorite haunt had Happy Hour from

5 to 7:00 p.m. We could get two-for-the-price-of-one drinks. I drank Black Russians—usually four, sometimes six. They served free cheese and crackers, so it's not like I was drinking on an empty stomach.

What happened at Happy Hour, stayed at Happy Hour. It must have because I don't remember most of those hours. I'm sure we never dined at that restaurant because we couldn't afford their prices. Actually, I'm pretty sure I never dined anywhere. I must have gotten home to my third-floor apartment and walked Humphrey, which was no small feat since he was huge and enthusiastic after being cooped up for twelve hours, and we had to navigate those steep, narrow stairs. Neither of us broke our necks, which qualified me as a responsible dog owner. Amazingly, I was always clear-headed and early for work the next day. I can't say the same for the others. That must mean that I was a professional drinker (whereas the others were amateurs) and an impressive employee.

For the first time, I was drinking for the buzz, not for the sex, but except for the after-work Happy Hour extravaganzas, I never drank more than a couple of drinks in public. I had an image to uphold. My friends and family believed I was pure as the driven snow. Pre-drinking, therefore, became my habit. I'd go out drinking with my friends and already be well on my way to drunkenness. I thus saved money and my reputation remained untarnished as long as my acting-sober abilities were spot-on—and they were.

Now I was Funny-Vivacious-Social-Drinker Lorna. When the music was good, I was also Sexy-Dancer Lorna. Dancing got me noticed, and being noticed was everything.

*****

Until Ex-Supposed Future Husband dumped me, I had only had relations with him. I may have been underage when I lost my virginity, but at least I was monogamous, so my Catholic upbringing wasn't a total waste. Mémé's admonitions about sex weighed heavily on my mind, too. In my limited experience, I though she must be right: sex was no good, and it was for men's pleasure, not mine. But I also knew from prodigious amounts of TV watching and reading steamy romance novels that the way to a man's heart was definitely not through his stomach.

Having always defined myself relative to someone else and never as my own person, I was alone and adrift. I was a sentence fragment. To the untrained eye, a noun is quite capable of standing alone, but to the trained eye, the noun (me) was obviously in need of a strong (masculine) verb to complete me.

Trying to find Mr. I-Hope-You're-Right was hard work. I lived in a small town. My self-esteem was in a constantly flushing toilet. I trusted Mr. Vodka more than anyone else in my life—except Humphrey, but dating my dog was out of the question. It was time for something new: one-night-stands. Why, I wonder, are they called "stands?" I don't recall a whole lot of standing.

My first one-night-stand was with one guy on the research assistant team. Four of us went out on a Happy Hour blitzkrieg one night and ended up in the only gay bar in town. The two other females on our team were lesbians, something I learned that evening. I'd just thought they *really* liked each other. We girls danced together during the fast dances, but when they danced the first slow dance together, I finally caught on. I'd gone camping with them the week before. All of a sudden, the sleeping arrangements (they'd slept in the camper's one double bed) and their insistence that I go skinny-dipping with them made a lot more sense. I'd only agreed to the skinny-dip after I was woozy from the wine, and they'd told me I should be proud of my body, which I wasn't. I should have listened to my gut and not exposed my butt.

I turned to the male in our group to see if he wanted to dance, but a man in the bar was hitting on him. I was beginning to wonder if I knew *anything* about my co-workers, who I considered fairly close friends. The other team member gave me a *help-get-me-outta-here* look, so I guess it wasn't a case of mutual attraction, after all. We left the bar and left the girl friends to their public or pubic or whatever gyrations. My apartment was just around the corner. Then the guy asked me, "Do you want to do it with me?" I figured he wasn't talking about dancing and that he needed to prove he was still heterosexual, so I obliged because I was his friend and I had nothing better to do. We only did it once. After that, we pretended like we didn't remember anything about the bar or the doing it. At least I pretended.

My second and last one-night-stand was with a guy I called Boston because he was wearing a baseball cap that had *Boston* embroidered on it. I was with some friends in a bar, and he strolled in…tall, blonde, beautiful, and buff. We noticed each other immediately. He sat at our table and bought us drinks. He was friendly to everyone. But I caught him ogling me every time I glanced at him, which was a lot. Again, my apartment was conveniently nearby. Location, location, location. He left the next morning promising to call. I'm sure he called someone, just not me.

STDs were, like pubic lice, making the rounds back then; but I managed not to run into any of them. Maybe my blood was sterilized from unusually high levels of alcohol. After my encounter with Boston, my period was late by an excruciating two weeks. I thought for sure his apology that he didn't have a condom was enough good will to protect me from the gentrification of my uterus. But just as I was about to reconnect with the nice people at Planned Parenthood, my period hit with a vengeance that I can only describe as a Warning From Above. (Actually, from Below.) I didn't want my "pure as the driven snow" image to turn into "pure as the driven coal," so I stopped trying to fill the void in my life with revolving-door men.

*****

The summer of my adventures in promiscuity ended. The lesbians went their separate ways to graduate school, and the other research assistants disappeared, too. I was the only one asked to stay on the project (probably because all the others came in with hangovers every morning). I also enrolled in graduate school for a master's degree in counseling.

A life plan was forming:

1. I worked as a researcher by day while learning to become a helper of human strays.

2. I reassessed my love life and opted for celibacy as the preferred alternative to heartbreak, desperation, and unwanted pregnancy.

3. I perfected drinking alone to the point of oblivion while still appearing sober and in complete control of my life.

Counseling was perfect for me. I certainly could empathize with my future clients.

Based on my experience, people who choose counseling for a career need therapy themselves. We were future helpers in desperate need of help. One guy in the program had serious "mommy attachments" and was struggling with his sexual identity. Another guy was trying to convince mommy's boy to spend the night with him—

just to settle the issue—but he was a shameless flirt with the ladies as well. As an added bonus, he felt intellectually superior to Einstein. A particularly promiscuous woman who was angry with men, women, and small animals alike rounded out the small group with whom I studied and partied. I was an alcoholic obsessed with perfection who craved the approval of others to feel worthy of the air I breathed. And we all wanted to help other people solve *their* problems. We spent most evenings at a local bar commiserating about our graduate school workload and how screwed up *other people* were.

Also based on my experience, professors in institutions of higher learning—especially those in counseling programs—are not saner/better/smarter than the average person just because they have advanced degrees in any one of the so-called helping professions. One of our professors was a sadist. He liked to make us cry—especially the men. He must have confused graduate school with his own psychotic upbringing. Another professor was so old that we had to wake him up to continue his lecture. Sometimes we quietly left while he was napping. He looked like he needed the rest. The others tried to teach us theories about helping people:

1. Active listening. This requires a knack for well-timed nods, mm-hmmms, and "I heard you say...tell me more...."

2. Behavior modification. "Every time you want to shoot someone, take a pillow and fluff it."

3. Existentialism. "What's the meaning of life and why aren't you getting it?"

Note that I have simplified these theories for those of you without a counseling degree. None of these theories for helping people has proved perfectly effective, but we had to master them because we were, after all, getting master's degrees in that field.

My studies, my research job, taking care of my loyal-but-lonely Humphrey, and drinking heavily every day kept me busy. I almost forgot that I was lonely and lost without a man to define me. Almost. During those "gab and crab" sessions at the bar with my fellow inmates at the asylum, I always kept my eye peeled for any man who might be looking my way. He had to show an interest in me first. If he saw something noteworthy in me, then maybe I was worthy of occupying his space.

Over a year had passed since I'd ended my experiment with casual sex, potential STDs, and the possible need for prenatal vitamins. Looking for men to notice me in bars got me nowhere but frustrated, which caused me to buy and guzzle more vodka in the privacy of my apartment. Would *any* man *ever* find me interesting and attractive so *I* could find myself interesting and attractive?

I had already taken a vow of celibacy, but that was when I was drunk. Now I was serious—still a bit tipsy, but serious. I decided to give up on men. They had repeatedly given up on me. My father had disappeared before I knew him. The boy I trusted with my virginity took it with him on his way to New York City with Sheba, Exotic Hussy. The two guys I'd had one-time-sex with had disappeared as if cloaks of invisibility were on sale the morning after.

I don't like sex anyway, I told myself.

"Boyfriends, and people in general, just get in the way of my drinking," I told Humphrey. He offered me a big furry paw in what I assumed to be a gesture of agreement.

If it weren't for that lingering feeling of being damaged because I didn't have a man to love me, which meant I was unlovable no matter how much Humphrey or my mom and sisters loved me, I would have been fine being a spinster. I preferred solitude to noisy gatherings. But too much isolation can be problematic. It can turn a person into a recluse—the kind the police discover after neighbors complain about the stench coming from her apartment. So I redoubled my efforts on the things that meant most to me: completing my master's degree in counseling, taking care of Humphrey, and being the best drunken Good Girl I could be.

*****

There is a very good reason I don't plan. My plans are generally foiled before they unfold. Perhaps a week into my seriously studious/happily celibate/perfectly sloshed new life plan, I met the man of my dreams in a most unlikely place. My heretofore limp libido jumped through the roof. And I was stone-cold sober.

It figures.

When I was a little girl and reached the age of pondering certain specimens of boys as "dreamy," I always pictured "tall, dark, and handsome." I never went for The Lone Ranger. The one I longed for was Tonto, his muscular, silent, mocha, wing-man. Robert Redford? No way. Tom Selleck? All the way.

So there I was, in the college library, my nose in a book, getting references for my master's thesis, when I looked up. Sitting at a table across from me was the handsomest man I'd ever seen in real life. He was The Man I'd Dreamed Of All My Life. Seriously! He looked like a thinner version of Tom Selleck, mustache and all.

And he was staring at me, which was a very encouraging sign. I quickly looked back down at my book, but I couldn't see a word. My heart was pumping too much blood away from my rational brain.

He can't be staring at me. He's too gorgeous. He must be looking at someone behind me. Either that or I'm dreaming this. This better not be a dream!

I looked up again. He was still staring at me. I turned around to see if he was actually looking at someone behind me. There was nothing but books behind me.

My God, he's looking at me. And he's smiling.

I smiled back. Then I self-consciously went back to my research, the quality of which was greatly reduced.

Then he spoke. "Do you have the time?" His voice was deep velvet.

The time for what, Mr. You're-Too-Sexy-For-The-Library? That's what I wanted to ask him, but all I did was look at my watch and report the time. My voice wavered. I hoped it sounded erotic, not spastic.

"Thanks." He sounded like Barry White. The "Oh, Baby, Baby," was implied.

I melted a few inches into the hard plastic chair I was sitting in. Or maybe the hard plastic chair melted from the heat I was generating.

A few more minutes passed. He folded the newspaper he was reading and stood up to leave.

Alas, I thought, *all good things must come to an end.*

As he passed me, he dropped his copy of *The Daily News* next to my books and said with a devilish smile, "You might be interested in reading this."

I managed a wobbly "Thanks."

He disappeared.

I didn't turn to watch him leave. I was afraid I would break the magic spell I was under. I lingered and half-heartedly finished my research. Then I picked up my books and stood up to leave. That's when I saw the folded newspaper he'd dropped on my table.

Well, he was nice enough to leave it for me, I thought. *The least I can do is look at it like he asked.* I was a girl who did what people asked of her. Especially men.

I opened the newspaper. On the front page was a headline about Diana Spencer, the future Princess of Wales. Written next to her picture was a message: *For a good time, call Phil. (Nothing personal!!)* He had also written his telephone number there. I slapped the newspaper closed, fearing that someone would see this naughty proposition. Then, blushing from embarrassment and excitement, I tucked the paper in my notebook and went to class feeling anything but studious.

Since I'd sworn off impersonal sex, I knew better than to call him for "a good time." But there was something very personal about our encounter. I had never had that kind of physical reaction to a man before. I'd learned about pheromones in my human sexuality course, but I was skeptical. Now I was convinced. We had a pheromone connection, which meant something. But what? I wasn't sure. There was one thing I was sure about, though. There was no forgetting that man.

I had his number, but I refused to call him for fear that I would be sending him the wrong message: *Lorna is a slut.* The more accurate message, however, was *Lorna is woman who really wants to get to know you so we can fall in love and live happily ever after.* What I wanted with him *was* personal. I wanted to get to know him and make sweet passionate love with him. But what if I never saw him again? I didn't want to ruin my chance with the man that might be "the one."

I wasn't yet aware that fate was (and always had been) working with me. Before that day, I had never seen this guy, whose name, I soon learned, really was Phil. All of a sudden, I started seeing him drive by when I was walking Humphrey or walking to campus. Since I'd noticed what kind of car he drove, I started looking for that car as I walked. I noticed it parked outside a restaurant near my apartment. He worked as a bartender there, a discovery I made when I peeked in and saw him standing behind the bar one night as I was walking Humphrey. My apartment was very conveniently located. I talked my sister Tina into dropping into the restaurant for a drink with me. Thus began my brief but steamy relationship with Phil.

Pheromones notwithstanding, he wasn't interested in having a committed relationship with me, so our sizzling liaison only lasted about six weeks. I spent that time blissfully exhausted. Our break-up was rather friendly. He said it was time for him to move on and I accepted the inevitable. No one this perfect for me could have been meant for me. I didn't deserve that kind of *oo-la-la* happiness.

I wasn't surprised it didn't last. Change was a constant in my life. Phil was like Halley's Comet. He came my way for a brief moment in time and, while he was in view, he was spectacular. But he was a force of nature and needed to move on, disappearing from my view, but not my memory. I held out hope that, like Halley's Comet, he would return. The impression he made on me was one that would last forever.

But was I his Halley's Comet? I wondered that almost every day of my life for many years. He once told me, "Lorna, you're the only girl I've ever been able to talk to. I mean, really talk to." I took this as a sign that maybe I was different enough from all the other women falling at his feet that he would remember me, too. It was a thin thread, but it was enough to keep me hanging on.

I was alone again. A happily married girlfriend of mine, who was beginning to worry that I was, indeed, headed down the road to Old Maidhood, had the bright idea to play match-maker. She said she knew a guy who would be "perfect for me." My raw instincts told me, "No way!" But the Good Girl actress in me only knew one answer that was sure to please her audience.

I said, "Sure."

CHAPTER 8: MY BLIND DATE WAS MEMORABLE. BUT NOT IN THE WAY I HAD HOPED

Oh, how I wished that my sight-impaired Humphrey would have talked me out of that blind date. I would have listened to him. He obviously knew something about not seeing things clearly.

My first and only blind date was with a guy named Dick. He was a new lawyer in town. I was finishing up my master's degree while working on a federal research grant. A mutual friend knew that we were single, young professionals. She thought that matchmaking might be exciting.

Dick called to make the initial contact and the arrangements. He chose our rendezvous—a local bar that had two floors—and suggested that we meet upstairs.

Upstairs was considered the hot spot for the white-collar class of our small rural city. Unlike first-floor folks like me—commoners who liked loud rock 'n' roll, cheap drinks, pizza, and eight-ball—upstairs people preferred jazz, expensive wine, hors d'oeuvre, and the sounds of their own voices.

Dick and I met upstairs for drinks, but as soon as I saw him, I knew he was not my type. He was short, blonde, and doughy, with a face that reminded me of the cartoon character *Underdog*. He wasn't hideous, but I certainly wouldn't stand up in court and accuse him of being "handsome."

Having been raised to be painfully polite or suffer the consequences in Hell, I stayed. We introduced ourselves awkwardly, found a place to sit, and ordered our first drinks.

"I'll have a Black Russian," I told the waitress.

Dick raised his eyebrows. I couldn't tell if he was impressed or distressed. "I'll have a glass of your finest chardonnay," he said. Either he was a light-weight in the drinking department or he was trying to teach me something about white-collar etiquette. Black Russians, apparently, were not appropriate first date first drink material. But I had already pre-drunk enough vodka to get me relaxed for the date. I was also smart enough to know not to switch my poisons. Of course, I wasn't about to tell him that. I was no expert, but I had a feeling that too much honesty on a first date just about guaranteed that it would also be your last date. As it turns out, honesty would have been an excellent policy on that date.

"Tell me your life story," he said. It sounded more like a command than an invitation.

Maybe he was mixed up, I thought. Maybe he thought he was interviewing a potential client.

"Oh, there's not much to tell," I said. "I was born here. Moved around a bit, but came back and spent most of my life here. I'm currently a grad student at the local state college studying counseling. But I'm really interested in social science research. I also work on a research grant."

"Anything else?"

I wanted to ask him if I neglected to mention something in the dossier he had on me, but all I said was, "Well, um, I have this great Old English sheepdog named Humphrey who lives with me." I didn't think it was wise to fill him in on my love affair with vodka, my experiment in promiscuity, or that I'd recently met and lost the man of my dreams.

"How about you?" I decided to take over the interrogation. "I hear you're a lawyer." That's all it took to direct his attention away from me to his favorite subject: himself.

Approximately two hours and three drinks later, I had learned quite a bit about my blind date. Private schools were the *only* academic institutions worthy of merit or mention. My hometown was, in his erudite opinion, the Most Abysmal Place in the Universe and its native inhabitants were the lowly bottom-feeders in the gene pool of life. He had yet to find signs of intelligent life among those who considered themselves "locals." The only redeeming value to this hell in which he had landed a job practicing law was the opportunity for the outdoor activities, upon which he thrived and fancied himself to be of Olympic caliber: hiking, cross-country skiing, and canoeing.

He didn't simply malign my hometown and me (as one of those moronic "locals"), he did it in exquisitely, painfully, excruciatingly lengthy detail. It must have been the lawyer in him. And besides the fact that he was arrogant and prejudiced, he also smoked. In my Dream Date

Department Store, he was located in the Bargain Basement, in the bin clearly marked *Nightmares. Reduced for Quick Sale.*

During his two-hour lecture, Dick spent some time on one topic that lifted his misery. He spoke at length about a woman he'd once known. She was the love of his life who had broken his heart but still was, in his mind, the Queen of All Womankind. She was perfection. She came from some Nordic country and her name was Ingrid or Elsa, or maybe she was the Icelandic Wonder Woman. He never explained why they'd parted. Or maybe I just missed that part of the story due to boredom, three Black Russians plus my pre-drinking vodka, and/or looking around to see if any other men in the bar were looking at me.

Three drinks weren't enough to help me uncover any charm in this man, but I figured that he was equally disappointed in my less than impressive showing in his Nordic Dream Girl Replacement Search. My first blind date was one long evening with a boorish snob in a place where snobs feel right at home. I longed to excuse myself to go to the restroom and sneak downstairs to get lost in the familiar chaos where the jerks were at least familiar.

But much to my surprise, Dick must have found something of value in me. Maybe it was the sincerity of my *um hums* or the hair-trigger timing of my knowing nods and sympathetic gestures that were the sum total of my contributions to his monologue on the deficits of my hometown and its dwellers and his ruminations on the exalted and amazing Icelandic Wonder Woman.

"So," he asked offhandedly after explaining that he always started off dating with "just drinks" in case he didn't care for the woman (he hated to waste his time and money), "would you like to have dinner sometime?"

I wasn't sure I'd heard him correctly. "What?"

He sighed and did a slight eyeball roll. "Maybe three Black Russians was too much for you. I asked you to dinner."

I was stunned. When I'm stunned, I'm often surprised by what comes out of my mouth. "Sure, this was fun." I wasn't sure if I'd heard myself correctly. Had I just accepted another date with this dick?

And so began a four-month, dysfunctional relationship that had its low and lower points. Even while dating and berating me, Dick continued longing for his Icelandic Wonder Woman.

*****

One of the items that Dick had lost in his break up with the Icelandic Wonder Woman was her extraordinary, irreplaceable goose-down comforter. He loved that comforter, but it was hers, and she took it in the breakup. He missed the comforter as much as he missed the woman. He found out that I was a fairly accomplished seamstress; therefore, he decided that, together, we could make a goose-down comforter just like the one he and the Icelandic Wonder Woman had shared together. If he couldn't have the comfort of the princess herself in his life, at least he wanted the comfort of the comforter.

To him, it seemed to be a fairly simple endeavor. After I calculated the amount of fabric we'd need, he bought the goose-down feathers and high quality cotton fabric. Never leaving an important task like design up to a mere "local," he also designed the precious thing and, naturally, supervised the construction.

The Icelandic Wonder Woman's Comforter Extraordinaire had a long tube, or channel, construction, meaning there were long sections into which the feathers were stuffed. Channels keep the down fairly evenly distributed. Dick's Nordic Fantasy Comforter had the same design. Against my advice, he decided that the channels should be sewn *prior to* the feather insertion process, whereas I was sure it would be easier to insert the goose-down into what was essentially one large sack and then sew the evenly spaced channels. Because he was a man and a lawyer and much smarter than a mere woman who had worked with fabric projects for many years, we followed his plan. I brought my Singer sewing machine to his apartment and dutifully sewed five perfectly spaced channels, leaving one end open in each one so that the feathers could be inserted. Dick had special-ordered five bags of expensive goose-down feathers to be poured into the channels. What could be simpler?

On the momentous day when his Nordic Fantasy Comforter was to be completed, I was wise enough to leave Humphrey at my apartment. He was a good dog who wouldn't have gotten in the way, but we didn't want to take any chances that pricey bags of goose-down and a large, shaggy, helpful dog might collide.

The procedure was supposed to go like this:

1. Dick opens Bag 1 of goose-down while I hold open Channel 1 of the comforter.

2. Dick puts the open end of the goose-down bag in the open channel and quickly and efficiently pours the feathers in.

3. I close off the end of Channel 1 and immediately sew it closed.

4. The whole process is repeated with Bag 2 and Channel 2 until all five bags are emptied and all five channels are closed.

Here's how the procedure actually went. Dick cut Bag 1 open, which immediately released the vacuum-sealed goose-down. Instead of the feathers flowing obediently into the perfectly spaced (but rather narrow) Channel 1, it was as if an invisible incendiary device had been silently detonated by an influx of oxygen. The tiny feathers exploded into the air around us. He quickly stuffed the bag's open end into the channel, which I was holding open as wide as possible (but not nearly wide enough), but it was too late. The feathers were released into his apartment.

Fun fact. Goose-down is unconcerned with the law of gravity. The more Dick tried to stuff the bag down the narrow channel, the more tiny feathers came flying out. It was a feathery prison break. Those feathers saw more action that afternoon than they ever had on geese in flight. Within minutes, Dick's apartment looked like a snow globe turned upside down. We were unprotected travelers in a blizzard of feathers. They were everywhere—in our hair, up our noses, on our clothes, on the ceiling and walls, on the furniture, in the carpet. Everywhere but in Channel 1 of the comforter. Since Dick had more facial hair than I did, his face was soon covered with little white goose feathers. Whatever dignity he thought he had was completely obliterated. Looking at the white fluffy feathers poking out of his nose and ears, dangling off his eyebrows and eyelashes, sticking to his glasses, and clinging to every whisker on his face, I might have mistaken him for an over-sized and unusually agitated snowy owl, and not a winged beauty in its natural setting.

Dick was angry. No, he was furious. Which made the situation all the more comical. An outraged owl-man was swearing at me with a tongue covered with feathers because whatever had gone wrong, it was my fault. Besides that, I was laughing at him. I was trying not to laugh too heartily because laughing required taking in air, and the air was filled with feathers, which meant sucking feathers, which wouldn't be good for my respiratory system. I was grateful that Humphrey was safely at home so that I wouldn't have to spend days plucking feathers out of his coat. Bad enough, I found feathers in funny places on my body for days and days. In an effort to restore calm, I recommended that we halt production of the comforter and use his vacuum cleaner to round up the feathers.

Of course Dick blamed me for the goose-down catastrophe. Because I had experience with sewing, he reasoned, I should have known better *and insisted that my plan was better.* That insight came about four months into our faltering relationship, and I was ready to part ways with him. I certainly wasn't making him happy. I knew that I would never measure up to the Icelandic Wonder Woman. My chances for that had flown out the door with the goose-down feathers.

Dick needed to feel in charge and superior, no matter the circumstance. I didn't mind that in a boyfriend. Some would say—even I said it, eventually—that I was looking for a domineering man, a father figure to take control of my life because I didn't feel capable of running my own show. I let Dick take control of our relationship, so I don't know why he continually felt the need to point out my flaws. I was smart, but he was always smarter. He corrected me in public and in private. I let him. I apologized for things that were his fault. The most memorable example of his need to be in control in this destructive relationship was also the most upsetting.

*****

Unlike Phil the library hottie, with whom sex was enjoyable and no alcohol was necessary to spark my libido, I needed to be drunk to have sex with Dick. One afternoon, he got it into his head that he wanted me to perform oral sex on him and complete the act. I had done a little of that before, but I'd always refused to let anyone ejaculate into my mouth. I found it repulsive. I didn't draw many lines in my life, but that was one of them.

But Dick wouldn't settle for no. "How do you know you won't love it unless you try it?" He was trying the soft sell first.

"I just know it," I said. "I don't want to do it. I'll get sick."

"Just start, and we'll stop whenever you want to." Now he was trying to get me to walk through the door he was holding open.

"I don't know."

"Sure you do." With that, he pulled my head down to his exposed crotch.

I was sloshed enough to begin doing what he wanted me to do. I was also drunk enough to trust that he would let me stop. After all, hadn't he promised? When I was ready to stop, however, he put both hands on my head and forced me to stay down there. Man-handling me must have gotten him further aroused because without my doing anything but gagging and flailing my arms, he ejaculated in my mouth. I didn't have a chance to fight back, bite down on his penis, or do anything to defend myself. I probably wouldn't have done any of those things, anyway. My brain and body lock up in dangerous situations, leaving me with the "freeze" response we see in rhesus monkeys in danger. Unable to fight or flee, the monkeys and I "play dead" and hope the attacker loses interest. It rarely works. Just watch any nature show.

So what did I do? I started heaving as if I were going to vomit. That's when Dick let go of my head. It's a rare man that finds vomit on his privates stimulating. I ran to his bathroom. Even after I threw up, I could still taste his semen. It was salty and putrid.

"Is everything all right?" he asked with cobweb-thin concern.

"No," I said, already crying, "I don't feel good. I'm leaving." I couldn't even look at him.

"I'll call you." He didn't even get up from the couch, where he was smoking his cliché after-forcible-oral-sex cigarette. "I love you."

I closed the door. (Slamming it would have seemed rude.) Then I ran home and washed the taste and repugnance away with whatever vodka I had left in my apartment.

It wasn't until years later that I defined what he did as rape. At the time, however, I just felt stupid for believing he would let me stop, and I felt like an awful girlfriend for being so disgusted by his semen.

The relationship was over. Why would he want a girlfriend who vomited after giving him head? He could do better than me, and maybe I could do better than him. Phil was gone, but there had to be someone out there who could love me, protect me, respect me, and not try to gag me with his Johnson.

I was beginning to understand why the Icelandic Wonder Woman had disappeared without a trace. She probably joined the Federal Witness Protection Program to get away from him. I was ready to vanish, too. But how?

Until then, every boyfriend had left me. I had lots of practice at being dumped; but none at being the dumper. I needed a plan. I decided deceit would work and made up excuses every time he called, hoping that he would eventually get the hint. I had headaches. My grandmother had just died. Twice. I thought I had an STD.

But Dick was no fool. He knew what I was up to. Dick could not stand to lose anything. I believe the Icelandic Wonder Woman had ended their relationship, and it was her power that made her so perfect (i.e., unattainable) in his mind. Whether Dick was talking about comforters or women (they were no doubt all the same to him), the one that got away was the one he coveted most. The one he had in front of him was trivial. In Dick's world (and there was no other), *he* would end the relationship or dispense with the object, not the other way around. For him, the upper hand was the only hand.

He wasn't ready to end his relationship with me, feather and oral sex debacles notwithstanding. It made no sense to me.

*****

One blustery spring day, he telephoned and he begged me to go canoeing with him. (Canoeing was one of his many self-proclaimed, outdoor Olympic-caliber accomplishments.) For several weeks following the gag and vomit incident, I had repeatedly but politely declined other outings or dinner dates, even though I felt guilty about making up false excuses. This new invitation was particularly objectionable, as I was leery of water sports in general and that particular water sportsman in equal proportion. I adamantly refused. But hanging up on him never occurred to me. He persisted. Exhausted, I finally gave in when he said he felt he needed to "make things right between us."

I was a sucker for making things right. Great in appeasement situations, I was pathetic in emergency situations. I still am.

Dick was bright. I have to give him that. I thought that we would go canoeing in one of the many small but scenic mountain lakes or ponds, which would be cold but calm and fairly shallow. But no. He took me out in the largest lake in the area, one that can grow waves up to six feet high and be very unpredictable because of its depth and size. Even on warm summer days, that lake can be intimidating to boaters in small craft. The lake is moody. Rarely do even the heartiest of nautical fools find themselves tempted by its cold, gray, menacing waters until, say, midsummer.

Dick knew I didn't like being in the open water in anything smaller than a forty-foot cabin cruiser. I am not a great swimmer. I've always been a klutz when it comes to anything that can rock, tilt, tip, or roll. Canoeing with anyone at any time anywhere becomes a gigantic act of courage on my part.

We and our yellow canoe "put in" in a quiet little river that fed into the lake. Although Dick assured me we wouldn't go very far, I should have known better than to trust him. We had the popular launching spot all to ourselves.

"Why isn't there anyone else here?" I asked.

Without answering, he assured me that his trusty canoe was up for bigger challenges than this or any lake could conjure up, that his masterful control of his vessel was an example of his pure genius.

I was not comforted by his self-confidence. "That's great," I said, "but why isn't there anyone else here?"

"Trust me. Get in. You'll love it." *Where had I heard that before?*

Brilliant summation. Case closed. He did not wait for the jury to come back with a verdict. We were on our way.

Getting into that canoe with that man was bad judgment. But I did it anyway. What possessed me? The easy answer is vodka. The harder to face answer is my low opinion of myself at that time, which is why booze and men were so central to my life. I felt empty and was willing to let self-destructive influences define me just to feel real. Well, I felt something very real that day.

The water was icy. I felt the breeze on the river, but the current was manageable. Then the river opened up into the broad lake. Dick kept paddling, assuring me that the view would be stunning "just a little farther out." With each stroke of the paddle, the canoe bobbled a bit more. The breeze became a blustery wind. The manageable current turned into unwieldy swells that became whitecaps splashing into our canoe.

Dick was absolutely right about one thing: the view was stunning. My life passing before my eyes was the most stunning thing I'd seen in a long time.

As the waves began tossing us more and more ferociously, we moved from sitting on the benches of the canoe to kneeling on the floor of that yellow death trap for maximum stability. Mr. Olympic-Caliber Canoeist stayed calm. He kept paddling farther into the open lake, assuring me of his nautical prowess. Suddenly deciding that there might indeed be a God, I began praying.

When we were far enough out for me to be totally panic-stricken, Dick finally stopped paddling. Waves were crashing into the side of the canoe. I'm sure I was a vision of loveliness. My fingers were claws, digging into the edges of the boat when they weren't cupped and trying to bail the water splashing into the canoe. My hair was sticking out in all directions and rigid from the sprays of icy water. My hysterical eyes were searching the heavens for either an angel or a Coast Guard helicopter to rescue me, then looking down at the floor of that swamped, yellow, piece-of-shit canoe that I was sure was going to be my sarcophagus.

How could this be happening to me? The news outlets occasionally ran stories about imbeciles whose cause of death was stupidity. Was I going to be the next imbecile on the news because I couldn't say no to a madman with a canoe and ex-girlfriend obsession?

As I was composing my obituary, Dick's voice broke through the din of wind and waves. "Lorna," he was saying, "it seems like you've been drifting away from me. I don't want to lose you. Will you marry me?"

All I could do was look at him. My face was as frozen as the rest of me. *Marry him?* The "until death do us part" seemed imminent. The rest of the deal was unthinkable. The only chance he had of spending eternity with me was at the bottom of that damn lake.

If I ever make it back to shore, I said to myself, *I never want to see Dick or his ugly yellow canoe again.* But I was facing a pretty serious dilemma. "Yes, I'll marry you" equaled safety. He wouldn't drown his fiancée, would he? "No, I won't marry you" equaled possible death. But drowning seemed preferable to becoming Mrs. Pompous Ass. I was figuratively between a rock and a hard place, but I would have given anything to be *literally* between any rock and any hard place because that would have meant that I would have been on dry land and could have done the mature thing: spit in his face and run.

I was Dick's seafaring, marriage proposal hostage. If that was his approach to wooing, it is no wonder the Icelandic Wonder Woman had dropped this guy and ran away with her precious comforter.

I was stunned, panicky, mortified, cold, desperate, ashamed, and anxious about who would take care of Humphrey after I drowned, so a bit of awkward silence wavered between us as I processed the proposal, my options, and the waves buffeting the canoe.

I finally replied. I had to yell to be heard over the howling of the wind and crashing of the waves. "Dick, this is a big decision, can you give me some time to think it over?"

It was pure genius on my part. I knew that my answer was an emphatic *No way in hell, Buster*, proclaimed in bright, blinking neon lights, but I wasn't about to tell him that in the middle of Death Lake. No, I was going to wait until I was back on *terra firma* to break the news to him.

"How much time do you need?" he bellowed back.

As if any girl in her right mind would leap up out of the water in the bottom of the canoe (assuming her frozen limbs would move) and hug him and thank him for picking her. He failed to calculate that any girl in her right mind wouldn't be out in the middle of a stormy lake in a canoe with a self-absorbed madman.

"A couple of days should be enough," I shouted back.

With a self-satisfied nod and smile as broad as his ego, he accepted my answer. He turned the canoe around, and we managed to return to shore. As soon as I stepped onto solid land, the overwhelming fear that had gripped me was replaced with righteous rage. *How dare he endanger our lives? How could I have been so stupid as to ignore my screaming intuition and agree to go out on the lake with him?* Humphrey could have been orphaned, and for what—his ego and my lack of self-esteem?

I finally admitted it: Dick was a control freak. In order to dominate me, he had to make me feel worthless and exploit my vulnerabilities. His proposal wasn't about love; it was about intimidation and control. But I'd foiled him. Pretty smart for a local girl. Why didn't I see him before for what he was? Why didn't I admit that he was a controlling jerk who felt he had to put me down to lift himself up because I was too good for him? Near-death experiences have a way of bringing clarity to one.

A couple of days later, as promised, I gave Dick my answer. I told him I would not marry him. My new self-confidence must have been apparent because he finally accepted something I had to say, though he couldn't resist telling me that I was making the biggest mistake of my life. But by now we both knew that that ship—and it was yellow—had already sailed.

When it was clear that it was over between us, he asked if he could visit Humphrey from time to time. Was it Humphrey he really wanted all along?

"Sure," I said.

CHAPTER 9: IT ALL BEGAN WITH THE DOGS

I was a dog person at heart. And dogs loved me without condition. I should have known to play to my strengths, but that would have made my life just too simple.

As a sociologist and twenty-five year-old single female, I was acutely aware of the cultural norms of my time regarding the course of life, how it was supposed to progress, and how *I wasn't progressing.* We were in the 1980s now, and women had more than the right to vote, wear pantsuits to work, and earn sixty cents for every dollar a man made. They had a little latitude to get an education and start a career. At the same time, women were told they had better have a sure-bet future husband on their arms well before middle age (thirty) came knocking.

I needed to find a stable, lasting relationship, preferably with a man I loved and who loved me. My wish list wasn't too stringent. I wanted my husband to be tall, dark, handsome, brave, willing to protect and defend me, and able to make important decisions for me. He also had to adore me and lavish attention on me at all times. I wanted to be The Center Of His Universe. In return, I would be what I had always been to anyone who loved and noticed me: the best version of what he wanted me to be. I would be his Good Girl, Wife, Lover, Friend…well, fill in the blank.

While working for the college as a statistical analysis research consultant, I met a young man who was working in the office that supplied clerical support to the project. On the surface, he was not my type. He was lanky and bookish. But he was also friendly and helpful. His name was Victor, and he was interested in me, which was my number-one requirement in a potential mate. As it happened, he was also a dog-lover, and our first non-office supply conversation was about his beloved German shepherd, which that had just died. I told him about my darling (and still living) Humphrey.

How could I not like a guy who loved dogs and was interested in me?

I made a point to need pencils or paper clips when I knew he was working, just so I could chat with him. He was always happy to see me and made me feel special by asking about me. He was a smooth talker. Eventually I looked past his glasses and skinny build and saw the person inside. Smart and ambitious, Victor was a man with a clear plan (to become a millionaire) and was self-assured enough to tell me about it. I was attracted to his air of self-confidence and the fact that a guy like that wanted to be with me.

We went to a hockey game on our first date. I was the third person he asked. (Two male friends were busy.) If that was an omen, my vision was blurred by my excitement about seeing a semi-pro hockey game. Hockey was the only sport I understood besides bowling and drunken flirting. The venue was a two-hour drive away, so he said we would have a picnic *en route*, which he told me meant "on the way," which I already knew but pretended I didn't to make him feel more impressive. I knew a lot about how to make men like me. I packed a lettuce sandwich, a can of Fresca, and a bag of popcorn for myself. He brought a wicker picnic basket filled with a smorgasbord of soft drinks, meats, breads, salads, and desserts to share. I tucked my paper bag of solo provisions under the seat and hoped he didn't notice. I guess he knew a thing or two about how to impress a date, too.

I pre-drank enough vodka to loosen me up for any awkward first-date banter. Silly me. He talked the whole time about the brilliance of Reaganomics. Listening took very little energy and required hardly any acting sober skills. Remembering the economics lesson was a bit more challenging, though. I still don't get the logic of Reaganomics, and I'm pretty sure I'm not alone in that camp.

Here's what I remember from the four-hour round-trip car ride/lecture:

1. He was a talkative, conservative, business/economics major who seemed to know a lot about every topic he himself brought up.

2. He didn't seem very interested in topics I brought up. At least we didn't spend any time talking about my topics.

3. His family was well-enough-to-do Methodist, which meant they had climbed to their upper rung on the social ladder through hard work.

4. He didn't ask me about my background. I guess my foreground (i.e., the cleavage) was sufficiently interesting.

5. He was a Freemason, which, from what I could tell, is a secretive, misogynistic cult masquerading as a community-minded organization. I could have been wrong, but learning more about that clandestine group meant I would have to be killed because I was a woman.

6. He thought I was odd (not adventuresome) to go so far away with a guy whose last name I didn't know. (I worked with his mother, so I finally did learn his last name.)

7. He was generous. The picnic provisions could have fed a family of four.

8. He knew zilch about hockey. That's where I got to shine. I explained "icing" and "off sides" to him. But Victor said he didn't care much for hockey, so my expertise was wasted on him.

9. He couldn't tell I was inebriated, which made him like every other person in my life.

10. He wouldn't share my popcorn because it was too salty. That, he said, was because he had hypertension. I didn't even know people in their twenties could get hypertension. What was he so hyperly tense about?

11. He kissed me on the cheek at the end of the date and didn't try getting to second, third, or home base. Maybe he was unfamiliar with baseball, too.

Was he a skinny, intellectual, talkative, Type A gentleman, or just a guy who liked dogs and noticed me, a Type B gal—blonde, blue-eyed, buxom, and brainy? After I got home, I went up to my apartment, glugged some vodka, and took Humphrey for a night-time walk, wondering why Victor was the only man I had dated who didn't immediately try to have sex with me. The whole date was odd but refreshing—kind of like Fresca or Dr. Pepper.

My plan to slip into the cultural expectations for a female of my advancing age wasn't looking good. I was supposed to be able to "have it all"—every magazine said so. Young women should be attentive wives (*wink, wink*), nurturing mothers, impressive career go-getters, tireless volunteers, gourmet chefs, and be able to upholster the living-room furniture in their spare time.

I could do that! Well, I could be an impressive career go-getter and, with the help of my old pal, Mr. Vodka, perform just fine in the "attentive wife" department. The other parts of "having it all" didn't suit me very well—especially without a husband.

Nurturing Mother? I never wanted children. My politically correct reason was because it was socially irresponsible to bring an innocent child into such a screwed-up world. The real reason? I trusted myself more with dogs than with children. I had the maternal instincts of a giant water bug, which sometimes eats its young. I never adopted a puppy because I was afraid I would traumatize it. Small, dependent creatures of any kind were best left to those who wanted them and would know what to do in an emergency, like if it needed a bath. I had a full-blown case of pedophobia (fear of children, which, I suppose, is a lot better than pedophilia).

Gourmet Chef? Once I discovered drinking, food was no longer a priority. I could eat the same thing (lettuce sandwiches) for months and not get bored. I was getting my calories and my satisfaction from vodka, which is made from potatoes, which are a great source of potassium. I could cook two special meals: meatloaf and a chicken/rice combo with some kind of cream soup over it. But cooking was rarely a good idea for me. All that alcohol and a large appliance that can explode should someone not pay close attention to the burners due to, say, passing out, was a recipe for disaster.

Volunteer and Home DYI Extraordinaire? That was just crazy talk. Being a show-stopper at work and charming on dates before passing out was exhausting. So was pretending to be sober. This girl needed her beauty sleep. I didn't have time for extracurricular activities beyond taking care of Humphrey.

Much to my surprise, Victor called and asked me out on another date. That time, I wasn't third on his list. I was first. We started dating regularly.

I was so good at pretending to be sober and that Victor probably figured he'd found a pretty special gal. I wasn't the Perfect Girl anymore, though. He found plenty of "rough edges" on me, which he obligingly helped buff away with constant and public "coaching" (i.e., criticism). His mother had gone to finishing school, but my mom had only finished high school, so I became *Eliza Doolittle* to his *Henry Higgins*. He didn't force me to go through his Lorna-Improvement Plan; I let him push and pull me. I knew I was in need of fixing, and he seemed to know how to fix me.

It was a match made in Purgatory.

As I saw it at the time, every correction was an act of love. He cared enough about me to fix me. He told me to crunch raw carrots more quietly. He said my clothing was "inappropriate." I was thrilled. He cared *that much.* He wanted me to be a better person in public because he wanted to be in the public eye with me. But first I had to change and become the person he knew I should and could be. If that wasn't love, what was? Having grown up with only a mom, how was I supposed to know what real romantic love looked or felt like? I had only my common sense to rely on, and that was like asking a tone-deaf person to hum a few bars of a song so you can hear the tune.

I did what came naturally. Believing Victor's criticisms of me were acts of love and my act of love was to change for him, I worked hard to please him. True to form, I was successful.

*****

During the short time we had been dating—about six months—I was accepted into a Ph.D. program clear across the country. Victor was happy for me but sad for "us." He wasn't willing to move to California because that was not part of his five-, ten-, or twenty-year plans. And a long-distance relationship was out of the question. (I suppose I wasn't worth the toll calls.)

As luck for "us" would have it, his idol, Ronald Regan, was elected President, and he immediately cut frivolous educational programs like the Ph.D. in gerontology I was going to get. The grant/scholarship deal I had worked out at the University of Southern California disappeared. Since I couldn't afford tuition and housing without assistance from Uncle Ronald, I stayed put in New York. Reaganomics trickled down all over me.

On Halloween night, 1982, Victor asked me to marry him.

But there were strings attached. Four thoughts entered my mind when he proposed:

1. That was my third marriage proposal. The first had been in fifth grade, but the boy's height suggested that he'd failed a grade or two. Big Boy meant business when he picked me for his bride, though. He chased me around the playground and tried to kick me. When he cornered me between some shrubs and the bus garage, he announced in a husky, breathy voice, "I'm going to marry you." Looking back, I guess it was more of a marriage command than a proposal, and my pouty silence, narrowed eyes, and crossed arms kind of discouraged him. The issue of our future nuptials never came up again, but he chased and kicked at me until sixth grade. I was a hard girl to get over and an easy one to corner. My second marriage proposal, of course, had been Dick's death-trap-canoe-proposal. Victor's proposal was civilized, on solid ground, and didn't involve any threat of bodily harm. I took that as definite sign of improvement.

2. Victor liked dogs, which meant he must have a good heart. He loved Humphrey. Unlike the numerous flaws he found in me, he found very few faults with my Old English sheepdog. If he loved Humphrey, I reasoned, he must love me because Humphrey loved me, so I should love him. Well, it made sense at the time.

3. My options were limited. It's not that I minded being a single alcoholic with no future, but how

long can that party last? I had a man with a plan willing to tote me along on his journey toward greatness. His goal was to become a millionaire. He always planned in five-year increments. Maybe I could use a little planning in my life and he was willing to plan my life as well as his.

4. I loved him because he loved me enough to want to make me a better person.

I was still a bit high from the bottle of wine we'd shared and the after-dinner drinks, but all these thoughts flitted out of my head quickly enough for me to give Victor an enthusiastic "Yes! I'll marry you!"

Victor soon announced the conditions I had to agree to before we would seal the deal:

1. I must bear him four children—two boys and two girls. I negotiated him down to one boy and one girl when I told him he could bring the four children to visit me on Sundays in the sanitarium when I was properly sedated. The thought of even two children scared me. I wanted him to forget about this excessive number of desired offspring. Alternatively, I could always hope that my uterus would get damaged in a freak bicycling accident.

2. I must be willing to move to a city where he could make his fame and fortune. The thought that he wasn't willing to move for me, but that I had to move for him, didn't strike me as unfair at the time. After all, his plan to become a millionaire seemed so much more realistic than my plan to earn a doctorate. I was fine with moving as long as our new home allowed pets and had liquor stores nearby.

3. I was, as a sign of my commitment to him, to take his last name. I wanted to keep my maiden name. He was firm. He wanted his surname to live on so that all future property transfers would be clear. In case of a war between landowners, there would be no mistaking that his lineage ruled over the kingdom. Wait— primogeniture pretty died out some centuries ago. Well, that didn't matter to Victor. He still wanted me to give up my name. Since I didn't want to start our married life with him resenting or doubting my commitment to him, I agreed to change my name.

4. I had to adopt Methodism as my religion and raise our children as good Christian soldiers. I had to go to religion classes and endure lectures by a minister about God, marriage, and forever. That minister is divorced now.

5. I had to learn to play bridge and stop playing strip poker. "Respectable" people who play cards in groups would rather bid their hands than drop their drawers. (At least that's what he implied.)

There were no prenuptial agreements in those days, at least none that I ever heard of. My word was good enough for him. He trusted me. I didn't tell him I was an alcoholic, but, to be fair, I considered myself to be only a heavy, closet drinker at the time, something hardly worth mentioning.

Excited that I was finally on track to be a grown-up, I shared the happy news with my family. "Happy," it seemed, was in the ear of the listener. My mom hugged me and said, "I hope you will be very happy, Lorna. You deserve the best."

But my sisters were mortified. "You can't," one exclaimed. "He's not your type," the other added. "He's not good enough for you. We don't like him." They added other, equally supportive comments. I thought they were just being overprotective of their middle sister, who, I had to admit (and based on my previous boyfriend misadventures), could enter a beauty contest and get the consolation prize of *Miss Guided*. They tried to talk me out of it, but I was firm in my commitment to Victor.

"Do you love him?" Lisa asked.

"Of course," I answered after only a slight pause.

"Why?" She would have made a great prosecutor if only she liked confronting someone besides her sisters.

After searching my heart for a bit longer than was comfortable for either of us, I finally replied, "Because he loves me."

"Well, that's just stupid."

I had no comeback for that. No one had ever called me stupid. I knew I should explore the topic further, but an overwhelming thirst for the bottle hidden in my bedroom closet suddenly gripped my throat and my heart. I just shrugged and walked away. I think Lisa started to cry.

My sisters eventually accepted the news of my betrothal and even agreed to be part of the wedding party. Lisa was my maid of honor and Tina was a bridesmaid. I guess they wanted to go down with the ship rather than watch her sink from a distance.

Victor and I were officially engaged on Christmas Eve, 1982. The wedding was set just before my twenty-sixth birthday. I was going to avoid Old Maidhood.

*****

"How did I get myself into this?" I asked Humphrey. He didn't have a good answer. Neither did I.

But I felt a growing sense of doubt weighing me down. Could I plan something as elaborate as a wedding? I'd never even planned a birthday party before. Being an intelligent and organized person who, so far, had excelled at everything I attempted to do (with the exception of anything involving physical agility and leadership dilemmas, predicaments, quandaries, or chaos), I knew that, theoretically, I was *capable* of planning a wedding. But I had a sinking feeling that I was in the deep end of an unfamiliar pool with weights rather than floaties around my arms.

Regardless of the all the checklists and do-it-yourself tips on the wedding of your dreams in *Brides* magazine, I needed a real live person to help me plan my wedding. That person had to have social savvy. She had to know about seating arrangements and color schemes. My family was as socially isolated as fringe sectors of society like the Amish, nudists, or the cast of *Survivors*. I knew I had to seek outside help to make sure my wedding and reception didn't make newspaper headlines because of some freakish disaster. I couldn't help but imagine the headlines: *Mass electrocution at wedding reception: electric guitar, extension cord and dewy cow pasture venue blamed.*

I had never asked for help in my high school or college years. I'd earned all those A's on my own. Every job I got was one that I was selected for because of my qualifications. I'd kept those jobs because of the quality of my work and my generally chipper demeanor. Even my job as charwoman for the apartment building I'd lived in as a freshman had been given to me for my unique qualification. (I was a girl the slumlord lusted after.)

It wasn't easy, but I began planning my wedding with help. First I turned to *Brides* magazine. It was helpful but discouraging. That is, the lists and tips were helpful, but the pictures and expectations they presented were for a wedding fit for Princess Diana. That was discouraging, even though I wanted to be Princess Di. Victor's family was situated much higher on the social ladder than my family was, so I was persuaded (by the magazine) to shoot for a wedding on the opulent side of affordable. "You only get married once, right?" I asked Humphrey. "You might just as well have the best wedding you can conjure up," He didn't disagree mostly because he was a very agreeable dog.

I also received help and advice from Victor's mother (who had gone to finishing school and was, thus, the only finished person I knew), my mom and sisters when they could or would help, and Victor himself, although by that time he was living in Washington, D.C., whereas I was still in New York. He was also very busy implementing his millionaire plan by starting from the bottom of a very steep ladder at a financial institution. I don't know how much my drinking helped in the actual planning of the wedding, but it sure helped get me through the process.

I had no idea what being a wife was all about, and the work of planning my semi-elaborate wedding kept my mind off what I was getting myself into. I was, in fact, so busy trying to figure out the details of the ceremony and the reception that I didn't have time to contemplate life after the wedding. Making my own wedding dress was a matter of survival. That satin and lace gown was the most complicated sewing project I'd ever tackled. It kept me focused on being a *bride,* not a *wife*. I had no satisfactory role models for wife, so imagining myself as one was nearly impossible. Mom never remarried, and my grandmothers behaved as if they lived with annoying uncles. All I had were TV, movie, or literary wives from whom to take my cues. I suspected they were pretty much invented for entertainment, not educational, value.

Before you can get a driver's license, you have to take classes and a test. Why don't they require the same for marriage licenses?

Since Victor had left town to find work in Washington, D.C., the place that would be our new home after the wedding, I was in charge of most of the decisions, based, of course, on his mother's approval. Since she was the expert on social protocol, I was grateful that she was a willing, involved, and free wedding planner. Between working full time, planning the wedding, and drinking myself into sweet oblivion each evening, I was a busy bride-to-be.

While this may seem obvious to most people, I learned that planning a wedding while drunk is challenging. I believed my drinking was medicinal. It was necessary to get me through the stresses of daily living. Victor called every night to check on the plans. I told him what his mother had decided, he said to ignore his mother. I drank and ignored the whole thing when I could. I was an adult and still felt like a middle child. As a result of not keeping score in the mother-son tug-of-war I was getting in the middle of, plus my therapeutic inebriation, some critical guests didn't get invitations, a few people weren't assigned seats at the reception, and the photographer was never told that we'd changed the reception venue. (He had to call all the local restaurants until he found our reception, already in full swing.) These may seem like minor snafus in the grand scheme of events, but each one was cause of great consternation with Victor and his mother, for whom any social gaffe at all was a black mark in the Big Social Registry in the Sky.

I've noticed that things in life seem to go their own way whether I plan them or not. My wedding was no different. *Almost* everything about the wedding went as planned. Invitations were sent out on time, gift registries were registered, my dress turned out beautifully and actually fit, the wedding party was properly attired, the buffet at the reception was delicious, the band played great songs, and all the other minutiae that make up a wedding and reception got done.

But some things went their own way.

Snafu #1: I chose an October wedding because I prefer cool and gray weather to hot and sunny. My wedding day was hazy and humid with temperatures cresting in the mid-80s. In our northern climate, this was rare, especially when no one was concerned about holes in the ozone layer from all the hair spray released in that decade. All of the women in my wedding party were wearing, at my selection, hunter-green velvet skirts with long-sleeved, fitted, heavy silk, ecru-colored tops. The only exception was my maid of honor, Lisa, who crocheted her top out of ecru-colored wool. By the time the dancing started at the reception, these women were two dress sizes smaller from perspiring. The humidity also wreaked havoc with many a hair style. Some hairdos flattened until they resembled well-trod grass, while others poofed out to chaotic cotton candy. And the women's hair fared no better.

Snafu #2: The wedding was at high noon. I didn't want to fret and fuss for a whole day in anticipation of an afternoon wedding. Noon meant that everyone had to be up and ready for action fairly early because we had to look our wedding best for the photographer. Trying to be helpful, my mom mistakenly ironed my sister's velvet skirt, which resulted in several perfect imprints of her iron on the front of her tailored skirt.

Mom called me in a panic. "Lorna, I am so sorry! I have ruined your wedding."

Since my mom was not prone to histrionics, I was worried that my sisters had gotten to her and they'd put a hit out on Victor.

"Mom," I said, "calm down. What happened?" I was unusually calm while sober in the face of an unknown potential calamity.

She explained about her unintentional iron decoupage experiment.

"Don't worry," I said. "Remember the skirt that the seamstress made by mistake? It's the wrong style, but I don't think anyone will notice."

Who was this level-headed Lorna and where had she been all my life? I had bought, at great expense to me, a whole bolt of the hunter green velvet fabric and picked a pattern with several skirt variations. Lisa had wanted the slim-line version. Since she was the maid of honor, I'd let her pick the style she wanted, even though it was different from the fuller version I wanted for the rest of my attendants. The seamstress had erroneously made Tina's skirt from the slim-line pattern, in effect giving Tina two skirts, since I insisted the seamstress make Tina's skirt match the others. That was the happiest mistake of the wedding according to my mom, who vowed never to iron velvet (or anything) again.

I had vowed to myself not to drink the day before my wedding, and not to drink until we were officially married. If only Victor had known how much a sign of love and commitment that was on my part, he would have been impressed. I sure was. Not drinking for all that time brought me a few revelations:

1. My head was clear, so time slowed down. What did people do with all this extra time?

2. I got very nervous about the sharp turn my life was about to take. Not because of who I was marrying (I believed that Victor was the guy for me), but because I was going to be a wife, move to Washington, D.C., and start a new job all at

once. Moving wasn't as much of an issue as was the fact that I was moving away from my family. We were a team—a group, like the Beatles, and I was breaking up the band.

3. Sobriety for a day and a half was a breeze. I could do anything with a time frame around it. When I was a teenager I had gone on mini-hunger strikes, only drinking water for three days in a row. That was my thin-Lorna maintenance plan. As long as there was a definite end in sight, I could do it. I stopped drinking before my wedding and didn't have a single craving or any physical blip. At that time, I was swigging about a liter of vodka a day— straight from the two-liter bottle always ready in my bedroom closet. In my clear-headedness, I had two questions that probably should have disturbed me, but didn't. *What is all this booze doing to my liver?* Oh, what the heck, everyone dies of something. And *How am I going to buy, hide, and drink my vodka once I'm married and living in a small apartment?* Not once did I wonder if I had a drinking problem or if I should tell Victor about how much I really drank. To him I looked like a girl who had one cocktail and drank a little wine with dinner.

In addition to the pocket watch that had belonged to my father and that I had had specially engraved with "Always and forever, 10/1/83, Love, Lorna," getting married sober was my wedding gift to Victor. I thought I was being very generous.

Standing at the back of the church at high noon in my beautiful dress, I suddenly asked myself, *What am I doing here?* Damn that sober head of mine! An image of me just walking away from the church and hitching a ride home in my white satin and lace dress flashed through my mind just as the organ began playing the Wedding March. Did you ever notice how slow and dirge-like it sounds? Maybe it was just me.

"Too late," I whispered to my bouquet. I had always trusted that things would work out just fine for me. So far, they had. Why should this be any different? Victor seemed to love me, especially the "me" he wanted me to be. I loved a man with vision, especially one who had a vision for me since I didn't have one. Neither of us knew each other or what we were getting ourselves into, but we were both people who stuck to our commitments. We knew that about each other. Maybe...hopefully...that was enough. And we both loved dogs.

I took a deep breath and stepped...paused...stepped...paused...stepped toward my future, anticipating the cork pop on the first bottle of cold champagne.

CHAPTER 10: WHO TOOK THE HONEY OUT OF MY HONEYMOON?

Mom and I were both feeling pretty stressed before the wedding...for different reasons. But when the photographer told us to smile, we obeyed. I did a lot of obeying that day.

We were married at noon on Saturday, October, 1, 1983. As weddings go, Methodist ceremonies are short because there are only music, vows, music, readings, vows, and music. The one special song I selected, "The Promise," made me sob in the middle of the ceremony. Victor handed me his handkerchief, a most gallant gesture that made me wonder why I ever wondered about getting married. Here was a man who would look after me. I felt nothing but pure love for him at that moment.

During the interminable receiving line at the church, he stood tall and proud—and a bit underweight—next to his flushed and buxom bride. Going through the motions of either knowing everyone or being "so delighted" to meet them, I was outwardly gracious and inwardly wishing I could ditch my uncomfortable shoes and heavy dress and sneak away to drink something strong enough to help me relax my tense smile muscles.

The first bottle of champagne was waiting for us in the vintage car Victor had arranged to putt-putt us off to our reception. I was so grateful that he'd had such a romantic forethought that I decided then and there that I loved him without reservation. I had indeed made the right choice for my life partner. The champagne bottle was empty well before we got to our destination. I'm sure I drank most of it. It was hot in that old car. I was very thirsty.

The reception went well. Cases of champagne were consumed that afternoon, and that was just by me. While Victor was doing what he did so well—being the gentlemanly host—I was acting like a member of the royal family: downing champagne and waving to people from my seat.

When the band leader introduced us, he not only mispronounced Victor's name but he got our last name wrong, too. Victor was not amused, but I was. I also suggested that we pay the band with a check signed with the mistaken name.

As would be the case in many situations in our marriage, I became the voice of moderation. My bridegroom finally saw the humor in the band leader's mistake and allowed himself to have a good time. We threw our shoes to the side of the room and danced with abandon. The official photographs had already been taken, so no one cared about appearances. At least I didn't.

Appearance always mattered to Victor's mom, now my mother-in-law. She kept her shoes on.

Two other parties had been planned for after the reception. I must have known about them, but they weren't foremost in my mind during the days preceding the nuptials. Tina hosted a small, informal gathering for the few friends and relatives on my side who came from out of town. One of them was my childhood friend, Skinny May, and her family. I really wanted to spend some time with them since there was no time at the reception. My new in-laws hosted a swanky affair at their large country home and invited a veritable who's who of local Somebodies, plus quite possibly every relative still living. Apparently there was no room at that party, however, for my family and my one group of friends. Victor wanted to spend every moment at his parents' gala event because that was the more "happening" place with food and drinks galore and because he wasn't in any mood to mingle with the enemies, who were my sisters.

Nevertheless, ever the gentleman, he obliged me and we went to Tina's house first. After about half an hour, he suggested we leave because his parents had people at his house waiting for us. I wanted to stay longer. We stayed about fifteen minutes longer. Since I'm a person not prone to confrontation unless unreasonably provoked while inebriated, I waited until we were in the car to mention to my bridegroom that Skinny May and her family had come all the way from Connecticut for our wedding and I wanted to spend more than forty-five minutes with them. Victor reminded me how selfish I was because his parents had gone to a lot of trouble and expense to throw a party we were impolitely missing.

Thus began our first fight as husband and wife. By fight, I mean I sniffled and looked out the window as he drove in stony, cock-sure silence. The drive took about forty minutes. Forty minutes is a long time to sniffle and stare out of the side window. I arrived at the swanky party with a stiff neck.

His parent's house looked like they were having the county's largest yard sale. Cars lined the road as far as the eye could see. Compared to the few people in Tina's living room, it was gigantic.

I turned to Victor. "I'm sorry," I said. "I didn't realize this was such a big thing."

"I told you they went to a lot of trouble," he said.

"Can we just forget about this?" I reached for his hand.

He let me hold it. Finally he squeezed back. "Okay," he said. "Let's not keep them waiting any longer."

We spent the rest of the evening—until midnight—at that party. I barely saw Victor. As the center of attention, he was in his glory talking and laughing with his relatives and his old family friends. I was happy that there were a few people I knew and enough chaos that the couple of extra public drinks I drank weren't noticed. The effects of the champagne had long worn off.

We spent our wedding night at my apartment, too exhausted to do anything but sleep.

*****

While we both would have loved to have a real honeymoon, with romance and travel and extravagant souvenir-buying in some exotic place like Italy, Hawaii, or the Poconos, there were a few problems that prevented us from enjoying a true, clichéd *Brides* magazine honeymoon:

We were young and poor. Even though my mom surprised us with an envelope full of cash to pay for the reception—something we had budgeted to pay for ourselves—we still had very little money with which to start our new life. We agreed that we would postpone our honeymoon until we could afford a "real" one.

We were moving to Washington, D.C., a very expensive city, three days after the wedding. Victor was fairly new to his job and could only get a few days off for the wedding. I started my new job the Wednesday after we were married, leaving us three days to pack and move Humphrey and me down to our new home. When I interviewed for the job several months prior, they wanted me to start as soon as possible. I didn't want to lose the job, so I suggested a date four days after my wedding, and they agreed. At the time of the interview, I was proud of my negotiating skills, but now, gawking at all the stuff in my apartment that I still needed to pack, I questioned my sanity. What was I thinking? Perhaps the better question was in this case and many more to come, Why wasn't I thinking?

We couldn't afford to hire movers. What we could afford was a U-Haul and a trailer hitch for my little Subaru sedan. We thus spent our first day of married life working as movers.

Late Sunday morning, the day after our wedding, Victor, Humphrey and I drove into the mountains to spend one night at his family's isolated, rustic camp. "Rustic" is realtor-speak for no insulation, no electricity, and no plumbing. It was, basically, a hard tent.

Humphrey wasn't the only non-human in our one-night honeymoon shack. A bat joined us for most of the evening. Our hurried before-the-bat-bites-our-naked-butts sex was more obligatory than celebratory.

I was happy to get back to my apartment to pack up the U-Haul. I've never enjoyed packing because it signals leaving the familiar and the comfortable behind. Moving to a city ten hours from home was especially difficult for me because I was leaving behind my mother and sisters. As a child, I had sometimes feared they would abandon me like my father had. But now, I said to myself, now I am the one deserting them. I wiped the tears from my eyes, which seriously hampered my efforts to label boxes accurately and legibly.

I packed my vodka last and made sure to put it in a convenient place for easy access during the trip to my new home.

*****

Humphrey, never a tranquil traveler, had to be sedated for the trip. I wished I could have taken some of what I gave him, though the occasional surreptitious swigs of vodka helped. Driving the New Jersey Turnpike with an over-full U-Haul pushing my Subaru sedan with its thinning clutch through the endless stop-and-go traffic was the most exciting part of my honeymoon experience. For ten hours I worried: *Would the brakes and clutch make it?* The anticipation was more spine-tingling than sensual.

For our first few weeks, we still had lots of extra cash in the form of small bills from the "dollar dance" at the reception, plus a healthy number of checks from wedding gifts. We used that money to pretend we were well-off enough to go out for dinner three weekends in a row and even some weeknights. When the cash ran out, we ate in. That's when I knew our so-called honeymoon was over.

It was back to business as usual for us, only I had one major problem—I had no idea what "usual" meant. I was lost in this new-wife life. The only two things that provided me any comfort in their familiarity were Humphrey and Mr. Vodka. One I couldn't hide if I wanted to in our new tiny apartment; he was too big, furry, and vivacious. The other I had to hide, but didn't know how. Space was both limited and shared.

If I was going to keep drinking—and I needed to keep drinking to survive my major culture shock—I had to get very creative. My only problem was that I'd never been known for my creativity.

CHAPTER 11: MY SASSY PANTS GAVE ME AWAY

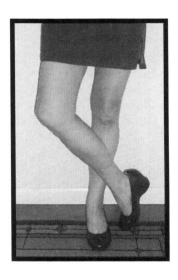

*That's me dressed inappropriately for our one month
anniversary trip to Ellicott City, MD, where showing off your
sexy legs is apparently against the law.*

Victor had found a half-basement apartment in
Bethesda, Maryland. Even though it was expensive ($550 a
month plus utilities, which was a lot in 1983), it was quite a
lucky find because the landlords allowed us to have
Humphrey. My bridegroom had had to find a place that
allowed pets; otherwise Mr. and Mrs. Us would be residing
in different states. Humphrey and I were a package deal.

Between us, Victor and I made less than $30,000 a
year. He had a job as a bookkeeper with a savings and loan
and I was working as a technical writer for Beltway Bandit,

an independent research firm that produced government reports. That's why I had to drink the cheapest vodka I could find—the kind that was best when tossed back quickly and never brought near an open flame, although my esophagus felt like a used fire pit after I drank the stuff. But what medicine isn't hard to swallow?

I went into immediate culture shock of course. For the first time in my life I was three whole states away from my family and, also for the first time in my life, married and living with a man. As a country girl, I was confused by the big city and all the traffic. As if all that weren't enough, my new job stunk. The work itself was fine, but the working conditions were foreign to me. No matter what I had been doing in my pre-big city life, I had always distinguished myself as the brightest and best among my colleagues. My bosses always said, "If I want a task done properly and efficiently, I'll give it to Lorna." But now I was a little worker-fish in a big, shark-filled pond supervised by Ms. Piranha Boss. And Ms. Piranha Boss wanted me as her mid-morning snack. She started by criticizing my clothing in front of other employees, then she told me I couldn't write, even though I had a major publication at the time. She also barged into my office at random intervals during the day to adjust the blinds to her liking and rearrange my desk while I was working. Everyone in the pond was expected to slave at least ten hours a day, plus work one weekend day. Ms. Piranha Boss considered anything less to be part-time employment. I dreaded work, all sixty hours a week of it. I had to dull my new, predator-filled reality. My drinking escalated.

Hiding a drinking problem was easy when the people around me believed I was perfect. But around people like Victor, who were looking for my flaws so they could fix them, keeping up the pretense of sobriety became nearly impossible. Plus we lived in such close quarters. I

145

drank quickly and heavily whenever the opportunity presented itself and passed out nearly every night. Even though I blamed it on hormones or stress, Victor knew that wasn't normal. He had two sisters. He knew about hormones and stress. As he started watching me more closely, I had to devise sneakier ways to drink. I'd send him on grocery shopping missions for unusual ingredients for recipes I told him I wanted to try. Since I actually knew how to make only two dishes, you'd think he would have suspected something, but he was such an optimist when it came to believing in his power to change me.

Distracting him with sex didn't help. He was too smart for that. In the mornings, when the booze was out of my system, I would reach over and start caressing his manly parts, the ones I figured he didn't want to remain private.

"Why do you only want to have sex in the morning when we have to get ready for work?" He sure knew how to kill a romantic gesture.

"I feel so alive in the morning—so full of life. Don't you?" I used my sultry voice and flirty eyes.

"No," he said. "I feel like I have to get ready for work. I prefer sex at night, but you're always asleep and I can never wake you up. Why is that?"

With him up and leaning on his elbow and talking down to me, I felt a bit like I was in an interrogation bed and the "good cop" was nowhere to be found.

"I'm sorry," I said. "My job isn't easy and it's hard being away from home—"

"This is your home!"

"I'm sorry. You're right. Maybe tonight?"

"We'll see."

And so went the not-this-morning-sex dance. Some nights, I managed to stay conscious for evening romance, but I always fell asleep quickly after he finished having a real orgasm and I finished acting mine out. Lest anyone think my orgasm-free sex had anything to do with Victor's sexual prowess, it didn't. It was me. I had never had an orgasm during intercourse with any of my previous partners. I have a few theories on the subject:

1. I was born with inhibitions when it came to anything involving my lady parts, as evidenced by not being able to refer to any lady parts by either proper or improper terminology.

2. The volume of alcohol I consumed to overcome my lady parts inhibitions may have drowned my orgasmatron, or whatever it is that makes a woman have an orgasm.

3. Creating a realistic fake orgasm so that the man in question feels good about his manhood takes a great deal of mental focus. All that mental focusing probably kept me from having my own feminine feel-good experience in my lady parts.

For a girl who liked to keep things simple, I certainly had a knack for complicating things.

*****

Everything fell apart on our one-month anniversary. By "everything," I mean my ten-year secret drinking career. Keeping my drinking a secret from Victor was impossible. For the first time since I'd begun closet drinking, I felt like I was hiding something.

I didn't wait for the perfect level-headed moment to admit to my drinking and carry on a discussion about it. I waited until the pot boiled over and the stove burst into flames. No one had to call the fire department when he and I both flared up. At least I don't remember any sirens.

147

Two clothing-related events precipitated the biggest fight of my life just one month after our wedding.

Victor had bought a pair of work slacks that were too long and asked me to hem them for him. Since I had sewn my own elaborate wedding dress, we both figured I could handle the task. I was eager to please him, especially since passing out at night all the time didn't please him. Because he didn't know about my drinking, he couldn't factor in my poor tailoring skills while I was hammered, and I wasn't a very good judge of my hemming-while-sloshed skills, either. I hemmed his pants, all right. They came out about three inches above his ankles. To my credit, both legs came out even and would've been fine if the latest trend in office attire for men was Capri-style dress pants.

Victor was livid. I was befuddled. Measure once, cut twice. *Where did I go wrong?*

The second incident, which involved my own clothing, followed about a week later. We had planned to go to Ellicott City, Maryland, for dinner to celebrate our one-month anniversary. He made a point of telling me he could not wear the new pants I'd just ruined. Although I didn't say anything, I noted the unromantic tone he'd already set for our romantic day. I chose to wear an above-the-knee jeans skirt. It was a mini-skirt, but not a micro-mini. That's all I remember. I'm sure I wore a top, but it was the skirt to which he most strenuously objected. He thought it was inappropriate (as in *slutty*) and insisted that I should change into something more conservative (As in "Thanks Grandma! I'd love to wear that old smock of yours.")

Once again, I noted the tone of his reply, but this time he was acting like my lord and master. Wearing my saucy skirt, I didn't feel like anyone's slave. This time I didn't keep quiet. I turned into a raving lunatic. I'd pre-drunk enough vodka to get me through the trip and was feeling as sassy as I was looking, so I told him, "You have no right to tell me what to wear. I don't tell you what to wear."

"Ellicott City is a classy place," he replied in his lofty tone. "That outfit is anything but classy. I don't want to be seen with you wearing that disgusting skirt. You have nicer clothes. You should wear them. And you don't have to tell me what to wear because *I know* how to dress appropriately."

"I like this skirt!" I insisted. "It's cute and it shows off my nice legs. You have to admit I've got nice legs." *How could he argue with that?*

"Cute? Maybe if you're trying to attract men. I don't want to walk around a quaint, family-oriented town with a wife who wants to show off her legs." *That's how he could argue with that.*

I couldn't think of anything else to say in my defense. I'd spent my entire life not defending my rights, so I was ill-equipped to win that (or any other) battle. Feeling angry, defeated, and drunk, I took Humphrey out for a walk, fully contemplating never coming back. I let the door slam behind me, hoping it sounded as final and dramatic as it does in the movies. But it was a screen door, so it probably lacked the *oomph* I was going for.

Victor was not the kind of guy a wife in a hooker-skirt walks out on. He followed me. What ensued is probably still the talk of our upscale Bethesda neighborhood. He yelled at me to come back. I yelled back that I wouldn't. (Don't ask for a transcript. Humphrey is dead now, and he was the only one rational enough to remember what really happened.) There was more yelling, then Victor walked away from me, leaving me and my "slut-skirt" to ponder our transgression. I really wanted to stay outside forever, but Humphrey finished his business and wanted his treats. Reluctantly, I went back into the apartment.

I felt like I had so many times as a little girl—small and helpless and, well, little-girlish. Victor gave me the silent treatment and the cold stare until I couldn't stand it any longer. I apologized for yelling in public and having bad taste in quaint town apparel. Then I changed my clothes.

"That's much better," Victor said as we headed for Ellicott City. "You'll feel more comfortable in that dress. You won't be sticking out like a sore thumb."

I'm sure he said this to make both of us feel better. Then he began to review the situation, with comments about how appalled he was that I had yelled openly in the neighborhood. He didn't mention his own yelling. That's when I, the Vanquished Bad Girl, ran out of excuses and energy. I told him the truth. Whatever the outcome would be, it had to be easier than my first month as his wife.

"Victor," I said in my calmest, most rational voice, "I *think* I *may* have a drinking problem."

"Thank God," he said. "I thought you were going crazy."

I wanted to say, "I *am* going crazy." Instead, I cried.

"Let's try to have a nice time in Ellicott City," he said. "We can talk about this tomorrow."

I didn't know if what I'd just confessed hadn't sunk in or if he needed some time to process it. Either way, we put off any mention of my "problem" until after our special celebration. To this day, I don't remember much about Ellicott City except that the streets were narrow and a large hoop skirt would surely have blocked traffic. I can't even remember what I had for dinner, although I'm pretty sure we skipped the drinks before, during and after.

The next day, and on into the evening, he lectured me on how to fix my drinking problem, if, indeed, I had a drinking problem. He did almost all the talking because he had so many questions, which I mostly answered with very short answers. I spoke only to answer his questions. I certainly owed him that. If he was going to fix me, he needed all the facts. He was a problem-solver. I was a doozy of a problem.

After I'd answered all of his questions, he assured me that he'd taken his marriage vows seriously. He wouldn't leave me, even though I lied to him about my drinking. I felt both relieved and ashamed. To restore his faith in me and to convince him that I took our wedding vows as seriously as he did, I assured him that I would do anything he asked of me.

Here's what he told me I had to do:

1. Stop drinking immediately. I could still drink coffee, tea, water, juice, milk, soda, and other crappy non-alcoholic beverages. I just couldn't drink anything that had the word "proof" anywhere on the label.

2. Pour every ounce of alcohol in our apartment down the drain. We had many bottles of booze. The glug-glug sound each one made as the various-colored contents swirled clockwise down the drain was wretched. Tragic.

3. Take the entire pile of empty bottles to the trash can. Victor must have thought that was a symbolic act of closure on my drinking problem. I thought it was laziness on his part after I'd already had to stand at the sink and empty all the bottles myself.

4. Breathe into his face whenever and wherever he commanded so he could sniff out any hint of alcohol or alcohol cover-up chicanery (gum,

mouthwash, or toothpaste in the middle of the day). My dental hygiene suffered, but that was the price I paid for my transgression.

In a cherished show of solidarity—I cherished the show much more than he did—Victor abstained from his nightly scotch before dinner and his glass of wine with dinner. We were poor, but not so destitute that we couldn't enjoy a few of the finer things in life, like high-brow liquid attitude-adjusters. I remained sober for two weeks. Amazingly, neither my body nor my brain missed the alcohol. I think Victor missed his drinks, though; I could tell by his sharpening edges. Alcohol had a way of softening him, and I missed his unsharp edges more than my daily mega-dose of vodka.

What was the worst part of those two sober weeks? The random breath-checks. I felt like a little kid showing my dad my fingernails so he could inspect them even after I'd told him I had indeed thoroughly scrubbed my hands. I understood why he didn't trust me and why he felt he had to check my breath to verify that I was telling the truth. But it was still demeaning. I felt like I was a child bride married to her father.

The up-side of sobriety was all the time I discovered in the evenings and on weekends. I read more books. I learned something from watching (and remembering) the news. I took longer walks with Humphrey and cooked more meals. The apartment never looked better. I'd been missing out on a lot of life when I was passed out or on my way there.

On November 14, 1983, my twenty-sixth birthday, Victor took me to a fancy local restaurant to celebrate my sober life and my success avoiding demon liquor. He was convinced that I was not a problem drinker because I had no problem, either physical or emotional, not drinking for two whole weeks. This was remarkable, given that I had spent the last ten years drinking like Truman Capote during his moody period. I wasn't a problem drinker; I just preferred drinking over other activities like eating, sex, or talking with people.

At that celebratory dinner, Victor ordered us each a single glass of wine. I sipped the wine slowly and didn't even finish it. Victor couldn't have been happier. I don't know if he was happy for me because I'd beaten that nasty lying/drinking habit or if he was happy for himself because now he could go back to having his evening drinks and not have to admit he had married a lush. He considered himself an astute judge of character, and it had to hurt that I had snookered him with my hidden drinking. Telling him that even those closest to me, like my sisters and mom, never suspected anything didn't smooth out the dent that I'd put in his perfectly smooth pride.

I was elated that I didn't have to keep breathing into his face, which should never be confused with a romantic gesture. I was no longer his lying-lush wife. We celebrated my twenty-sixth birthday with unparalleled joy.

Perhaps a day went by, or maybe it was an hour. Like a camel that had just reached the other end of the desert without stopping for water, I got mighty thirsty...and not for water. Something inside me snapped or fired or exploded. I needed a drink of something alcoholic. Fast. Heck. I needed *a lot of drinks*. A trigger was pulled and the need to drink shot straight through me. *If I hadn't had those sips of wine, would the craving have been triggered?* I'll never know. All I know is I had two-week's worth of heavy-duty drinking to catch up on and I needed to get started. Right now.

For the next two months, I drank more per day than I'd ever drunk before in my life. If I couldn't buy bottles of vodka for myself, I snuck into my landlord's house, found their stash of booze, and drank as much as I dared. I was desperate. My cure went totally down the drain.

*****

My job as a technical writer lasted just shy of three months. I wasn't cut out for that kind of writing, nor for that kind of boss. Ms. Piranha Boss's demands were impossible to meet. She was the high-heeled, platinum-blonde version of a boot-camp drill sergeant, and I was the hapless recruit who'd signed up without a clue about what "character building" really meant. I could never please her. She told me I wrote like a high school dropout and dressed for failure. (This was in the days of that famous "dress for success" book.) If she was trying to motivate me, she did—she motivated me toward a nervous breakdown. But I quit before she had a chance to kick my butt into a psych ward.

The month of January, 1984, was a blur. I was at home all day, supposedly looking for work. Each day started with a good-faith effort at reading the multiple pages of "help wanted" ads in the *Washington Post*. I even sent out some resumes. But by mid-morning, I had already started spiking my orange juice with vodka. By noon, I didn't need any more orange juice. Plain vodka was fine. Then I started following the daytime line-up of soap operas with great interest. Those characters had lives much more interesting and complicated than mine. I found that refreshing.

Since I was home all day, I was expected to be the domestic one, but this was a role I neither enjoyed nor was able to accomplish with much proficiency. I never understood why the women in commercials seemed so happy and satisfied with their shiny floors or clean toilet bowls. They would just get dirty again and have to be cleaned again. Housework, in my opinion, was an exercise in futility, but I had to make an effort. Dusting or vacuuming while drunk helped me cope with the senselessness of housework. As an added bonus, I usually finished in record time and wasn't bothered by a home that looked like the Merry Maids had gotten way too merry and forgotten to finish what they started. Which was exactly what happened.

Although Victor was worried about how we would make ends meet financially, he didn't want me working in another place that so obviously made me feel suicidal. I'm sure he was worried that I might revert to my former coping mechanism. Little did he know that I had already crossed that bridge, blown it up, and jumped into the river head-first. Victor never confronted me about excessive drinking, so I didn't have to tell him that I was experiencing a wing-dinger of a relapse; nor did he ask me to blow in his face. I can't believe that he didn't recognize the telltale signs. He was such a smart man who cared deeply about our marriage. I think he just wanted to believe his wife was normal.

*****

When you're sloshed most of the time, you have to keep things simple. That trick got me by for many years, but it tripped me up in the end.

On Valentine's Day, 1984—our first and most memorable romantic holiday as a married couple—we had the biggest blow-up of our marriage so far, bigger than the slutty-skirt debacle. That time, I ratcheted up Victor's Anger Meter from Floozy-Fashion-Faux-Pas to Culinary-Cataclysm. The vortex of the storm was Meatloaf. I'm referring to the ground beef comfort food, not the portly rock star with the hit "Back to Hell," which, given our fight, is kind of ironic.

I have never claimed to be a master chef. Victor knew that about me when he married me. What I could do was bake chicken and make delicious meatloaf that was, even according to him, the best meatloaf he'd ever tasted. That was all the encouragement I needed to make meatloaf a regular menu item. I loved being able to do something for which I could get genuine praise.

Victor was the glory cook in the family. Whenever company came over, he used pans, dishes, bowls, and utensils we didn't even own to whip up impressive meals. I would be in charge of clean-up.

A pattern emerged that seemed to work. I did "utility cooking," making one meatloaf (among my chicken-related meals) each week of our marriage (thirteen weeks at that point). Since we were too poor to go out for lunch, meatloaf sandwiches also made for great lunches. Just about the time one meatloaf was gone, it was time to make another one.

I was unemployed and gerboozled with alcohol, and wanted to make our first Valentine's Day special. An idea of such brilliance came to me that I needed sunglasses to avoid being blinded by my own ingenuity. I called Victor at work and told him I was going to make him a Very Special Dinner as my Valentine's Day gift to him. He was very happy. Ward Cleaver happy.

Driving drunk wasn't illegal back then, so I drove to the grocery store. My portrayal of a vodka-swilling lush playing a sober holy-roller with a driver's license deserved either an Oscar or an arrest warrant. Shopping drunk was perfectly legal, too (and I believe that it still is). Then I hauled my swerving, grocery-laden butt back to the apartment and began an afternoon of Special Meal Preparation. I called Victor again, tantalizing him with the notion of a fancy, romantic meal made especially for him. He was giddy. Herman Munster giddy.

The Special Meal Menu was a study in old-fashioned, hands-on kitchen wizardry: twice-baked potatoes, cauliflower *au gratin*, home-baked bread, home-baked apple pie, and the centerpiece of the meal...a fifteen pound heart-shaped meatloaf. Magnificent! *Bravura!* Right? I had learned to bake bread, pies, and the other menu items, but that was my first attempt at *shaping* a meatloaf. For some reason (probably my pickled brain cells), I thought that my meatloaf sculpture:

1. Required three times as much ground meat as an ordinary loaf

2. Was the ultimate romantic gesture

3. Would impress Victor's culinary sensibilities

4. Would taste exponentially better than the normal log o' meatloaf

Yes, my *chef-d'oeuvre* was huge—just like my heart. I slathered it with nearly an entire bottle of ketchup, so it was also good and red. The thing took hours to cook, giving me plenty of time to prepare the rest of the meal and drink plenty of vodka in preparatory celebration of a fine and fancy meal. I waited in schnockered anticipation for Victor to come home to a nicely set table and this magical meal.

He came home all smiles until he smelled that familiar odor. His smile vanished. "Please," he said, "please tell me you made spaghetti and meatballs."

"No, Honey. Look! I made a heart-shaped meatloaf. Isn't it perfect for Valentine's Day?"

The gargantuan, ketchup-smothered, labor-of-love sat on the table surrounded by the other dishes I'd lovingly prepared.

He looked at it, then at me.

He walked away.

"What's the matter?" I was truly baffled by his reaction.

"You have the nerve to call me at work *twice* to tell me that you're making something really special for dinner tonight and all you make is another meatloaf?"

"But it's heart-shaped!" I exclaimed. "And look at all the other good foo—"

"The smell in here is sickening! I can't eat any of this. And I never want to eat meatloaf again. Do you understand me? Never! I've had enough of your meatloaf to last a lifetime."

Sometime during my tearful apology, I bench-pressed the platter displaying the meatloaf just to get it out of his sight. I ate alone, taking no comfort in one of America's most popular comfort foods. The rest of that evening is only a blur. I think Victor ordered a pizza. Maybe he had some apple pie later. I was passed out in bed by then.

Humphrey and I ate a lot of meatloaf over the next few weeks. I didn't know it at the time, but that was the last meatloaf I would ever eat.

CHAPTER 12: LAST CALL

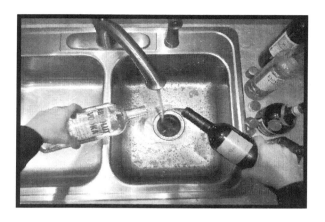

I remember the fumes from the booze. They were both delicious and tragic. Unlike a former President, I inhaled. Oh, I inhaled.

Exactly two days after the 1984 Saint Valentine's Day Meatloaf Massacre, one of my lives ended and another began. I'll never forget the date. February 16, 1984.

I didn't plan to stop drinking. Quite the contrary. It was a normal day for me. The moment Victor left for work I began to blur reality with daytime TV and vodka. Keeping up with the soaps had become my full-time job. Vodka relieved the stress of all those simultaneous melodramas and the pressure to keep those crooked plot lines straight in my loopy mind.

But that evening, February 16, something happened that blew up my dulled-down world. A neighbor's house caught on fire. I knew it wasn't a booze-induced hallucination because both Victor and I heard sirens.

Curious and concerned, Victor dashed outside to assess the situation. Knowing I was a liability in emergencies even when I was sober, I stayed away from the hubbub. Victor popped back into the apartment from time to time and reported on the progress of the fire and firefighting efforts. He also encouraged me to come out so I could stand among the other Curious and Concerned Neighbors in a show of spectator support, but I declined, telling him Humphrey looked upset and needed company. I also reasoned that more people on the street would only get in the way of the firefighters. Victor was not the kind of man who would get in the way of professionals doing their job, nor would he simply spectate. Someone surely needed him and he had to be there whenever someone needed the something that only he could give.

My reasons for staying inside, however, had nothing to do with Humphrey or my civic duty to keep the area clear. I had rare Victor-free moments that evening, and I wanted to take full advantage of them to drink. Since he kept appearing at random intervals to stock up on refreshments and supplies (cookies, coffee, blankets, towels—anything we had that might help the people outside on a cold, damp February night), I had to be smart about my drinking. Humphrey was helpful in this regard. When he heard footsteps coming toward the door, he raised his head from his normal sleeping position. That would be my cue to jump onto the couch and look casual but alert.

"How are things going?" I always asked with as much sober concern as I could muster. I leaned forward to appear more anxious for his news.

"The house is going to be a total loss. You should see it. It's so sad. They've lost everything and that house was just gorgeous." Victor shook his head with an odd mixture of remorse and exhilaration. Then back out he went as if his presence might be missed if he were gone too long.

He went back armed with more supplies. The man was generous with our stuff, I'll give him that.

The moment he left, I got up and headed for my stash behind my shoes in the closet. Knowing he'd be gone for maybe fifteen minutes, I couldn't waste any time.

Sitting on our living room couch about two hours into the situation, I entered into a woozy kind of pondering. One very clear question made its way through my hazy brain: *Who am I?* I was kind of glad that the neighbors had arranged a crisis to keep Victor out of the apartment so I could drink freely. It's not that I wanted them to lose everything in a fire, of course; they could have invited Victor over to play bridge, and that would have been just fine with me. But the fact remained that my neighbor's house was burning to the ground, and all I cared about was that I was able to drink as much as I could without Victor scrutinizing my every move. While my husband was being a chivalrous, generous neighbor, I was being a selfish drunk.

And in a rare moment of clarity while skunk-drunk, I realized just how self-centered, heartless, and deceitful I had become. I no longer displayed the qualities I wanted others to think of when they thought of me. *Where was Lorna, Everyone's Good Girl and The Perfect Child?*

Shamed to the core, I started sobbing. Alcoholics in recovery always talk about their "bottom," the searing event that is so bad they can no longer deny their addiction to alcohol. Well, that night I hit my bottom.

When Victor came in again, looking for more things he could hand out to the people shivering in the cold outside, he saw his wife in a tearful, messy lump on the sofa. That got his attention. Both concerned and frustrated, he asked what was wrong.

For several minutes, I wasn't able to speak at all, then I was finally able to eke out something sounding like words between my sobs. "I've been...um...drinking... [*sob*] ...you know, um... [*sniff*] ...vodka...since my...my...birfday."

"What?" He just stood there looking down at me. I really hoped he'd heard me because I didn't want to repeat it.

"Yeah. Uh huh. Um. A lot. I'm...um...real...sorry, but... [*sob*] I...I have a...really bad...prolem with... [*sob*] ...with halcolol." I figured there was no sense in trying to sound sober at that point. The effort it took to pronounce words correctly was best used to make a clean confession.

He narrowed his eyes. "How much have you been drinking? Has it been every day? Why didn't you tell me sooner?" He was launching rapid-fire questions at an unarmed suspect who had already waved her white flag.

"Whoa. A lot of drinking... [*sob*] Every day. I'm... [*sob*] ...sorry, Victor. I don't know who I am anymore." *Sob, sniff, sob.*

Once again, he surprised me. "Well, I guess, deep down I knew it. I just didn't want to admit you were *that* sick."

I guess I wasn't as clever at hiding my addiction as I thought. Most alcoholics aren't.

The neighbor's fire took the back burner. Victor turned his attention to helping the "someone" he'd married. The New Deal was that I had to go to Alcoholics Anonymous (AA). He stood there while I trembled uncontrollably and watched me search the phone book for the number for the general help line for AA, dial the phone, and talk to someone and learn the details of The Program, including the next meeting in my area. That wasn't easy because:

1. The phone book was thicker than the U.S. Tax Code and I was too weak to pick it up and hold it. I heaved it up on my lap and leaned over it,

turning pages a handful at a time. Since "AA" was at the beginning of the directory, all that page turning was unnecessary. But I was traumatized from facing reality and had forgotten my basic command of the alphabet.

2. The listings were tiny and my eyes were getting a headache and having trouble focusing on moving numbers, even when they weren't moving.

3. I was so upset my telephone comportment deteriorated to that of a whimpering toddler with a speech impediment.

As I dialed the phone, I was on my way to becoming a certifiable alcoholic. Before I picked up the phone, I was just a woman who drank too much.

*****

I knew this about Alcoholics Anonymous: it is a group for alcoholics who want to remain anonymous. And not drink. See? Vodka hadn't killed all of my brain cells.

Here's what I didn't know about AA but quickly learned:

1. The Program consists of twelve steps you have to "work" more or less in order, with the understanding that truly completing any of the steps is impossible. That seemed defeatist to me, but I was in no position to judge. I had two immediate problems with the twelve steps. One was that "God" or a "Higher Power" was mentioned in seven of the twelve steps. I was what most religious people would call a "heathen." While Victor had tried his best to

convert me to Methodism, I shunned both God and structured religion. If becoming sober meant finding religion, I was worried that I needed to find a Sobriety Plan B that Victor would buy into. The other thing that bothered me about the twelve steps was that there were twelve. Twelve seemed an excessive number of steps to remember. Couldn't the people who came up with this program boil them down into, say, three easy steps? Did they really expect alcoholics' brains to work that well?

2. To stay sober, they say, you have to attend meetings regularly. All anonymous alcoholics emphasize that going to meetings keeps them sober. Since there is no alcohol at the meetings, I could see the logic in this rule, but it seemed to apply only while you were at the meeting. Some anonymous alcoholics had been attending meetings for twenty or more years. As a virgin to AA, I was told I had to attend "thirty meetings in thirty days" as a minimum, for starters, and then as many meetings as I needed so I wouldn't drink. Forever. Until I died. Which seemed imminent. Victor, unfortunately, overheard that rule and made me promise to attend thirty meetings in thirty days. I promised to do it out of equal measures of fear and hope. Fear of what? Hope of what? I'm not sure, except that both were related to Victor.

3. Having a Sponsor is mandatory. You need someone who has, as they say, "been there before" to call upon when you are inevitably tempted to swallow a bottle of Nyquil or mouthwash.

4. Anonymous alcoholics love to be Sponsors. They say it helps to keep the sponsor sober. I had a whole pack of men and a few women rush up to me after my first meeting and volunteer to be my Sponsor. They handed me slips of paper with their first names and phone numbers and assurances that I could call them at any time. I wondered if AA was where single people who lost hope in the personal ads went for possible dates.

5. These people love slogans. "One day at a time." "There but for the grace of God go I." "One drink is too many, and a thousand is not enough." "Let go and let God." "Live and let live." "If it's not one thing, it's three." (Okay, I made up that last one.) Many conversations were just strings of slogans loosely tied together with nods, "oh yeahs," and slurps of coffee. On the up-side, small talk is easy at the meetings if you know a lot of slogans.

6. Anonymous alcoholics require prodigious amounts of coffee, donuts, and cigarettes. People with addictive personalities don't just stop their addictive behaviors; they substitute them. Back in 1984, smoking was permitted in nearly all public places. My virgin lungs seized up within the first five minutes of the smoky hour-long meeting. If I get lung cancer, I blame my first few AA meetings. I only made it through the thirty days/thirty meetings by discovering non-smokers' meetings. They still had plenty of donuts and coffee, though.

7. The meetings (at least the ones I went to) consisted of an opening prayer, discussion about

one of the steps, volunteer "alcohol war-story-telling," announcements of attendees—including "anniversaries of sobriety" and new anonymous alcoholics in the room—and a closing prayer (complete with hand-holding). After the meeting, there was a general kibitzing time over coffee and donuts where you could pick up a sponsor or trade more "I got so drunk..." stories. It was all very communal and *kumbayah*-ish.

8. Having a mandatory, anonymous social network for life didn't thrill me. I liked my privacy. You'd never find me in a gang—not the Brownies, the 4-H, or the Girl Scouts. Serial best friends, that's how I lived my social life. I didn't even like big family gatherings. The thought of socializing regularly with a cadre of alcoholics in various stages of recovery for the rest of my life made me want to take up smoking.

9. Some AA meetings are "open" and some are "closed." Anyone can attend an open meeting, so normal people can support their alcoholic or just observe alcoholics trying to stay sober and anonymous while they smoke, drink coffee, and eat donuts. Closed meetings are only for alcoholics. I never went to those meetings because I was afraid I might be bumped up to a higher class of anonymous alcoholic. That was one kind of promotion I didn't need.

*****

AA and I got off to a bad start. My first meeting was held in a church basement, which I should have taken as an immediate *wrong way* sign. With Victor by my side, I sat through that first meeting, shaking so much he asked me if I was cold. I wasn't. I was scared. I don't remember which of the twelve steps the speaker was lecturing about. It wouldn't have mattered because I didn't know about the steps yet and I was too busy studying my shoes to look up or ask any questions. What I remember are the stories people told. They were dreadful. The bottoms people spoke about were all much lower than mine. I wasn't there by court-order, at least. But many of these anonymous alcoholics spoke about their bottoms with humor— something I didn't expect. They also spoke of multiple relapses and how the meetings kept them sober between those relapses. Every one of them said that this time their sobriety would stick and, if it didn't, they knew AA would be there when they came to their senses. I didn't know whether to feel inspired or depressed.

When the time came for announcements, people stood up and declared days, weeks, months, and years of sobriety—each followed by applause and amens from the crowd. Some received much-coveted chips, which are coins that mark certain sobriety milestones. I supposed they carried the chips in their pockets as reminders when a temptation arose, but I also wondered if anyone ever confused the chips with regular change when they were buying a pack of gum. That would be something I'd do. Then the leader—there's always a leader—asked if there was anyone new in the group. That was my cue. I stood on legs so weak and wobbly I must have looked like a newborn calf standing for the first time. And I said the most difficult sentence of my life to date, "Hi, my name is Lorna, and...I'm an...an alco...coholic." The people there must have thought I also stuttered. Then they applauded me. *Applause? Really?*

After the prayer circle, happy, caring people swarmed me. I got all kinds of advice (thirty meetings in thirty days, tips for quelling cravings by sucking on hard candy), many offers for sponsorship, where to buy *The Big Book* (their Bible, which was written by the founders of the program, Bill Wilson and Bob Smith), and encouragement to stay for coffee and donuts. I was polite and listened…and begged Victor to get me out of there as fast as possible. He made sure we bought a copy of *The Big Book* before we left. I was now an official anonymous alcoholic.

Once out in the fresh air, my head and lungs clearing, I knew in the deepest part of me that the AA program wasn't for me. But I wasn't about to share that revelation with Victor.

I had promised him I would stop drinking alcohol. I'm a woman of my word. I'm not a quitter—well, in the case of drinking, yes, I *was* a quitter. But he didn't trust me. I understood why. I had withheld my drinking problem from him before we got married—although I hadn't defined my drinking as a problem at that point, so technically I hadn't lied to him. Technically, I had lied *to myself.* I had also deceived him for months when I went on my post-birthday drinking rampage. I'm sure he wondered what else his adeptly deceptive wife was hiding from him. My greatest secret was now revealed to him: *I was a great actress.* I couldn't imagine a more frightening thing to learn about your spouse. Many men would have ended the marriage due to lack of trust, but Victor wasn't like any man I had ever known.

He told me he wouldn't leave me, but he added that he would *never* have children with me until he was sure I'd beaten my alcoholism. Hadn't I told him I wasn't the maternal type and never really wanted children? I'd certainly meant to tell him. If he wanted to dangle that sobriety carrot in front of me, he should have picked "no more dogs." But his "no children" threat hooked me, anyway, because it was a direct challenge. He was telling me that I had to prove I was worthy of him and his legacy. My whole life was about proving my worthiness to anyone who cared to pay attention to me. I needed to show him I was worth his while.

*****

Ashamed of having lied to so many people in my life, especially to those who loved me, I asked Victor one favor. "Please let me tell my family in my own way and in my own time."

"Of course," he said. "But you know you should do it sooner rather than later."

"I want to tell them in person and when I can find the right words. Just let me do this my way. I kept this secret from them. I need to make this right."

"Okay."

A few weeks later a got a phone call from my sister Tina. She was very upset. "Lorna, what's this I hear about you being an *alcoholic*? What's going on? It's not true, is it?" I could hear my mom in the background.

I was stunned. Victor was standing there when I answered the phone. I just stared at him. *How else could they know?*

I stumbled through an awkward explanation about my drinking, my covering it up, and any other crimes and misdemeanors I could think of, including why I hadn't told them sooner. "I was waiting until the thirty days were behind me," I said, "and I could see you in person so that you would know that my drinking was behind me, too."

After a few moments, Tina said, "Well, I just don't believe it. When Jim told me Victor called him to talk about it, I just didn't believe any of it. And I still don't. You're fine now and you always have been," I heard my mom agree.

"Well, Tina, it's true. And we'll talk all about it when I come home, okay?"

I finally got off the phone. That ended one excruciating conversation with my older sister and mother. Then I began another equally agonizing one with my husband, my Judas.

"Tina said you called Jim and told him about my alcoholism."

"Yes. I did," he said with an air of defiance.

"I asked you one favor. One. Just let me tell my family in my way. And you took that away from me. How could you?" Maybe I was still reeling from the shock, but I was uncharacteristically calm, coherent, and dry-eyed.

"*Your* alcoholism has been hard on me, too, you know. I needed to talk to someone about what I've been going through." He made it seem like alcoholism was some kind of prize that he wished he had won.

"And you had to pick Tina's husband? You're not even that close to him. What about anyone in your family?"

Silence. This was as rare as cruising through all green lights during rush hour. So I took advantage and continued.

"You knew telling Jim would be the same as telling my family. You did this on purpose. To hurt me. Well, congratulations. You hurt me and my family. Well played."

He responded, a little less defiantly, "Let's just say we hurt each other and now we're even."

I didn't know it then, but Victor had only just started filling out his Lorna Wronged Me scorecard.

*****

And thus began my AA odyssey. Hoping to avoid lung cancer on top of any cirrhosis of the liver I might already have developed, I asked about different meeting places and times, hopefully smoke-free meetings. There were AA meetings in the greater D.C. area running day and night in more places than there are slot machines in Vegas. Stopping drinking was an epidemic in that city.

I found non-smokers' meetings in non-churches. That helped to reduce my truancy fantasies. I tried meetings at different times of the day and in different venues, hoping to find less ardent members. No luck. Everyone was kind and helpful—bordering on solicitous—but most of the people I met were also stuck in their pasts while hoping not to screw up their futures. They didn't strike me as optimistic about their chances for success. *Shouldn't I be hanging out with more confident people, people focused on their bright futures and not their sketchy pasts?*

I had plenty of time to contemplate my alcoholism during those meetings. I listened to the lectures on whichever laudable-but-never-to-be-completely-accomplished step, but tuned out the story-telling time after hearing essentially the same stories each time. These people spoke with a certain badge of honor about their DTs and their constant internal struggles to fight the cravings for alcohol. I wasn't like them.

After the Olympic sized pool of vodka I'd drunk, I never had any physical withdrawal from stopping cold turkey. Not once did I have an urge or a craving to drink—not even when I saw others drinking at social functions. On the morning of February 16, 1984, I was possessed by booze. I didn't care about anything else but getting buzzed. By the evening of that same day, I knew I would live alcohol-free the rest of my life. It was as if I was the 1920s poster princess for Prohibition. The kind people with whom I spent thirty meetings in thirty days and who were supposed to be helping me kept warning me that I would "start craving alcohol any day now." They seemed to be waiting for me to become like them. But as I saw it, it was that kind of uplifting attitude that created the only constant craving I developed. This was to get away from these people and get on with my life.

The door to my drinking life was closed and forever sealed. There were no more self-delusions. I *was* and *always would be* an alcoholic, but I was an alcoholic who feared drinking, had no cravings for booze, and didn't need AA meetings to keep me sober. Those meeting kept other alcoholics from taking the next drink. Maybe. But not me, because I knew I would never drink again and I was as sure as I was breathing smoke-free, donut-and-coffee-scented air. I learned later that, in very rare cases, alcoholics experience what some people in the alcohol recovery business call a spontaneous recovery. I believe that is what happened to me. Some people in the alcohol recovery business don't believe in such a thing. They probably don't believe in aliens, reincarnation, or effective facial hair-removal techniques, either. All I know is that the burning desire to drink had been lifted from me. *Poof!* It was just like that.

But Victor still had his doubts, so we went to meetings so he would feel better. On our way out of the meetings I tried telling him again and again how useless these meetings were for me. He still had serious doubts.

"AA is a program that works," he kept saying. "Look at all the people it helps in there. You need to do it for our sake. For your sake and my sake."

"Yes, I know," I always said. "I'll keep going. It's a great program for the people who need it. I'm just not one of them. I'll stick with it for you. But I don't need it for me.

The only time I think about alcohol is during these meetings. I may be an alcoholic, but I'll never be a drinker again. I know it."

"How do you 'know it'?" He actually used the air quotes.

"The same way you 'know' things when you're sure you're right." I couldn't resist using the air quotes back at him.

"Well," he said, "this is different. This is our life and our future we're talking about. And this is a disease you can't just make disappear because you decide you're going to." He was never at a loss for words in a debate.

"I know this doesn't sound logical," I was trying to address him logically, "but I know in my heart that I don't need AA to keep me sober. That part of my life is gone. It's like it was lifted away from me the moment I admitted my problem to you the night of the fire. I knew then I would never drink again."

"It must be nice to be so sure—especially when you have your revelation when you're drunk. I think you better stick with AA."

That tone meant our discussions were over, even if his words suggested there might be room for more dialogue. Yes, that discussion was over. I was staying in AA, reading *The Big Book* from cover to cover, and "working" the steps.

When my thirty-day sentence ended, Victor asked me to keep going to meetings, regardless of my assurances that I was better off without them. I negotiated him down to one meeting a week, and we eventually found a meeting held more like a stand-up routine, with an entertaining speaker doing his forty-five minute shtick on one of the steps. He was the only storyteller. We both enjoyed attending a program called "Sunday Morning Live," which was a parody of *Saturday Night Live*. And being able to quickly exit the "show," which was held in a hospital amphitheater, was a real bonus.

My new biggest problem as a wife was that my husband didn't trust me. Every time I was moody, which was at least for a few days each month (often more, depending on circumstances and Victor's mood), Victor asked me if I was drinking again. Or he began searching the apartment for liquor bottles. If I couldn't remember something quickly enough, he asked to sniff my breath. Under this constant scrutiny and suspicion, I got a sense for how bad children, zoo animals, and people on the Official Registry of Sex Offenders must feel. No matter how much I changed my ways, once he discovered I was a lying alcoholic, I supposed he would always see me as a lying alcoholic. I understood it, but it still seemed unfair. Where was his Christian forgiveness?

Victor failed to understand something fundamental about his wife: I wasn't as predictable as he thought I was. Or maybe I wasn't predictable in *the way* he thought I was. He saw me as vulnerable and weak. Okay. People who are butt-toasted on booze aren't the type most people want as their leader in a battle. But Victor didn't see that, in my core, I was strong, determined, and needed to be loved. He never fully understood how resolved I was to fulfill others' expectations of me as a Good Girl. If being good meant being sober, then being sober was what I would do without question. But he didn't know that, and I wasn't self-aware or self-confident enough to tell him and, even if I had, would he have believed me after all I'd just put him through?

My husband was willing to stay married to me, but he didn't trust me. Not once did I question whether I was willing to stay married to a man who couldn't trust me and violated my trust. Doggedly, I ramped up my efforts to prove to him I was both good and worthy of his trust.

This makes me remember my one philosophy class in college, where I was discouraged by the logical argument that *you can't prove a negative*. How could I convince Victor that I *wasn't* drinking? I just had to keep *not drinking*. Which is exactly what I did.

But not drinking had its problems, too.

CHAPTER 13: MY CREDIT SCORE WAS FINE...BUT MY CREDIBILITY SCORE WAS A PROBLEM

When life plopped me in a bucket, I eventually found a way out of it. But it wasn't always pretty.

It was tough to be perfectly sober and have such a low credibility score with my husband. Would he ever believe that my drinking days (and nights) were behind me?

Unemployment wasn't helping my situation. Because I had way too much time on my hands, Victor began to worry that I might relapse into daytime TV dramas, daytime drinking dramas, and the deceit both TV and drinking inspired. Without even one reply to all of the resumes I'd sent out to research firms and educational institutions within an hour's commuting distance, I was ready to inquire about the skills required to operate a deep fryer and began rehearsing, "Would you like fries with that?" Underemployment was better than unemployment for our bank account. And our relationship, too.

When Victor saw that I was willing to take any job to kick start my re-entry into the sober, workaday world, he finagled a clerical job with his employer, one of the banks that would go under in the infamous savings and loan debacle in the mid-1980s. I didn't work in his department, which was good. I worked for a woman who looked and behaved as if she hadn't yet graduated from high school, which wasn't good. I wondered, in fact, if her parents drove her to work. Until I came to be her Office Slave, Gidget was the department's Office Slave. She enjoyed her promotion, but I felt her hostility toward me. I was older and smarter than she was. How could I not correct her grammar so that she would sound more professional the next time she spoke with her superiors? I always did the correcting privately, but she didn't seem to appreciate my helpful suggestions. Instead, she would assign me a task like alphabetizing index cards for eight hours a day. Her constant presence over my shoulder didn't help me remember if U came before or after V. I suppose we made each other nervous.

The work was mind-numbing, stressful, and humbling. That was actually great news for both Gidget and me. It motivated me to find a job better suited to my talents, which now included professional alphabetizing. Surely I had enough functioning higher-level brain cells to land a job doing something closer to what I'd done in my former professional life, the one in which I had been so successful, even while boozing it up off the job. What I needed was to have faith that things would work out as they always had in the past.

It's a truism that no matter how many resumes you send out, all it takes is one getting to the right person. When that one resume I sent out landed on the right desk at another company, I was proud and elated to announce to Gidget that I would no longer be working at the savings and loan. She breathed an audible sigh of relief. Perhaps supervising was not her destiny, at least not until after her prom.

I'd landed a job as a research assistant for an organization that collected and analyzed government data. The organization was a large and reputable firm in the heart of downtown D.C. For the first time, I would be commuting into the capital that we'd only visited as occasional tourists. I became an urban working girl in a respectable profession.

Victor was happy: for me, for him, and for us. I had a job in which I could use my professional talents and hopefully shine. With any luck, he would trust that I was competent, and if he was confident in me, all would be right in my world. If that sounds convoluted, it was. Our relationship was not a simple one.

In preparation for my first day at work in the big city, Victor and I did a trial run and drove to and from my new office at 500 5th Street, NW. This was somewhere between N and K Streets and located precariously close to the city's nefariously large and speedy traffic circles. We did it on a Sunday. On Monday, with me behind the wheel and during rush hour, nothing looked the same. I had flashbacks to my little-girl days when I'd gotten lost coming out of the corner grocery store, only now I was behind the wheel of an automobile in what felt like NASCAR trials. The only difference is there was a lot of honking and obscene gesturing. Because I left for work approximately two hours early, I arrived for work in plenty of time to wipe the sweat from my brow and under my bra so I appeared excited to begin my new job.

Commuting became easier as I became a savvy, sassy city driver. I wasn't obnoxious, just effective at getting from Point A to Point B without letting anyone cut in. Driving became my way of venting my daily frustrations at my new boss, who was the embodiment of the Peter Principle, which is that a person will rise to the level of his/her incompetence in a bureaucracy and stay there. Ironically, my boss's name was Peter. He had begun as a research assistant, like me, and had been promoted to project director, where, although he stopped getting promotions because he was a horrible manager, he had been with the organization for so long that no one wanted to fire him. Although I didn't know it when I was hired, Peter went through assistants like bad guys go through police blockades in action films, with similar levels of drama and collateral damage. No one in upper management seemed to notice or be concerned by the turnover among Peter's assistants. Assistant after assistant hit the pavement, and what did Peter say? "Good help is hard to find."

I imagine Peter treated me no differently than he treated my predecessors. My job was to produce specific reports from a national data base for any number of clients around the country. Academics or politicians would call and ask for certain information. Peter's job was to "handle the clients," which meant he would schmooze them for his own entertainment while making sure everyone knew the "big gun" with whom he was now chummy. He was also supposed to get a clear picture of what information the client wanted from the database. My job was to write programs to create tables from the database that gave the clients (Peter's new pals) what they needed. In between running various reports for Peter and His Homies in High Places, I also had to fetch his lunch and make him coffee.

Peter was neither well-liked nor respected in the organization. While I wasn't a person anyone would call "the life of the party," I made friends easily and got along well with the people with whom I interacted most frequently, especially the people in Information Technology (or, as we called them back then, The Computer Guys). Peter didn't it like that I was more popular than he was. Although we were well past high school, I still fell victim to his jealous-cheerleader, movie-villain capers. When data requests came in, he always withheld key pieces of information from me so that I would fail to produce what the client wanted.

Next, I would overhear him saying to the client, "I can't tell you how sorry I am that your report isn't complete. My assistant still needs my help in getting up to speed. You must know how *that* is. I will personally make sure the report is done properly as a personal favor to you."

After he hung up the phone, he would call me into his office. "Lorna, this report is wrong." And here he would give me a bulleted list of what I had to do to get it right and explain each step as if English was my third language.

"Okay, Peter," I always said, "but I remember this request. This item right here?" That's where I pointed to the key element he had "forgotten" to tell me. "This wasn't on your original request to me."

"Oh, yes, it was."

"I'm pretty sure it wasn't. I can pull your note to me."

"You don't have time to do that. I want you to run this report immediately. It's late enough already." He was adjusting his too-big glasses and bobbing his shoulders up and down—his "tells" that he was edgy.

"Okay," I always said. "You'll have it before I leave today."

"Fine."

If he was on vacation, he also called in at random times of day just to see if I was at my desk.

The topper, however, was when *I* wrote a paper based on data *I* had analyzed but he presented it as *his* work at a professional conference. My name wasn't even in a footnote.

I knew I had to quit when I could feel my heart pounding when I heard Peter coming down the hall. He didn't stomp—he was the size of an underweight jockey—but he whistled. I can still hear that shrill whistle in my head. It said, *I'm the most important person in the world, Lorna. And today I'm going to prove it to you all over again.* I was always watching out for the next trap he was laying for me. When he rescued me from this trap, he wanted me to crown him Master of the Universe. What I wanted was to toss him out the window, but, as in most city high-rises, the windows were hermetically sealed to prevent employees from becoming murder suspects. I endured his management style for one year. This was because I was determined to show Victor that I was the responsible person he needed to believe I could be.

So no one was more surprised than I was one day when Peter called me into his office and, instead of chiding me for some mistake he'd set me up for, gave me a promotion! I was promoted from research assistant to research associate. I was now earning over $35,000 a year. With Victor's income, that meant we could afford our own home and leave that claustrophobic basement apartment we were still living in.

Looking for a real home brought us closer together. We finally had a common goal other than wanting him to trust me again. My getting a promotion at work, I think, gave Victor greater faith in my sobriety. That was a start to the healing process between us. It felt real. It felt good.

*****

Even though our credit was good, we didn't have enough of it, or enough cash in savings, to buy a modest home. Houses anywhere within a hundred-mile radius of Washington, D.C., were priced way out of our reach. Even houses described as "cute as a button" (realtor code for "the size of a tool shed"), "has great potential" ("probably missing some windows, doors, and the toilet might be in the kitchen"), or "charming" ("the second bedroom is really the crawlspace under the basement stairs") were too expensive for us to contemplate because they were single family homes in a time when property values were inflated and interests rates were, too.

New townhouse developments were appearing as if Johnny Townhouse-Seed were sprinkling corrugated wood chips and vinyl siding pellets all around the area. But we couldn't afford those either, no matter how many times we visited the model homes and pictured ourselves in them. Those were disappointing days for us, but they revived our marriage. Victor and I were on a mission to build our future. Together.

We finally found an older condo in Hyattsville, Maryland. Victor and I had about equal commutes to our jobs—thirty minutes on a good day, forty-five on a not-so-good-day. People in cities measure distance in minutes, not miles. As a white couple with no children and a big Old English sheepdog, we were a triple minority in the condo complex, but the neighborhood seemed quiet, the building was clean and secure, and it was a two-bedroom, two-bathroom home that we could just barely afford with my new, larger income. We bought it.

Two months after we moved in, I quit my job.

Victor knew I was extremely unhappy at work. Each night I told him what rotten stunts Peter had pulled or what degrading comments he had made to me. We fantasized about the day when Victor would get a big promotion and pay raise at work so that:

1. Victor would feel proud of himself.

2. I would feel free to look for a humane job with a sane boss.

Victor agreed that I needed to get out of Peter's clutches as soon as possible, but the financial perks of my promotion altered his definition of "as soon as possible." For him, the higher salary offset the office abuse. Had I been more of a capitalist, I might have understood Victor's reasoning, but I was unable to see the up-side of more money and more denigration. All I could envision was my pathetic obituary:

> *Lorna died doing what she was trained to do—research and servitude—for a vile boss with a Napoleon Complex. The cause of death is officially listed as blunt-force trauma due to repeated attempts to hurl herself out of the hermetically sealed window in her office. Absent a suicide note, her death was deemed by family and coworkers as a self-induced mercy killing upon hearing her weasel-boss whistling as he moseyed into work. Lorna expired before she had a chance to write her sure-to-be-best-selling book,* Little Men, Big Problems. *In lieu of flowers please send donations to Workers_for_Windows_that_Open.org.*

On the day I decided to quit, I

1. Told Victor that I was quitting and that everything would be fine. Then I left before he had a chance to say anything to talk me out of my decision.

2. Calmed my heart down when I heard Peter whistling his way into the office and bark his coffee order at me.

3. Marched into his office, sans coffee, and said, "This is my last day." After several awkward moments of him staring up at me, he told me I couldn't quit. I replied, "What are you going to do? Handcuff me to my desk?" And I walked out. That day, I think Demure, Polite Lorna vacated my physical body and Powerful, Astonishing Lorna took over.

4. Made an appointment to speak with Peter's superior about the need to include "daily humiliation" in the next job description for the position I was vacating.

5. Cleared my desk and said my farewells to my friends.

6. Left the office for the first time without Peter hovering around me. I don't think he uttered a single word the entire time I was there. For Peter, that was highly unusual.

I was free! But now I had to make sure that Victor and I would be financially secure. It's a good thing I had already been working on a plan. For me, that was highly unusual, but I was sober and had plenty of sober time to ponder things like my future.

*****

I wanted to get a Ph.D. in sociology and had already made inquiries at one of the many universities in the D.C. area. Where did I enroll? In a private institution...let's call it Pretentious University, or PU, because that's what it was. After my experience with the cut-throat world of business and bosses, I longed for the security and camaraderie of academia. While I wasn't adept at climbing a corporate ladder with all the back-scratching and nail-biting (or was it back-biting and nail-scratching?) that was required to get from one rung to the next, I knew what I was doing in a classroom environment. I knew how to do it very well. I was a Grade A, Number One Student. Hopefully, someday I would make a Grade A, Number One Professor of Sociology.

Based on the strength of my application, the financial deities at PU gave me a full scholarship and a teaching assistantship. They wanted me as a student and were willing to pay to have me attend their university. My tuition (nearly $20,000 a year in the mid-1980s) was covered in full, and the job they gave me as a teaching assistant for the research methods professor, Dr. Dreamy (because he was very nice and very nice-looking), covered books and commuting expenses. There was even some money left over to help with daily nourishment. I also landed a part-time job as a research assistant for a physician at PU's affiliated hospital. He was studying treatments for venereal diseases, which was a bit outside of my professional area of expertise, but, hey, research is research. Combining both part-time jobs, I contributed about $20,000 to our household income. The money was nowhere near the $35K I gave up when I quit my job with Peter, Peter, Assistant Eater, but I felt my dignity was worth the cut in pay. Victor agreed, or so I thought. Plus, I clipped coupons and shopped at thrift stores for clothes. I economized as if the roof over our heads depended on it. Which it did.

Victor worried about finances, but that was nothing new. He also worried about all the pressure I would be under now and insisted I keep up with my weekly AA meetings. I understood this, but begrudged the time those meetings took away from studying, working, and sleeping. Victor was proud of my determination to realize my lofty Ph.D. dream, even though my timing was atrocious given our new mortgage debt. He seemed to trust that I had control over my alcoholism and seemed to be watching me less for signs. Or maybe I was so busy with my new and varied commitments that I didn't notice that he was still watching me.

We seemed, once again, to be on the same path. He was at a different financial institution after the S&L scandal broke and was moving up in the ranks. Unlike me, he knew how to climb a corporate ladder and brought a greater measure of financial stability to our lives. I think he enjoyed the feeling of being the sure and steady one in our relationship. I appreciated his willingness to support my decision to go back to school and made sure he knew it. He was gracious about my gratitude. He did say, however, "Lorna, your time will come." I nodded, not knowing what he meant and not wanting to know, either.

During my first semester at PU, my time was already beginning to reveal itself.

CHAPTER 14: ONE PLUS ONE EQUALS THREE

When I said I didn't have any maternal instincts, I wasn't kidding. Pregnant Lorna definitely did not "glow."

In the fall of 1985, something—I mean some*one*—unexpected came my way. I've never prided myself on precision-timing, so getting pregnant during the first semester of my Ph.D. program shouldn't have come as much of a shock. Although Victor was ready for the family I'd agreed to before our wedding and feeling confident that the mother of his children wouldn't *lush-out* on him, I didn't expect that Mother Nature would completely disregard my blatant lack of maternal instincts, especially with my Ph.D. work already in progress. My heart wasn't into parenting. Apparently my uterus was.

187

Our sex life wasn't very life-like; it was more wax-museum-ish. We looked healthy and vital enough, but we just weren't able to make the moves on each other very often. I blamed it on stresses due to jobs, finances, housing, traffic, AA meetings, and Victor's greater interest in my sobriety than my sexuality. Maybe there were some trust issues underlying our lack of intimacy, but we didn't feel comfortable talking about that. At least I didn't. And Victor never brought up the subject. So for the first year of my sobriety (which was also the first year of our marriage), we lived basically as platonic, civil, supportive partners.

Also, sobriety made me hungry. I gained about twenty pounds, which made me officially "big-boned." My body still craved the simple sugars that alcohol metabolized into, so I had to oblige it by feeding it non-inebriating quick carbohydrates like bread, pasta, cookies, cake, and candy, which kept my brain happy and expanded my wardrobe. Victor was concerned about my weight gain and tried to inspire me to lose weight by buying me beautiful new clothes several sizes too small. His strategy only helped me to reduce my self-esteem, which didn't weigh much.

After my first year of sobriety, Victor declared himself ready to try for a family. At the beginning of the summer of 1985, therefore, I stopped taking my birth control pills for two reasons:

1. I had made a pre-wedding promise to Victor that two children was something I could live with, so I felt obligated to comply.

2. Given the infrequency of our intimacy thus far, I figured that pregnancy was pretty much hypothetical.

But I miscalculated two things:

1. How much Victor wanted a child. He was willing to have sex with his overweight wife (whom he still didn't quite trust) every time he thought I was ovulating. He even researched ovulation indicators and made me take my temperature. I did it, but it wasn't romantic. I pictured us in lab coats "doing it" on a metal table.

2. How fertile I could be when I was taken off guard by a romantic moment.

We planned a vacation to visit our families in August. A whole week in the country and fresh air did wonders for us. We relaxed. One night we were so relaxed that we forgot how fractured our romantic relationship was. We made love before going to sleep. That was one sweet summer night.

About three weeks after we returned to the city and I was about to begin my Ph.D. program, I mentioned to Victor that I felt strange.

"How so?" He was probably wondering if I was about to confess that I had been closet drinking for the last year.

"I don't know. Something just feels different. I feel…I don't know…heavy inside."

"Heavy? Like you have something on your mind that you need to tell me?"

"No. Heavy in my body. Something isn't right." I never gave a thought to that one night of love-making.

"Maybe you should see a doctor. You could be pregnant," he said, suddenly brightening at the thought of fatherhood and proof of his virility.

"Oh, I don't think it's that," I said, "but if I don't feel more like myself in a few days, I'll call my doctor."

I just said that to placate him. I didn't want to go to my physician and step on the official scales that always displayed a weight five to ten pounds more than my scale at home, which was depressing enough even after I'd jettisoned all ballast in my bowels, bladder and wardrobe. And I really didn't want to have some physician tell me I was pregnant just as I was beginning a Ph.D. program.

But within a few days I knew I needed to see a physician, and not my regular physician. My period had been due a week earlier, and now I was officially, suspiciously *late*. I had to find a new OB/GYN. I picked one out of the yellow pages. He turned out to be a gem of a man from Spain or Portugal or someplace that made him say, "Eeez so nice to meet ju, Lorrrrrna." The way he rolled the R in my name sounded so wonderful that I immediately fell in love with this man who would guide me though the inconceivable journey that my body was taking.

*****

Dr. Spaniard soon confirmed that there was a person growing inside of me that would eventually come out and rely on *me* to survive and grow into a contributing member of society. Actually, what he said was, "Lorrrrna, I haf soom berry goud news for ju. Ju are prrrregant." That "berry goud news" took me some time to process. Was I ready to be a mother? How would I balance my goal of getting my doctorate with caring for a baby? Would Victor and I become closer because of this little life I was now carrying?

With all these questions swimming in my head and a fetus swimming in my uterus, I called Victor at work to tell him the news.

"Hi, Honey," I said casually.

"Well? Are we or aren't we?" He was all business, whether he was at work or not.

"I'm pregnant!"

I had rehearsed that part so that I sounded genuinely happy. And I was happy on some level. Having a baby is a miracle not everyone experiences, and I was feeling grateful that I was able to fulfill another one of our mutual goals, even if it was Victor's goal, not mine. But I resented the new trend of saying "the couple" is pregnant and references like "we are pregnant" bugged me. "We" definitely were not pregnant. *We* had made the baby. *I* was pregnant. *I* would be having all the interesting experiences:

1. My belly was going to stretch beyond recognition and reason.

2. The itchy, bothersome hemorrhoids would be all mine.

3. I would be lying on a table disguised as a bed, with my legs in some unnatural and undignified position feeling the pain.

4. The baby would be coming out of some orifice of my body.

Where was the "we" in all that? I can't chalk these feelings up to hormones because I still have them. The feelings and the hemorrhoids.

Pregnant women are supposed to "glow," right? I didn't. Victor glowed. I could hear it in his voice.

"Let's go out to dinner tonight and celebrate."

"I'd love that." I felt kind of nauseous, but I hoped it would pass by dinnertime.

"I love you," he said. And he meant it. Maybe Victor would start seeing me as his treasured wife, now, not as his alcoholic. An asset and not a liability.

This pregnancy thing could be a very good thing.

Victor was happier than he'd been before he knew he'd married a drunk. I was terrified but cautiously optimistic. I really liked Happy Victor, though, and didn't want to do or say anything to break the spell. To him, I became a precious vessel—the woman who would bring forth his descendants (mine, too, but *mortality* was more my issue, not *immortality*). I had a person growing inside of me that had to come out of my little lady parts—a place not large enough to pass a decent sized lemon without major bodily contortions, mystical expansion cream, and major opiates. Screw "natural" childbirth. I wanted to be unconscious when this creature passed through me and out into the world.

I wasn't totally without feelings, of course. The welfare of the child concerned me greatly. S/he would have me for a mother. Santa Claus, Tinkerbell, and my maternal instincts could be classified in the same category: comforting to believe in, but purely mythical.

I was a better dog mother. Humphrey had come to me as an ill-mannered adolescent from a broken home, but soon I had him behaving like an Old English gentleman. He even did impressive tricks at a mere hand signal from me. But infants and children? Forget about it. *I should know something about raising a child,* I told myself. *I was one, for God's sake.* My next thought was, *But living in a house doesn't mean you're good at fixing the things around the house that break.* I had an inkling that babies needed repairs, or at least general maintenance, from time to time. If only I were having a puppy…but that would make me a bitch, and I had worked too hard for too long to avoid that label just to get stuck with it because I was going to be a mother of a something.

*****

The worst parts of the first trimester were:

1. Giving up caffeine. I had a week-long withdrawal headache, which seemed odd since I'd never had the DT's when I stopped drinking after ten years of hard-core boozing. My body rebelled when the caffeine was yanked. The brain and body are mysterious and not meant to be understood. I think it's kind of like why reality television shows are so popular or how drive-thru funeral homes work.

2. Adjusting to the shock of my new role as mother along with my other new role as Ph.D. candidate/part-time research assistant studying venereal diseases. I tried not to think about dealing with conflicts of interest or consequences, at least until I started to show.

As the proud father-to-be, Victor took great care of me. He watched what I ate and made sure that every food craving was satisfied. Even mine. As I grew in girth, so did our mutual anticipation. It was when the baby first moved, well flutter-kicked, that I finally embraced motherhood. For the first time, I felt privileged, not just pregnant. Little Bugger (as we called him at the time) and I bonded. Maybe I had some maternal instincts hidden somewhere in me, after all. They were just waiting for a fetus to kick-start them into action.

During the second trimester, I started reading the popular parenting books. I never finished them. They were more convoluted than my quantitative research methods texts. With my newfound affinity for Little Bugger, I figured we would figure it out. How hard could it be? I did learn one thing from those books: reading aloud to your unborn child is good for its cognitive development. So I read my sociology articles and books aloud. This child was destined for social consciousness.

Although being pregnant didn't interfere with my Ph.D. studies, I found another job as the research coordinator for a large nursing home in the D.C. area. The nursing home seemed to be a much safer environment in which to work, and the subject matter of my research exposed me to fewer potentially life-altering substances. Researching the social issues of institutionalized elders seemed much safer than being around Petri dishes smeared with the consequences of other people's unfortunate decisions.

Little Bugger was due on May 10, 1986, just a few days after my second semester at PU ended. At least timing was on my side for once. I wouldn't have to miss classes to experience the painful joy of childbirth. Thanks to the hormones and all the love I was getting from Victor, my attitudes toward all things maternal had softened, so Victor and I went to Lamaze class with the silly notion that we would attempt natural childbirth. Natural childbirth had been all the rage in Medieval Europe and now, in the 1980s, everything old seemed to be new again. In the Lamaze class, we were told we could breathe our way through anything. Maybe the coaches could, but I had my doubts about all the walrus-sized women with aching backs on the floor.

Victor remembered everything about those classes—even the name of the nurse who taught them. What do I remember?

1. Focusing on my protruding belly and wondering how I was going to get Getting-Bigger-Bugger out of me without dying a stunningly loud and bloody death.

2. Watching the Birthing Film. Like The Texas Chainsaw Massacre, I could only watch part of it. But Victor watched all of it. He was fascinated by the miracle of childbirth "we" were going to experience.

3. Stopping at Baskin-Robbins for a butter pecan ice cream cone after each class. Butter pecan calmed me. The promise of ice cream kept me attending class each week.

*****

My pregnancy was a by-the-book affair until sometime in the seventh or eighth month. I was a busy graduate student at the time, studying, going to evening classes, and working two part-time jobs (as a teaching assistant and as the research coordinator for the nursing home). My days began with a 7:00 a.m. Metro ride into D.C. and ended with a 9:30 p.m. Metro ride back home. Since I was in a medical facility nearly every day, I had my blood pressure checked regularly. Dr. Spaniard had said it would be wise, and I did everything he said just because of the way he said it. I had my consistently low-end-of-normal blood pressure monitored just to keep Victor and Dr. Spaniard happy.

But no one was happy when my reading started going up from "low normal" to "normal" to "high normal." When my blood pressure reached "borderline high," Dr. Spaniard ordered me into bed. Which wasn't as appealing as it sounds. In order to keep Getting-Bigger Bugger and/or me alive, I had to lie in bed all day until his/her birthday. I still had one month left in my second semester at PU, plus my two part-time jobs that I couldn't lose. Besides, daytime TV wasn't nearly as entertaining when I was sober and I could read only so many novels and magazines until my brain turned to mush. I spent most of my horizontal time worrying about my classes and jobs. And that was just the first week. Lying in repose for a month or more wasn't for me, at least not while I was still alive.

But I tried. I talked to all parties concerned, including Getting-Bigger Bugger. Everyone seemed to understand my anxiety about my other responsibilities, but they also reminded me of my major responsibility, which was to deliver a healthy baby. There is a reason that "liberty and the pursuit of happiness" comes after "life" in the Declaration of Independence. My child's life should have been my number-one priority. It certainly was everyone else's number-one priority. My needs, as the cargo ship springing leaks, were secondary. Pregnant women gain weight and lose their identity. That was really problematic in my case, as I had precious little of my own identity to lose.

I spent two long weeks in bed worrying about what I was missing at school and at work and if anyone was missing me. Getting-Bigger Bugger owed me. S/he would, I vowed, hear stories about *my* sacrificial lounging in bed while Victor made all of our meals, cleaned the house, and took care of Humphrey.

After two weeks of torturous bed rest and against Dr. Spaniard's orders and Victor's warnings, I resumed my schedule. My blood pressure miraculously went back down. Now I only had two more weeks before the semester ended. While at work at the nursing home, I checked my blood pressure several times a day. Although it stayed higher than normal, it didn't escalate like before. I also called Victor frequently to report how great I felt.

One night I came home, more exhausted than normal. I didn't feel like eating, so I went straight to bed. My rest time was always Getting-Bigger Bugger's cue to start acting up, so I got ready for kick-ball time inside my belly. But that night was different. No activity. I waited an hour before I tearfully told Victor about the stillness and that I was pretty sure I had killed our child. We began using my belly like a Ouija board, moving our hands around and asking Getting-Bigger Bugger probing questions.

1. "Are you sleeping, little one?"
2. "Are you ready to kick Mommy in the ribs?"
3. "Are you all right in there?"
4. "You don't want to worry Mommy and Daddy, do you?"
5. "Did your Mommy kill you?"
6. "Should we call an ambulance or the coroner?"

We tried to keep the questions simple. Any sign of movement would have been the answer we wanted.

Soon we both felt a flutter, then a regulation kick. I was relieved that I wasn't going to start my career as a mother with a manslaughter—make that babyslaughter—conviction. Now bed-rest wasn't such a hard sell. I finished my semester by mailing in my term papers, getting a temporary leave from my two jobs, and scheduling twice-weekly appointments with Dr. Spaniard.

On May 8, two days before my due date, Dr. Spaniard told me that Getting-Bigger Bugger wasn't budging.

"That's not possible!" I replied. "I can't be pregnant anymore! I've done my time. I want my body back. He doesn't even fit in there anymore." I was nearly hyperventilating by the time I finished giving all the reasons why being pregnant another two weeks (his estimate) was unacceptable.

He smiled. He chuckled. He had heard this before. "Eeez okay, Lorrrrna. You do juss fine." As he spoke, he was examining me. My legs were spread and my swollen feet were propped in stirrups of his cold metal table, and all I could see over my belly were his curly Latin hair and dark Latin eyes staring at my probably swollen lady parts. The rest of his Latin face was covered by his surgical mask.

"Baby come when baby come," he said. "Eeez dee way of nature, no?" His voice was Ricardo Montalban-smoothing.

"I suppose so," I said. How could I argue?

Mother Nature is wise. She has a plan for wimps like me who are terrified of the pain of childbirth. The thought of keeping a growing human imprisoned inside your torso forever is much worse than somehow getting that growing critter out of you. You can't let that imminent person stake a claim to your territory and squat in there forever, right? Landlords have rights, don't they? Fish gotta swim, birds gotta fly…babies gotta breathe on their own.

When Victor got home from work that night, I told him that the baby hadn't dropped, wasn't turned in the right position to make a graceful exit, and probably wouldn't be ready to do either for two weeks.

"I already look like an elephant," I said, blowing my nose and wiping away tears of despair. "I might just as well have the gestation period of one."

Victor was sympathetic. "How about if I give you a nice back massage to relax you?"

"That would be great," I said, "but I can't find a comfortable position except reclining on my back. This kid is taking up every damn inch of available real estate inside of me."

"Well, I could try to massage your neck and shoulders. I just know that I have to keep away from your feet."

"My feet? Why?"

Victor shook his head. "Don't you remember anything from Lamaze class? We were told not to massage the feet because there are pressure points in the soles of the feet that could induce labor if stimulated."

"Oh...*really*?"

I am hyper-sensitive when it comes to tickling. My feet are no-man's land. But desperate times called for desperate measures. On the evening of May 8, I asked Victor to massage my feet. "Massage," I said, "like your life depends on it."

"Are you sure about this?" He was facing an odd predicament. He didn't want to violate the rules the nurses had given him, especially given the news that the baby wasn't close to being ready for birth; but neither did he want to face the consequences of his obviously grumpy, desperate wife turning into a blubbering whale. He began massaging my feet, probably hoping that the nurses were just passing on a silly old wives' tale.

Old wives are not silly, and their tales should not be taken lightly. In the wee hours of May 9, my water broke and contractions started. At about 3:00 a.m., we called Dr. Spaniard to tell him the glorious news. We woke him up.

"Oh," he said, less smoothly than usual, "how manny minootes apard are day contract-jons?"

"It varies," Victor told him. "Ten, twelve, fifteen minutes."

"Are day getting quicker or fur-der apard?" *Yawn.*

"It varies, but they aren't coming more frequently."

"Okay. Go back to bed an call my office at 8:00. I'll see ju in da morning, okay? Eeez fine. [*Yawn.*] Call back if da contract-jons coom less than ten minootes apard."

"Okay, Doctor. Thank you so much and sorry for waking you up."

He probably only heard the first part of what Victor said because he'd already hung up.

We tried to get some rest, but it was impossible. The contractions slowed down to every half hour or forty-five minutes, but my water had broken and that baby was coming out sooner rather than later.

The enchanting details about birth aside, I learned a few things about childbirth that Lamaze class had failed to mention (or I failed to remember):

1. Pitocin, a drug to make contractions occur more frequently and with greater intensity, was probably devised by Josef Mengele. A normal contraction felt like my ovaries were being used like the brake pedal on a fast moving vehicle, stomped on hard, but quickly released. Breathing exercises, done more by the coaches than the students, generally work well because there is time to recover between contractions. A contraction when on Pitocin, however, felt like my ovaries were being twisted out of my body with pliers, then captured in vise grips and squished until they were no longer recognizable. Breathing exercises didn't work at all. I was too busy trying not to die. Victor dropped the breathing coaching and spent his time contemplating a celibate future.

2. Demerol is a great drug if you have time to rest between contractions. I was told I would drift off into a dream-like state and feel relaxed. Since I was given Demerol with the Pitocin, I never had time for drifting. I had to use every ounce of self-control I had not to go freaking ape-shit from the pain. Demerol took the edge off my ability to control my sanity in the face of

unending excruciating pain. Never accept Demerol while you're on Pitocin and expect to come through it with your dignity intact.

3. Breathing exercises work quite well after the epidural. After my epidural, it didn't matter if I did "who, who, who, ha" or "ha, ha, ha, who." Indeed, breathing exercises were unnecessary. I said, "Turn up the Pitocin! I can't feel anything and it's wonderful."

4. Epidurals were invented by Divine and Merciful Angels. The delivery method of the magical epidural could, however, stand some improvement. I had to lie cadaver-still in a fetal position while a neurosurgeon (or anesthesiologist) took a six-inch needle and pumped a vial of magic juice into my spinal column. Getting into a fetal position with a Monster Baby inside me was no easy task. Just as the physician told me to "not move a hair because if he hit a nerve, I could end up paralyzed," a Pitocin-induced contraction came on. The only thing that kept me temporarily paralyzed during the minute it took to inject all that magic juice was the thought that I could end up permanently paralyzed and my dancing days would be over.

5. C-sections have a bad reputation, but mine saved two, maybe three, lives that night. Dr. Spaniard let me labor for twenty-three and a half hours. The baby inside me liked his/her digs and wanted to stay put. After seeing a slight elevation in the baby's heart rate and more than a slight deflation in my facial color, however, Dr. Spaniard suggested a Caesarean section. I

would have agreed to an exorcism if it would bring that birthing experience an end. I'm glad Victor agreed. If he hadn't, as soon as I was able to move again, I would have killed him. I would have blamed it on Colonel Mustard in the dining room with the dagger inside my body. Trying to get out.

Alexander, nearly ten pounds' worth of him, was born at 1:23 a.m. on May 10. Now all I had to do was learn how to be a mother.

CHAPTER 15: CRYING ISN'T JUST FOR BABIES

Okay, so maybe I had some maternal instincts. Look how good Humphrey's coat looks. And I knew enough to keep my shirt protected from this little human's leaky parts. What a Mom!

I knew I was in baby-love the minute I saw Alex. I'd never before considered newborns especially beautiful or even cute. To me, they are strange-looking at best and scary at worst. Alex's face was bulbous and terribly blotchy, and what was most startling was that he looked Asian. Both Victor and I are from Northern European stock, but our son's hair was black and his eyes were dark and almond-shaped. I didn't need to have Victor wondering if I'd "done the dirty" with the delivery guy from *Wong Hong Lo China Delight*, but daddy hormones must have been swirling through Victor. All he saw was *his son*, a newborn whose chin looked just like his. Just to make sure that we wouldn't be on some switched at birth exposé on TV, we double-checked the identity bracelets. This baby was ours to keep. Nevertheless, I hoped that some Asian couple wasn't having the same doubts about their blonde, blue-eyed infant.

Once I got past his resemblance to Jackie Chan, I thought Alex was beautiful. The moment I held him, I decided I wanted five more just like him. (Later, I decided that a one baby versus two parents ratio was pushing the limits of fair play and my temporary delusions of wanting a half-dozen children was proof of either a post-partum baby-crush, a hormonal-tsunami, or the pain-control medication. I chose the baby-crush theory.)

I enjoyed the warm glow of the Demerol for as long as I could until the nurses told me I had to get down to the business of mothering. While I was recovering from major surgery, Victor took charge and learned all about infant care. Nurses' instructions, which wafted into my foggy brain then evaporated, were etched into his brain. He was an enthusiastic father and soon became an expert changer of soiled diapers, whereas I was the boobed one who was supposed to offer life-sustaining nourishment. If my mammary glands had been clued into their new role to start behaving like mammies, things would've gone more smoothly. Incantations like "Let the milk flow!" and "Produce, dag-blammit!" weren't effective. Where were wet nurses when I needed them?

Once I was off the barbiturates and Alex was regularly getting what he needed from my breasts, the hospital kicked us out. But I wasn't ready to leave. Did they understand they were sending this innocent infant home with a woman who knew more about teaching her dog to fetch than changing a baby's diaper? Where were Child Protective Service workers or nannies when I needed them?

Because Alex came into this world looking like a three-month-old, I was pretty sure I wouldn't damage him easily or right away. With the best of intentions, we muddled through each day. I knew I had to be careful. There were so many soft parts. Soon I was focused on some aspect of his survival every waking moment of the day and night, losing myself in bumbled mothering. At the same time, exploring Alex's new world helped me see my old world differently. That part was fun. I felt little tingles of wonder when he discovered something amazing, like his toes or my nose. The world was new, and new was nice.

Alex and I did our fair share of crying when we were raising each other. After an hour of his suckling on my breasts, two outcomes were guaranteed:

1. My nipples were swollen, red, and raw. They felt as if someone had decided to rub a Brillo pad to them, then douse them in rubbing alcohol. Merely washing them made me cry because of the physical and emotional pain. I had beautiful, symmetrical breasts. Now I was sure they were ruined for life.

2. Alex wouldn't just burp. He projectile-vomited anything he swallowed. Reruns of breast milk are only slightly more unpleasant than the first show. The fact that the vomit was splattered on everything within a six foot radius (depending on his head movement and my reaction to it) made the reruns both dramatic and disgusting. Although he was immediately hungry after his very productive burb and gush, there was no

way he was going to suck on my closed-for-business nipples. He would start to cry because he was hungry and I would cry because, well, I wasn't coated in Teflon.

I began expressing my breast milk so I could add rice flakes to it, thus making Alex's meals from a bottle more substantial so they would settle in his stomach rather than on our drapes. Even as my nipples slowly healed and the vomit fountains ended, I was still crying. Why?

1. I had failed as a nursing mother. I couldn't give my baby what he needed. Mothers of all mammal species feed their infants by suckling. But not me. Alex rejected my milk in a clear and unmistakable way, and thus I felt he was rejecting me in favor of a bottle with cereal added to it. Now that I finally warmed up to the idea of motherhood, my baby vetoed me. Was this payback for not wanting children?

2. I had to sit down several times a day with a pump hooked up to each bare breast and watch as milk collected in the container. Growing up near a dairy farm, I had seen the automatic milking machines attached to cows' udders. I felt as if I had been reduced to a "milker." Could I be less feminine? No wonder farmers had to artificially inseminate their stock. If Old Bessie felt like I did, she knew no bull would ever be interested in her sore saggy boobs and stretched out belly. I cried in mourning for the last vestiges of my dignity and my blue-eyed blonde hotness quotient.

How much of their waking life are infants supposed to cry versus coo and make lovey noises? I had no idea, but it seemed to me like Alex cried a lot. When he cried, I had my checklist of tear-stoppers—change his diapers, offer him some food, pick him up, rock him, sing to him, distract him with a toy or game, and/or let him watch me dial the phone for help. My first call was to Dr. Lollipop (his pediatrician). When Dr. Lollipop began screening my calls, I called my older sister and my sister-in-law—each had at least one child and both were infant-specialists compared to me. Usually, I just cried along with Alex. I was modeling empathy. The synchronized sobbing seemed to soothe both of us.

Victor often came home to a puffy-eyed, blotchy-faced family. How did I greet him? "Here, take *your* son. I need a break." He was happy to oblige. Being a great father was everything to him, whereas being a wife and mother was only part of me. Victor filled his evenings with Alex-time until we fell asleep, exhausted, until Alex woke in the wee hours, hungry and in need of a diaper change.

Although both the feeding and diaper changing could be done by either of us, I was usually the one to take the wee-hour shift. Victor worked. At a real job. For money. Theoretically, I could catch up on my sleep during the day. Theoretically, in some parallel universe, mothers who stayed at home with their demanding infants took restful naps while necessary household chores completed themselves because, in the parallel universe, magic happens.

Loneliness and loss swelled inside me during that first summer home alone with Alex. I needed intellectual stimulation beyond what a butterfly mobile and conversations with a drooling baby could provide. When I stared into the mirror, I saw a bloated, exhausted creature that barely resembled a woman. I decided I'd looked way better during my Lorna-the-Lush days. Was I looking at the person I had become or the person I would always be?

I made a note to buy more facial tissues the next time I was at the store. There were a lot more tears left inside me.

*****

Alex thrived in spite of my sub-par maternal skills and self-pity. His diapers may have been crooked, but his curiosity and language skills were impressive. His giggle was priceless, too. I had him shaking hands and "sitting pretty" in no time. No. Wait. That was dog training. Dr. Lollipop was pleased with Alex's three-month, off-the-charts growth and social development.

Still, I was the mother who longed for the day when I could:

1. Measure his age in years, not months

2. Communicate with him via words, not just sounds and gestures

3. Travel with one tote bag, not a carload of baby gear

4. Carry snacks, not whole dinners complete with full place-settings

5. Entertain him with books, not the entire stock room of *Toys R Us*

6. Leave him in the care of someone who knew about babies so I could resume my doctoral studies.

Wanting to be the best Ph.D. student, mother, wife, employee, daughter, friend, pet owner, and woman I could be, I was ready to attack year two of my doctoral program with a carefully considered plan. If the plan was a stool, its three legs were these:

1. I had to find suitable daycare for three-month-old Alex.

2. Victor had to be supportive both of having Alex in daycare and me back in school and my pre-Alex professional life. That was tricky because his job now required him to travel more often. I couldn't just hand Alex over at the end of the day to his loving father's arms. When Victor was traveling, I had to be both mommy and daddy for days at a time. For me, parenthood was like spending an afternoon with an insane but lovable aunt—tolerable and sometimes actually fun. Single parenthood, however, was like having the crazy aunt living with me. It was distressing and potentially dangerous to everyone concerned.

3. I had to juggle more balls than I could count. If I failed at any one of my roles, I failed big. But failure had never been an option for this Good Girl. If I couldn't do it, I could act like I could even if it killed me or gave me a nervous breakdown.

Knowing Alex would benefit from the exposure to someone other than his inept but determined mother, we decided to put him in daycare. He would probably miss his sobbing buddy, but I felt confident he would find an adequate substitute. After calling fifteen certified daycare providers and hanging up after hearing the eardrum-bursting din in the background, however, I began doubting our decision. My loving ineptitude had to be better for Alex than eardrum-bursting chaos in a stranger's home.

But Victor knew a woman from his church who watched children "on the side" (code for "not certified"). Since she was Methodist and grandmotherly, she was as certified as we needed. Saint Marge was a Godsend. I marveled at her ability to take in six children of varying ages, care for all of them, do things she needed to do (like pee and sew, although not simultaneously), and still appear sane at the end of the day. Maybe she was an alien or a Divine Being. She was wonderful and worth the $100 per week we paid her, even though Alex was only there part time. Saint Marge potty-trained Alex and told us the exact night he would take his first steps. Yes, she must have been just visiting earth.

*****

With Saint Marge taking such great care of Alex, I could focus on my studies and my work. Returning to campus, I discovered that I wasn't alone when it came to major changes. The Sociology Department had hired a big-name sociologist as its new chair. Tides had turned. The air was thick with arrogance. During my first year, every faculty member had loved me, the brainy young researcher who'd already been published. I was their Golden Girl. But now, under Dr. Arrogant's reign as Supreme Master of All That Was True, my skill-set was deemed useless.

Dr. Arrogant used his power as chair of the department to yank my job as a teaching assistant away from me and gave it to another student he wanted to serve as his lackey. The money I earned from that part of my fellowship package was meager, but it helped us pay our ever increasing bills. Teaching a class or two didn't hurt my resume, either.

"You don't need the money as much as that other student does," Dr. Arrogant told me, as if he had access to my bank statements.

"But my fellowship includes the TA position," I said. "And it is based on merit, not financial need." I was looking at my shoes because they weren't as intimidating as Dr. Arrogant was. Throughout my life, my shoes have been my confidantes and confessors. They have always been there when I've needed comfort in a sticky situation. For me, going shopping for new shoes is like going in search of a new best friend, but it's more about the emotional support than the style.

"Need I remind you that I'm teaching your qualitative research methods class?" he said. "You don't want to start off on the wrong foot with me, do you?"

"No." My shoes couldn't believe his poorly veiled threat.

"And I have every right to appoint myself to your dissertation committee," he said. "I can be a very difficult person to please if I want to be. Are you sure you want to fight me on that?"

At that point, I was using all my courage to hold back my tears. I didn't want to let that scoundrel see me cry because he would just define me as a weak woman, which I kind of felt like at that moment. So I said, "Fine."

"Good," he said, "See the secretary. She already has the papers for you to sign. You still get to keep the tuition waiver, so don't worry about that. I'm glad we came to this agreement. You won't be sorry."

That was a first. I had never been blackmailed before. As I waived and waved my teaching assistantship goodbye, I wondered if he had been the bully on his playground or the kid the bullies had picked on.

I ran into Dr. Dreamy's office and sobbed out what had just happened to me, his involuntarily retired teaching assistant. I could get away with crying in front of him because we had a great relationship. I couldn't hold in the overwhelming feelings of powerlessness and betrayal without risk of internal damage.

It took him a few minutes to translate my sobbing into English, but once he got the story, he was livid. He was also ready to march down to Dr. Arrogant's office and fight for me. But I stopped him. He was up for tenure, and I could see that dirty, rotten scoundrel, Dr. Arrogant, ruining Dr. Dreamy's career. I assured him I would be fine. Had I not been weeping into a fist-full of tissues, I would have been more convincing.

Year Two of my Ph.D. program wasn't going as smoothly as Year One had. And this was only the first day.

I missed Alex's first Halloween (he probably did, too, being only five months old) because I was sitting in Dr. Arrogant's class. Victor dressed him in Superman pajamas and flew him around to the few homes of people we knew, just to show off our super little man. I vowed to make all of his costumes for the rest of his life.

Despite my best efforts in Dr. Arrogant's class qualitative research methods, he gave me a B—the only one in the sea of A's that populated my graduate school transcript. I had sacrificed precious time with my little boy only to be cheated by that terrible professor. He used his position of power to bully those who weren't in lock-step with him and were thus (in his august opinion) intellectually weak. Did I get the B because I didn't drink or smoke pot during the last evening class, which he held at his apartment, or was it because I refused to pose as a homeless person on the streets of D.C. to help him with his newest research project? Dr. Arrogant mistook my integrity for weakness.

*****

Pursuing a Ph.D. is challenging in the best of circumstances. The best of circumstances might exist if I:

1. Were independently wealthy so I could afford every book I needed to study and every toy I needed to relax in luxury.

2. Had no distractions so I could focus exclusively on my studies.

3. Were related to someone with political pull so I wouldn't have to worry about the partisan shenanigans that are rife in any academic department. Yes, the hallowed halls of higher learning are as vulnerable to political chicanery as any public office, private workplace, or loving family.

4. Were male and always taken seriously. Although the social sciences were less sexist than the natural sciences, female students pursuing advanced degrees still faced subtle discrimination. I heard comments from male faculty members that female students were taking away opportunities from more deserving male students who were more serious about their careers. They assumed we women were trolling for husbands or would abandon our careers for a family. The fact that I'd gotten pregnant didn't help.

I didn't have any of those things going for me, so my road to the doctorate was rocky. Unlike the tough times during my master's degree program, now I didn't have the after-class drink-and-gripe sessions with compatriots. I had to commute home to my family after working my part-time job, spending quality time in the stacks of the PU library, then going to evening classes. I don't know how I did it. And I certainly couldn't have done it without Victor's support.

My doctoral program required two years of coursework, which supposedly prepared me to pass two seventy-two-hour comprehensive exams in my chosen areas of specialization: quantitative research methods and gerontology (the study of aging and its impact on the individual and society). The program allowed students who completed the requisite coursework one year to pass both exams and only *one try* to pass each exam. A master's degree in philosophy was the consolation prize for failing either exam.

By the end of my second year (May, 1987), I had completed all of my coursework. Classes ended just before Alex's first birthday, so I was able to give him a proper party, complete with a chocolate cake he smashed to smithereens.

While I was working and studying for my comprehensive exams, Alex spent most of his days at daycare with Saint Marge. I dropped him off and picked him up, often mid-afternoon-ish. We went grocery shopping, practiced words, walked Humphrey, and pretended to clean the condo until Daddy came home. Then Daddy took Alex, and I vanished into our bedroom/study room until dinner time. Together, we ate the meal Victor prepared, and I disappeared again until it was bath-time for Alex. Victor never liked to bathe him, but I enjoyed that bubbly time to splash and tell him silly stories. The fragrance of a freshly bathed and powdered baby was intoxicating (in the most wholesome way). Then Victor entertained him before his bedtime, and I often, but not always, rocked him to sleep.

Wanting to get the exams over as soon as possible, I continued working part-time and preparing full-time for my exams through the summer and the fall. Alex didn't see much of Mommy. Neither did Victor, but the PU librarians and the D.C. Metro workers and I became quite chummy.

At home, I seemed to be a magician's assistant who disappeared into the bedroom. That was my special talent.

Leave it to children to snap us back on the road when we've veered into a ditch. I knew I was shirking my maternal duties while I was cramming for those make-or-break exams, but Alex hit me over the head with just how much of an Absent Mommy I had become. One evening, I emerged from the bedroom/study room earlier than usual. As I strolled in to the kitchen to make myself some tea, my son, who was playing build-something-with-blocks-and-Daddy's-socks, looked over at me with wide, questioning eyes. He was clearly confused.

"What's the matter, Buddy?" I asked.

He responded, "Mama? Dada's ch-chin [kitchen]?" He thought I didn't belong in his father's kitchen. While we laughed about his observation, I got the message: Mama's a great student and can do better at everything else she was supposed to do.

By Thanksgiving, 1987, after I passed both grueling exams, phase two of my doctoral program began. This was devising a research idea that would add to the body of sociology literature in a meaningful way, justify my proposed idea, design the research methodology, conduct the research, write up my findings, and defend my results. Because there were no classes in that phase, which was like independent study, I thought I could make up for lost time with Alex, cook gourmet meals for my family, and pay more attention to my supportive husband by showing him some wifely gratitude (*wink, wink*). I hadn't lost any weight, but my nipples had long since healed.

My plans to finally make amends to my husband and child were premature.

*****

I had one year to write a dissertation proposal and get it approved by my dissertation committee (three faculty members whom I selected). If my proposal was not approved in one year, I would have to take those damned exams again. It was a perfect incentive to write a brilliant proposal in less than a year. For ten months, I did my research. Then I wrote the proposal of a lifetime. It had to be approved. I didn't give myself much time to redo it, but I wasn't about to take two more three-day exams.

The dissertation is what stops many a graduate student from obtaining their coveted advanced degree. Many, including me, approach it with the naïve notion that they can devote their precious time and energy to a research question that both interests them and has social significance. Some, including me, learn that the faculty members on their dissertation committee each have their own agenda, none having anything to do with what interests the graduate student. Completing the dissertation, therefore, is as much about navigating very tricky political academic waters as it is about research acumen or writing ability. Those who don't understand that fact (or refuse to accept it) end up with the letters ABD (All But Dissertation) invisibly after their name on their curriculum vitae and either give up or continue in Phase Two Purgatory for years via the magic of extensions granted by the dean. In that way, getting a Ph.D. is not all that different from any of the competitive reality television shows that clog up the air time. The winners aren't necessarily the ones with the most talent. They're the ones who know how to play the game or are very quick studies. I was a quick study.

In September, 1988 (three months shy of the year deadline), my 150-page dissertation proposal was approved. My reward? I got the privilege of doing what I said I would do in the proposal. The program allowed me four years to complete that task. Easy-peasy, right?

Wrong!

I suddenly got that familiar strange feeling in my core. It was either an extended case of gas or, despite my post-Alex weight gain, libido loss, and more fatigue than air-traffic controllers suffer during the holidays, Victor's pre-planned family was going according to *his* schedule.

I was about two months pregnant.

How could this be? I don't remember having sex? Did we do it while I was sleeping?

Victor was elated. I was deflated (before I started to visibly inflate). Just before Thanksgiving, 1988, when I was flying to San Francisco for a sociology conference, Victor made plans to come with me. His idea was to surprise me with a "proper" honeymoon five years after our wedding.

"You deserve it," he said. "You gave me a son." He got points for being romantic, but I had to take away points for chauvinism.

One week before the trip, I started to "spot. That's medical jargon for ruining the three panties I owned that still had some elastic sass. Dr. Spaniard advised against flying with or without the benefit of an airplane.

The honeymoon was canceled.

We decided to spend Thanksgiving with Victor's family, a full day's car trip away. Sometime between the turkey dinner and the pecan pie, I began to feel crampy—which is not to be confused with *cranky*, which I was as well. Too many mashed potatoes, perhaps? I went to the bathroom. Being a female and occupying the bathroom for more than twenty minutes without bath salts, candles and soft jazz sent up all kinds of red flags. Various people knocked gently and asked if everything was okay. I imagined a small crowd forming outside the door as I replied, "I'm not sure." I'm sure they wondered if I plugged the toilet with a gigantic turd or if I was experimenting with bulimia to finally lose a few pounds.

Victor finally ventured into the bathroom. He found me sitting on the toilet, pale, and staring blankly at my chubby thighs. No husband should ever have to see his wife like that. I told him that there was a lot of blood and... a blob. Not one to panic, he assured me that everything was fine. He called Dr. Spaniard. I kept bleeding. I was panicked enough for both of us. Even though I didn't want to be pregnant and do the mommy-thing again, I didn't want to kill my baby, either. I was a Catholic at heart. I could muster guilt for any occasion.

When we returned home, Dr. Spaniard confirmed that I had miscarried. Victor was disappointed, and I pretended to be, too, but I was really perfectly fine with it. The fetus had been so small that it was infinitesimal compared to a regulation baby, so I wasn't emotionally attached. Dr. Spaniard ran a hormone test just to be sure that the miscarriage was complete. It indicated that I was still pregnant. *Huh?* Another test. Same result. A sonogram. Pregnancy number two was actually twins. One had aborted naturally; the other one was lodged in my right fallopian tube, which required emergency surgery before one of us exploded. Emergency surgery it was. The alternative (my parts exploding) I considered only briefly, not wanting pregnancy—especially twins—stalking me for the rest of my reproductive years.

I had seven miscarriages during the sex-for-reproduction portion of our marriage. Alex was truly the Miracle Child. My body had only one childbirth experience in it and the data isn't all in yet regarding whether or not my disposition was favorable to parenting even one human being. If I had to be a parent, I'm relieved that I had only one, as opposed to more than one, child. Alex is all I ever needed or wanted. I'm glad he was the one that made it through my inhospitable womb.

*****

Even with only one child, that time in my life was chaotic. Here's what I faced:

1. My precious Humphrey had a stroke. Within a few months, I had to make the decision to euthanize him. He was a little over twelve years old, and I could barely remember life without him. I'd always considered Humphrey my first child and the scar on my heart over losing him still hasn't faded.

2. I had a dissertation to write and defend.

3. I was promoted to working full time as a researcher for the nursing home.

4. Alex reached his Terrible Twos about six months early and seemed to be planning to extend them because he seemed to be really enjoying himself.

5. I was recovering from emergency surgery and dealing with all kinds of conflicting emotions— mine, Victor's, mine and Victor's.

6. I picked up the linguistic tic y'all, which was shocking for a Northern girl with unsullied grammar, diction, and vocabulation.

7. We eventually decided to move back to New York State, where we'd both grown up and still called home. That meant completing my dissertation long-distance. The chances of completing a doctorate are small to begin with.

Layer on raising a child, moving away from my scholarly support network, nesting in a new home, and starting a new job, and my chances became as infinitesimal as those twins that were never meant to be.

The only way to cope with everything that was piling up on me was to live on auto-pilot. Deal with the day-to-day stuff and stuff the troubling stuff away. Which is what I did. I was really good it. An expert. I'd done it all my life. Only now I had to do it without the benefit of booze. I wondered aloud to my reflection in the bathroom mirror, "Can I handle all of this?"

CHAPTER 16: CHA-CHA-CHA-CHANGES

Home, Sweet-Jesus-What-Was-I-Thinking, Home

Six years in the city was enough for us country bumpkins. The more Alex grew and formulated noises that sounded like words, the more concerned I became about having to home-school him rather than set him loose in the danger zone called the Prince George's County public school system. Whether it would be Alex and me fighting about why I was better at teaching than the gang at *Sesame Street* or it would be Alex lecturing the tough kindergarten gang about proper manners—someone was going to get hurt. Victor and I made moving back to our bucolic roots a priority. Nothing important was keeping us in D.C. except my dissertation research and our jobs. Victor was confident that we could find professional jobs "back home" where cows outnumbered humans; and my dissertation could be completed anywhere. That's what he believed, so that's what I believed.

The hunt for jobs was on and we sold our condo.

Two steps forward, one step back, *cha-cha-cha*. As long as Victor was leading the dance and we remembered to smile for the crowd, he wouldn't let the restless rhythm inside him stop us from being everything he wanted us to be. All I had to do was stay out of his way and keep up with him at the same time. Soon I became hypnotized by the music and didn't even notice the blisters forming on my feet. *Cha-cha-cha*.

During the fall of 1989, I contacted the professor with whom I had previously done grant research during my swinging, swigging, single days. She was thrilled to hear I was returning home because she received another grant and was looking for a reliable research assistant. She didn't know I was sober this time around, but then she hadn't known I was drunk when we were such a wildly successful team years before. The grant wouldn't begin until the summer of 1990 and we just sold our condo, so we could move any time. We sub-let a condo in our development on a month-to-month basis while I looked for a temporary job until the grant started and Victor looked for permanent employment.

Even though Victor's employment history was as stable as a mountain, whereas mine was a wobbly as a toddler on rollerblades, I had more luck finding work. I was hired as a full-time temporary sociologist at the one community college (let's call it Local Community College, or LCC) back home. There were two highly unusual circumstances surrounding my getting that job: teaching positions in that small college were rarely vacated (the man I replaced had been there for over twenty years), and the

222

search committee interviewed me over the phone and hired me sight unseen because I'd refused to travel up at my own expense for the on-site interview. Either I was that impressive or they were that desperate. Beginning in January, 1990, I left D.C. to go home and teach six sociology courses (five courses was a full-time teaching load) for the spring semester at LCC. Until that time, I had only taught one course for PU and had been a guest lecturer three times. *Preparing* for six courses was an absurd amount of work to do while also packing and preparing for a major life move. *Teaching* six courses was even more absurd. I don't know if my students learned anything that semester, but I sure did. I learned that I could be talked into anything and, given the proper incentives, I could bamboozle anyone. I should have already known both of these things, but they seemed like newsflashes to me.

By January, we hadn't found our own home yet and Victor hadn't found a job. Until he found a job, he commuted nine hours each weekend to see us and to house-hunt. Alex and I moved in with Victor's parents, who lived in a renovated sixteen-room farmhouse. My mom still lived in an unrenovated five-room trailer. I like to attribute the decision to live with Victor's parents purely to physics, but I have a sneaky suspicion that he wanted to be on his turf.

It was awkward at first, but we eased into a routine where I tried to fit into their routine. My in-laws were very gracious and generous. They loved being Alex's live-in grandparents and Alex loved being their live-in grandson. When Grandpa and Grandma wanted their privacy, they had a vacation cabin in the mountains on a small lake. When I wanted my privacy, I closed my eyes. The life of privacy I conjured behind my eyelids was quite lovely, though always fleeting.

Work on my dissertation stalled because my responsibilities as an amateur college professor teaching more courses than seasoned or sane professors ever took on were overwhelming. I considered myself ahead of the game when I was one week ahead of my students.

The upside is that, since I wasn't distracted by my dissertation, I managed to spend a great deal of time with Alex. He was almost four years old and I discovered that maybe I wasn't such a doofus-mother after all. I remember one evening as particularly special. It started off like almost all others:

1. I was exhausted, Alex was revved up.

2. He needed to go to bed, mostly so *I* could get some rest. We splashed through his bath,

3. I cajoled him to accomplish the dreaded brushing-of-teeth.

4. We flipped and wiggled him into his footed pajamas.

5. It was finally time to read his favorite book for the two-hundredth time. That was the last hurdle before prayers and blissful "lights out."

By now, we were sitting on the edge of his "big-boy" bed and I was working up some enthusiasm in the face of reading the same old words, pointing to the same old pictures. Then I got an idea. And here's what made the evening both special and memorable.

"Once upon an elephant, there was a hamburger named Todd and a bathtub named Copper…"

Alex looked up at me, wide-eyed. He took the book from me and looked at the cover to see if it was different. "Mommy, *read it*." He pointed to the first page. He knew the words by heart and these new words were wrong.

"Okay." I nodded and started again. "Once upon a donkey, there was a hiccup—"

Alex's laugh erupted from his toes and burst out in bubbles of uncensored joy. A contagion of laughter infected the room. He threw himself backwards on the bed, laughing so hard his little-boy body bounced up and down. I threw myself backward to join him in horizontal hysterics. Laughter morphed to tears of joy washing over our faces, pooling in our ears.

"Mommy, I love you," Alex said, looking at me through blue-gray eyes blurred with his sweet tears.

"Oh, Honey, I love you, too," I hugged him hard and squeezed a few more giggles out of him.

I wished Victor could have been there to share in this silliness and sweetness, but that moment was obviously meant to be shared between this unlikely mother and her miracle child.

"Read the funny way more, Mommy. Please?"

I did so until our nights of reading aloud sadly ended.

*****

Victor moved in with us in late February, when he got another job in the financial sector. We were finally able to start our house-hunting in earnest. After living in the D.C. area, we expected homes here to be reasonably-priced, but we were buying in a small seller's market. My luck in getting good deals in the real estate market was about as good as my chances of winning the lottery. Let's review:

1. I'd rented a slummy apartment for six years, during which time mine was the only apartment that wasn't burglarized. I can thank my big, happy-to-bark Old English sheepdog for keeping my worthless possessions safe.

2. We had bought our condo located on the edges of a suburban ghetto when interest rates were in the twelve percent range.

3. We broke even when we sold our condo. "Buy high and sell low" was our unfortunate practice.

4. We were living in Victor's parents' home—a lovely home, indeed—and facing another situation of buying a home that, whether it needed work or not, was priced beyond our means, with high interest rates (the nine to ten percent range).

Then Victor got an idea. Actually, he was fixing to make his childhood dream come true: to own an abandoned house about three miles from his parents' home. I knew about the ramshackle structure because he made a point to drive by it nearly every time we came home for a visit.

"I'm going to own that house someday," he told me. He had also told himself that very same thing as a child. A lot.

When Victor had shown me his abandoned dream house in the past, I'd always nodded in polite support. I was agreeable because I figured his aspiration was preposterous. To me, it looked like a haunted house that even ghosts had abandoned because it was unfit for the living or the dead. To Victor, however, it was a piece of local history that he could revive. His vision for that house was grand. Since I thought his dream would never come true, what was the harm in supporting him and his vision? That was my first serious miscalculation in what would turn out to be a stunningly long series of Victor-related miscalculations.

Since habitable homes for the living were proving impossible to find and residing with his parents was turning from temporary to semi-permanent, Victor's idea of buying the abandoned house was beginning to sound tempting. That may be an overstatement. More realistically, I was willing to listen to the possibility of buying a haunted house in lieu of living with my in-laws forever. In my own home, I would be living with *my* husband and son; in my in-laws' home, I was living with *their* son and grandson. Generous as they were, I'm sure my in-laws wanted their home and privacy back, too.

On a frigid, gray day in late February, 1990, the owner of the house that had been abandoned for twenty-five years agreed to show us the place. Icicles resembling fangs hung from the roof. He came with the "key"—a crow-bar he used to pry the plywood off one of the doors. (Most of the doors and windows had plywood covering them.) With flashlights illuminating our way, we entered the cold, dark house. Victor and his dad were giddy with excitement. I was apprehensive and cautious. With each step, I wondered, *What's all the crunching about? Bones? Teeth?* What we were crushing were walnut shells. For over twenty years, squirrels had called the place home and carried in black walnuts from the trees on the property.

As we proceeded through a maze of rooms, I fully expected skeletons and/or ghosts to jump out at me. We eventually entered a room that the owner called The Parlor. Shining my flashlight around the room, I saw exquisite woodwork around massive windows and doors. It was in that room that I finally saw the "potential" Victor had envisioned all along. Maybe it was a magic spell, but the old house somehow "spoke" to my heart. I was sold. If Victor was crazy to want that house, then so was I.

He wasn't surprised at my positive reaction, but then he'd thought I was on board with his idea all along. That I don't have an Academy Award for my various performances is a mystery. But I also surprised myself. I truly loved that old beast (I'm referring to the house, not my husband). My mom and sisters, on the other hand, couldn't believe what they were seeing when I took them to see the wreckage after we bought it. They did their best at being supportive, but I can only imagine what they said when I wasn't around. I may have grown up in a trailer, but at least our accommodations were up to code.

True to our tight bonds, my family was there to help during those first months when we were struggling to make the old house habitable. Tina and her husband Jim had a camper that they parked on the property when they came over to help with demolition projects. The camper gave us private bathroom facilities and a working kitchen—the only modern amenities on the property for many months.

We bought a house built in 1810 and fancified in the 1870s by the same builder who had built Victor's parents' home. (The circular staircase design gave the fancification away.) Through its history, the house had survived three fires, the last in the mid-1960s, and had been deserted ever since. Even though they had modern conveniences back in the 1960s, the house lacked:

1. Running water

2. Indoor bathrooms

3. Electricity that wouldn't kill you if it worked, and it worked only in certain parts of the house

4. Windows (all smashed or unusable)

5. Insulation (unless you consider newspapers from the 1800s as insulation)

What did the house have plenty of? Never mind. If there was a Demolition Derby for houses, it would have been the hands-down loser.

At the closing, we got word that the well-driller finally struck water, but they had to drill down 580 feet to get it. That was just the beginning. For years, we sank stacks of money deeper than that well into our dream house. It was more money than we had ever imagined having. Or spending. To save money, we did much of the demolition work ourselves with a lot of help from our families. Victor did the heaviest lifting—he was Business Man by day and Demolition Man by night and weekends.

In August, eight months after Alex and I had moved in with my in-laws, we moved into our own house. All three of us slept in a tent in one of the bedrooms because the new windows hadn't arrived yet. A blanket served as the bathroom door. A used claw-foot bathtub served as both a place to bathe and a place to wash dishes. We had a charcoal grill, a hot plate, a microwave, and a refrigerator. Camping inside that 4,000 square foot house, we were a bit rough around the edges but happy. It was, as Victor continually reminded me, An Adventure and A Learning Experience. I'd never liked camping as a kid, and now camping as an adult wasn't any more attractive just because it was inside our big old house. Imagine getting presentable for work when your bathtub is also where you have to wash your breakfast dishes.

Cha-cha-cha.

In June 1989, I started my new job on the grant, which included teaching three courses at the Local State University (LSU). With the clock ticking on the amount of time I had to complete my Ph.D. research, I also resumed my dissertation work, but I had to analyze my statistical results and write up my findings in the middle of the construction site that was my home. Victor never hesitated to summon me to help him hoist sheet-rock or hand him tools. I was supposed to know which ones he needed, so there were many tense moments when he got upset with me for not being able to read his mind and know exactly which tool to hand him. Apparently, I wasn't the perfect

Demolition Man's Helper, and he let me know it. But I'm not a man and I don't think like a construction worker, traits you'd think he would have appreciated in a female, so I frustrated him more often than not. If he had let me know which tool he wanted as easily as he let me know how unhappy he was with me, the home improvement program would have been a lot more pleasant.

As it was, I was simultaneously apologizing for not anticipating his tool needs, listening to a lecture on how anyone with half a brain could see what he needed, and (when he was finished with me) trying to get my half-a-brain back into dissertation-writing mode. I decided I really didn't like construction. (I still don't.) It had a very destructive effect on my self-esteem.

We borrowed money to bring the house up to code and hired a contractor to do the major work. I always assumed the resulting product would be a beautifully restored 4,000-square-foot home that we would happily live in until "they took us out feet first." Within a reasonable time-frame. That was my second serious miscalculation.

*****

The limbo rock was a popular dance when I was young. Two people held up a bar or a pole and people vulnerable to pack mentality shimmied under the pole, bending backwards. The winner was the most flexible fool who made it under the pole without falling down or breaking her/his back. I was getting so good at the *cha-cha-cha*, and now I had to learn another dance. At least it had a Latin beat.

I always noticed that the pole was held pretty high in the beginning. Victor was a great planner. He knew the rehabilitation process because he had been through it before when his parents bought and restored their old farmhouse. I was blissfully ignorant of what it took (financially, physically, emotionally, and mentally) to live in a house that was being restored. My role was to be supportive wife, mother, and wage-earner. We both had inspiring visions of our beautiful historic home. It was easy to shimmy under the pole then.

Victor devised construction phases, time-lines, and specific budget allocations. I trusted in his detailed written plans. They seemed so thorough and logical. What did I know? I was raised in a trailer. You go to the trailer store, pick one out, get it delivered, and move in. Simple.

But there was nothing simple about what four-year-old Alex soon dubbed the Broken House. After he nearly fell from the second floor because the balcony was missing, I cautioned him never to wander around the house without adult supervision (something I never did either) because there were too many things still broken in the house.

"Is this house broken, Mommy?"

I smiled and hugged him. "Yes, Honey, it is kind of broken, at least right now."

Thereafter, whenever he referred to his home, he called it the Broken House. He stopped calling it that sometime before he turned ten.

I still call it that.

The faux-limbo pole was first lowered when two astronomical and unexpected expenses had to be dealt with: the well that reached the earth's core and the massive roof that needed to be replaced, not simply resurfaced, as we had budgeted for. Money for minor luxuries—like real insulation and interior doors that closed—disappeared. But I was still flexible enough to bend under the descending pole.

When the construction crew left, the pole dropped further. I looked around. To my untrained eye, not much had changed. The exterior of the house was the same, except we had real doors, windows and an entry way that had stairs rather than sloping planks. The interior was still skeletal, with wires poking out from everywhere, framed-in walls (some with insulation, some without) but no sheet-rock on most of them (or on the ceilings), and floors that were still exposed, rough-hewn pine planks—the kind where splinters were just gunning for your feet. Our domestic limbo rock dance was getting uncomfortable.

We created a modest kitchen when we purchased a used one from some lucky person getting all new cabinets and countertops. The refrigerator was new, but the stove and sink were hand-me-downs. Our "new" kitchen didn't have a dishwasher (if you excluded me), either.

We eventually had two serviceable bathrooms…if you focused only on the fixtures and not the surroundings, like ceilings or walls. At least each bathroom had a door that would close. A new heating system and updated electrical wiring made the house habitable for the colder days of autumn and winter. By this time, I sincerely missed our condo back in D.C.—the one with painted walls and no wires sticking out of places that could hurt you. Even when we heard that a drug-related murder had happened just down our hall a few months after we left, I looked around the Broken House and felt a twinge of nostalgia for that finished, albeit crime-scene, condo building.

Victor picked away at insulating, wiring, and sheet-rocking the walls and ceilings after work and on weekends. He became, understandably, burned out. After the place was carpeted and some of the ceilings and walls primed, work ceased. I, understandably (at least to me), became frustrated. The structure I was living in was not the home I had envisioned when I'd jumped on board for this home renovation project. Victor's "good enough," however, trumped my "but it's not finished." Thus began the years of living in the Good Enough Broken House. Victor ignored my attempts to point out all the unfinished work.

"Focus on all we've done," he kept saying. "Be more positive."

The pole was ridiculously close to the ground and still I tried to squeak under it. Hurting from the contortions and ignoring the pain, I tried to see things his way. *I should focus on the positive*, I kept telling myself. *That means Alex, my work at LSU, and completing my dissertation.*

But I was positively sick of living in a house with exposed insulation and wires. Was I asking too much to live in a house that felt like a real home?

Apparently I was.

Cha-cha-cha. Bend over backwards. *Cha-cha-cha.* Maybe I could start a new dance craze. Well, it *was* crazy.

*****

One AA hangover that has stuck with me is the Serenity Prayer. Alcoholics didn't invent it, but they chanted it like they did.

> *God grant me the serenity to accept the*
> *things I cannot change;*
> *the courage to change the things I can;*
> *and the wisdom to know the difference.*

It asks a lot, but God, I've always heard, is known for fulfilling impressive requests. Reluctant to invoke God, I just sent out a general SOS. *Please grant me...* Then I made my *Help!* list, which was colossal. At the top was something time-sensitive.

The clock was ticking on my dissertation. I'd moved home after my proposal was approved, giving me four years to complete my data analysis, write up my results, get my final draft approved by my dissertation committee (hopefully they remembered me), and defend my work to the committee and selected experts in the field of my subject matter, which involved predicting the likelihood of consuming alcohol. No surprise there. If you want to know a person's secrets, ask what they would love to learn more about or what major they selected in graduate school.

Without email or texting available to me in the early 1990s, I communicated with my committee via Pony Express, otherwise known as the U.S. Postal Service, and expensive toll telephone calls. In 1991, there were also no cell phones with "anytime, anywhere minutes." I had to balance completing that last leg of my doctoral marathon while I was also working full-time as a researcher/college instructor, caring for Alex, coping with the challenges of the Broken House, trying to be Victor's good wife, and keeping up with my personal hygiene. Notice that my personal hygiene is last on this list. That's because it was last on my "to do" list. Yes, I was looking and feeling as broken as my house.

The final chapter of my dissertation was the hardest one to write. Synthesizing all existing knowledge in the relevant academic literature on the drinking behavior of adults in light of my research results and offering insightful directions for meaningful future research on what factors might predict whether any random person is likely to start drinking or not isn't as easy as it sounds. My dissertation presented a complex statistical model for predicting whether any random person was likely to be a drinker or an abstainer. As long as I was going to delve deeply into the topic, I thought I might as well explore something personally relevant. It was that old "kill two birds with one stone" approach to picking a dissertation topic.

I wrote the final chapter at home, in fifteen-minute intervals with constant interruptions by Alex and Victor, each needing me for various urgent matters: story reading, inept tool handing, telephone answering, beverage service, coloring, video tape changing, meal preparation, and/or transportation to find better meals. In addition, there was laundry to do and the following loud noises:

1. Hammering (not the fun drinking kind)

2. Screwing (not the fun, bedroom kind)

3. Summoning of the "Lorna-bring-me-a-torque-wrench" or "come-here-I-need-you" kind (not the fun, call-to-the-bedroom kind)

To this day, I wonder if men writing dissertations have these challenges. Of course not! They always have someone like me to insulate them from distractions and general household/construction commotion. They have important intellectual work that needs their undivided attention and they cannot be interrupted. I was a wife and a mother, meaning I was perfectly interruptible. Even though I dropped my dreams of being a perfect wife or adequate mother, I still succumbed to the interruptions because I didn't want to fail at either role. I knew I could somehow pull a decent dissertation together in spite of my unfavorable, not-exactly-scholarly environment.

As interruptible as I was, I completed my dissertation within a year of moving home and my committee approved it. In April 1991 I went down to PU in Washington, D.C., to defend my original research. Maybe it was adrenaline, maybe it was nerves, or maybe it's PTSD, but I don't remember much about the defense. I hardly slept the night before, which worried me because I wanted to dance as nimbly as Gene Kelly through the questions those experts and scholars would be tossing at me. When I arrived, I found about fifteen people sitting around a huge table with my manuscript in front of them. I think the "dance" lasted about two hours, but it felt more like two days. The chair of my committee escorted me out of the room so they could deliberate on my future. He came back out in about twenty minutes—or was it two days?—later.

His exact words were, "Congratulations, Doctor. Is there anyone you would like to call?"

Victor was waiting at his sister's home in nearby Virginia. I called him.

Then I cried.

All the way home on the Metro train, I kept saying to myself, *I did it. I earned this. The hardest of hard ways. No one can ever take this accomplishment—this validation of my capabilities, fortitude, and courage—away from me.* I edged toward a Lorna that stood a bit taller that day.

*****

There are four possible outcomes of a dissertation defense:

1. Approved with no changes (rare as a Sasquatch in Manhattan)

2. Approved with only minor changes (the result graduate students only dare to dream of and few get to realize)

3. Approved with major changes (the most common outcome because most professors like to make students suffer for the longest time possible)

4. Not approved (rare, as this only happens if someone at your dissertation defense has a

personal grudge against you but can't afford to hire a hit man).

My dissertation was approved with only minor changes. I had dared to dream and the dream came true.

I had to make those minor, mostly cosmetic, changes between the time I defended my dissertation and Graduation. Victor helped me go through the approximately 300-page manuscript to make sure I addressed all the changes noted by the committee. Then he pointed out a sentence that *he* wanted me to change, but that the committee hadn't flagged.

"What's the matter with that sentence?" I asked him.

"I think it sounds sexist," he said.

The sentence was in the Results chapter. It was a factual sentence about men drinking more than women regardless of any intervening factor.

"I can't change the sentence," I said. "It states what the data revealed."

"Well, you could make it sound less biased. You're a sociologist. You should be more sensitive to prejudicial statements." His tone suggested he was doing more than making a helpful suggestion.

And here's where I crossed a line with Victor, the man who had to be right but was also willing to have a wife with a Ph.D., while his highest level of education was a bachelor's degree.

"A whole panel of experts in the field read this entire dissertation," I said, "and they didn't have a problem with that sentence. *Who are you to complain about it?*"

Another serious miscalculation on my part.

"Who am I?" he asked, and not rhetorically. "*Who am I?*" he asked again in his trademark sanctimonious-but-wounded tone. He was able to intimidate me with both his absolute certainty that he was right and his vulnerability.

"Are you going to lord your advanced degree over me now? You couldn't have gotten where you are without me, and you know it. How dare you think you're better than me just because you have a 'Piled Higher and Deeper' [Ph.D.] degree now?"

After sending all those rhetorical questions zinging past me like poison arrows, he walked out of the room and began hammering on something other than me.

I sat there fuming, fighting with myself about whether I was right to stand my ground or wrong to have chosen words that apparently demeaned him. In the end, I sought him out and apologized to him for insulting him.

"I never meant to 'lord' my degree over you," I told him. "I know I wouldn't be where I am today without your support. You're a smart man and I love you. I'm sorry."

"Are you going to change that sentence?"

"Sure."

I never did. But saying I would do it made him happy. Making things right between us was the only way he would keep dancing with me. And dancing with him was all that I knew how to do now.

*****

There's an old saying attributed to the most quoted author of all time, Anonymous: *My karma ran over your dogma*. Anonymous knew what he or she was talking about.

A good definition of "dogma" is: a principle or set of principles laid down by an authority as incontrovertibly true, as in Victor (an authority) asserting the incontrovertibly true principle that he was always right. If I disagreed with him, I either had to keep quiet or suffer the consequences of his ire. But anger was never an emotion with which I could deal effectively in myself or others—it

238

scared me for reasons having to do with my disappearing father. So I learned early on to squelch my opinions and silence my voice in my conscious attempt to create a peaceful relationship. When I expressed my contrary views, I ended up apologizing for them just to restore harmony.

A good working definition of "karma" is "what goes around comes around," as in sooner or later Victor's dogmatic approach to life and the resulting stifling of my spirit either by keeping me silent or by my eliciting my constant apologies when he felt threatened was going to come back and bite him. Sooner or later, I was going to find my voice and use it without the predictable act of contrition.

Karma was coming for Victor. He got a taste of it when I defended my scholarly work, but could either of us take a whole meal of it?

(Cue fading Latin rhythm.)

CHAPTER 17: TURNABOUT IS FAIR PLAY...I SUPPOSE

My baby was growing to a darling little boy who I was beginning to understand. I was also growing, not just as a better parent, but as a bigger parent.

My life in the Broken House was stabilizing. I was becoming accustomed to the half-rooms and learning the syncopated rhythm of being a mother, researcher/lecturer, imperfect handy-woman, and supportive wife. Then things just had to change. If they hadn't changed, I would have wondered whose life I was living.

Federal research grants end, unlike the government entities that fund them. I knew that, but I also knew about grant extensions and the always popular, "need for further research" new grant applications. I thought about familiarizing myself with Wiccan full-moon ceremonies to conjure spells that might bend time, space, and the federal budget, but having had some very creepy experiences with a Ouija board as a teenager, I decided that simpler positive affirmations for continued funding might be my best course of action.

It didn't work. I was out of a job and I had to find work that would help to pay the ever-increasing, nightmarish bills that Victor's dream home was bestowing upon us. I still wanted to believe in the dream that the house would someday reach its potential as the grand home we envisioned, but my imagination, faith, and optimism were dwindling.

Remember my Job Fairy? I didn't, but she remembered me. And she was still on duty. Two full-time, tenure-track sociology teaching positions opened up at about the same time. We lived in a small town with one local state university (LSU) and one local community college (LCC). The chances of one (let alone two) sociology full-time faculty positions becoming available at the same time were about the same as being almost hit by lightning twice. Wait. That happened to me, too.

I applied for both positions. My preference was the faculty position at LSU, where I was already teaching and doing research. The faculty knew me well and I was a popular member of the department—even the students liked me. The bridge to LCC was still strong, too. My teaching evaluations for all six courses were high and the professional staff, both teaching and non-teaching, remembered me fondly. I was a college professor who knew how to teach and play well with others. Never having been turned down for a job for which I had applied, I felt confident that I would soon be a full-time assistant professor at the school smart enough and fast enough to snap me up.

The application and interview process proceeded quicker at LSU. During my time teaching there, I had the highest teaching evaluations in the sociology department. I knew every professor well—many of them had been my professors when I attended there as a student. I even knew the dean and the Vice President of Academic Affairs, with whom I had interviewed. I felt sure I would get the job. But I wasn't very psychic back then. They hired a woman with no prior teaching experience who was from some exotic part of the country, like Peoria, Illinois.

I would learn later, from self-reflection and inside information, why they chose a single, childless, inexperienced, caustic woman over me:

1. I threatened the predominantly male faculty members. Seeing me as a mini-version of the woman who brought all the grant money and notoriety to the department, they didn't want the female equivalents of Batman and Robin in their midst. Batman was quite enough. Along with my mentor who, thanks to her research, rarely taught, I was the hardest working and most popular (among the students) faculty member in the department—and I wasn't even a real member of the department. The male members of the faculty search committee must have had a hard time with my current and future success as an educator. Yeah. I might make them look bad.

2. Since the decision to hire came down to the recommendation of the faculty search committee, and many of them had been my professors several years back, I think the fact that I was a former student colored the way they

viewed me as a potential colleague. Except for Introduction to Sociology, which was as stimulating as watching your grandfather clip his nose hairs, I'd aced all my sociology courses. So it wasn't competence that was an issue. Maybe I made them feel old.

3. I had a small child. They were no doubt sure that the demands of a full-time faculty position plus the requirement to publish for tenure might have been "too much" for little me to handle. That paternalistic and blatantly discriminatory discussion took place during the final decision-making process between Dr. No Experience (but no family either) and me. Someone leaked that to me. While I could have slapped these sociologists with a discrimination suit, I didn't have enough money for a lawyer or enough proof beyond hearsay and a "sorry you didn't get the job" phone call that I didn't have the means or wherewithal to record.

Doing what countless victims of unfair hiring and labor practices do every day, I turned my attention to trying to find another job. Lucky for me the LCC faculty position was my fallback option. The pay and chances for advancement were deplorable, but it was a teaching job and that's what I needed. Teaching is the focus of faculty at a community college, so there is no pressure to publish to be awarded tenure. All I had to do was immerse myself in every committee ever created, teach my classes, and not make waves with the ultra-conservative administration. Since I'd spent my life so far pleasing people, I learned quickly how to please the administration, my colleagues in the faculty, and, most importantly, my students.

Search committees in academia are curious, large varmints. I didn't know if everyone wanted to examine the new kid on the block before I got to be the new kid, or if they simply didn't trust each other, but they recruited half the staff to hire me. I made it past each hurdle. Even the janitors liked me. Most of them remembered me from that one grueling semester when I'd taught six courses. I had learned back in my days of being piddled upon by arrogant people (which described most of my life to that point) that it is wise to be kind to every person with whom you work, no matter what their position. The lower in the organizational chart their position is, the more they likely know about what is really going on, thus the more power they really have, whether they know it or not. Plus, it's just better form to respect people. Until they give you a very good reason not to.

I was invited to LCC for a first interview and then a second. The second interview was a full-day affair, the pinnacle, a gang-bang interview. Fifteen or more faculty members from various academic areas ganged up and fired soliloquy-questions at me. Too many faculty members love the sound of their own voices. They also tend to lack that much-admired quality of humility, so they ask protracted questions that are really essays expressing their own copious knowledge. Never had I noticed these traits more than in search committee interviews. Many of their interview questions to me were fairly obvious attempts to impress the other people in the room.

One professor prefaced his question with an oration about the importance of students coming to class prepared by having read the assigned material but not having done the reading. He blathered on about his frustrations at that unsolvable problem and the anarchy it created in his lecture plan and in the world as we know it. He ended his monologue-question with, "How would you *guarantee* that students come to your classes prepared?" Before I reveal my answer, please keep in mind:

1. I was exhausted from a day of being interviewed.

2. He had just told everyone in the room that, in his expert opinion, there was no way to guarantee that students came to class prepared.

"I agree that your concern is a grave one," I responded. "I have no idea how to ensure students do their assigned reading. What ideas do you have?"

The room rippled with suppressed amusement. The rather prim-looking English professor sitting next to me said under her breath (but loud enough so a few of us could hear her), "Oh, I love this woman!"

After the tittering went quiet, and I could tell he was quite uncomfortable, I offered the ideas about pop quizzes at the beginning of class and short assignments based on the readings to be handed in at the beginning of class that would be required as entry to the class. Of course, attendance would have to be a factor in the students' final grades.

He recovered nicely.

And I got the job. I even managed to negotiate my salary up a couple thousand from the normal starting salary for an assistant professor at LLC. I had a Ph.D. and was making $28,000 per year. There was no pay differential in the contract for my advanced degree, research experience, or publications. And no faculty member was ever hired at anything but an assistant professor level. It just was never done, thus it was impossible to even contemplate. I was working for an institution of higher learning that was founded on the principle of "even if it *is* broke, don't fix it."

I shared an office the size of a walk-in closet with a long-timer faculty member who taught biology and hoarding. During my first week there, I rarely saw her because she was hidden behind stacks of papers and files yellowed from exposure to decades of academic hot air. But one day she emerged to give me this sage piece of advice: "If you want to be happy here, keep your head down and just teach. They'll leave you alone and you'll be fine. Whatever you do, though, don't get involved in the politics around here. They'll grind you up like hamburger and eat you for lunch."

"Okay," I squeaked.

What kind of college was this? I'd come back to academia to get away from conflict, smarmy bosses, and back-stabbers. Had I jumped from the electric chair onto a bed of nails? But given my experience with the only job I wasn't hired for, why was I surprised? Politics, it seemed, was everywhere.

At least I had a job. My home and financial life were stable again.

Then Victor decided to switch careers.

*****

Victor always said that major events in our life came along every three years: married in 1983, child in 1986, beginning of Project Relocate to Broken House in 1989. It made perfect sense, then, that 1992 would be another year of change. My Ph.D. and my new job had happened in 1991, but they involved the word "my," so they didn't count as Major Life Events. Something bigger, more memorable, and relating to directly to Victor had to mark 1992.

Victors was unhappy at his current job where advancement was impossible and where he felt underappreciated because he wasn't in charge. Then an opportunity collided with him. He bought a business involving sales, about which he knew nothing. Well, he always liked a challenge. He was confident that the thing he knew nothing about couldn't be *that* hard to learn. After all, *he was always the victor*.

He wanted very much to be his own boss and let his creative, entrepreneurial spirit fly unencumbered by the bureaucratic machine that provided security and stability (SaS) to us. He had me providing the SaS now—health insurance, a pension, and a guaranteed job once I got tenure. We discussed his potential opportunity at length until he talked me into believing the certainty that it was a fantastic idea. He reminded me that he was "the anchor" when I pursued my dream. Now it was his turn. Victor was a smooth talker. Arguing with him was like throwing Jell-O on Teflon. My points about the security of *two* guaranteed pensions and income just didn't stick.

SaS was now my responsibility. How could I argue with that? I figured if he used that kind of smooth-talking with his clients, he'd make us the ton of money he envisioned and the Broken House would be broken no more.

How many miscalculations am I up to? Four?

*****

His business overhead was low. That's because he set up his office in our house and some of the rooms didn't even have ceilings. Victor was selling *concepts*, not vacuums, Tupperware, or encyclopedias. Because clients would theoretically come to his office to hear about Victor's concepts, he had to fix up at least a few parts of the house. That's when I learned a great deal about "business expenses" and "tax deductions."

Here's what was great about Victor owning his own business and having it in our home:

1. He was happy and energized. He looked forward to going to work—some days without pants.

2. Some rooms that were broken got fixed, although they were decorated in Modest Office Sterile rather than Dream Home Comfortable.

3. If Alex got sick, Daddy was there (most days) to stay with his son while I was in class. But Victor had done regular Daddy-Duty for sick Alex in his former job, too, because it was hard for me to miss classes.

Here's what was *not* great about Victor owning his own business and having it in our home:

1. Before we could afford to fix enough of what was broken to make a decent-enough office for him and his minuscule staff, he set up shop in various locations in our home. In the middle of the living room. In a vacant space outside our bedroom. While mostly it was just him and Kay, the assistant he hired to answer our phone (our personal number and his business number were the same for a while), file, and generally keep him organized, there were often awkward, underwear moments…his and mine, but, thankfully, not Kay's.

2. As his business slowly grew and the private spaces in our home could no longer accommodate the occasional client and a growing staff (two or three support people), a whole section of the house was renovated into

his office space. The part of the house that had the most charm was cordoned off and filled with desks, file cabinets, and computers. I was no designer, but I was sure that was not the best use of that potentially grand space. I had envisioned a library with leather chairs and floor-to ceiling wooden shelves populated with classics, not a call center with cubicles.

3. The other, "private" areas of our home, except our bedrooms, were fair game for strangers. Employees and clients had to use the bathroom. Lunch and coffee breaks were kitchen affairs. In the summer, I couldn't be seen in just a bathing suit; it was unprofessional. If I baked cookies for Alex's class, I had to make enough to share with Victor's staff. I couldn't sing or play music; it distracted the "work flow." My personal life became the business's business.

For me, the most difficult and unforeseen result of Victor's foray into small business ownership was that nearly all of our resources (and more) went into the hungry mouth of the business. After renovations to his office area, any work on "my part" of the house was halted because the business needed the money. We became indebted to the business with the promise that, in the future, the rewards would be vast.

"Be patient, Lorna," Victor said with the conviction of the determined entrepreneur he was. "The first three years of a new business are the hardest. Once we make it past that, we'll see the money come back to us. Then we can finish the projects you want finished around here."

"Three years??" I stopped listening after I heard that. I'd be dead of exasperation by then.

"It will all be worth it," he insisted. "I promise. We invested in *your* Ph.D. Now we need to invest in *my* business. Together, we can do anything. Alex is proof of that."

"If you say so."

I said he was a smooth talker.

*****

Victor worked incredibly hard to build his business. It devoured both him and our money. At the end of very long days of very long weeks, he had little energy for anything but eating and sleeping. When he could still conjure up some mojo, it was devoted to Alex, his pride and joy. The house and the wife that rattled around inside it were equally abandoned and broken.

I was working steadily, too, of course, investing my energies into activities that rewarded me. My little-girl need for attention didn't go away just because I grew up. I still craved to be noticed. Teaching gave me what I needed on a professional level, at least. My students loved me, the administration respected me, and most of my colleagues in the faculty admired me. Some were jealous of my immediate success, but even they had trouble rounding up a posse to try to run me out of Dodge.

Alex needed me in the way that all little boys need their mothers: to keep them fed, clothed, entertained, safe, clean, and out of serious trouble. I also got him ready for school and made sure his homework was done. I signed him up for sports. Even though I am allergic to team sports, I attended his games and cheered when the other parents did. He turned out to be as allergic to team sports as I was, but at least we both gave it the "old team try." I was, in effect, a married single parent. That is how Victor must have felt when he took on extra Alex Duty while I was working on my doctorate. But his duties were evening only, whereas mine were virtually full-time.

Not only was I waiting for the three-year business start-up period to be over so that the money would start pouring in rather than just leaking out, but I was also hoping that Victor's dogged attention to his business would moderate and he would remember he had wife and son. I gained "I'm not happy with my life" weight during this time. Maybe if I was a bigger target, he'd notice me. If he did, he didn't say so. Alex did, though. He asked when his little brother or sister was arriving. I told him to enjoy being an only child.

Enter Pseudo Brother, a guy Victor met through a client. Pseudo Brother became the brother/buddy/confident/collaborator Victor never had but always longed for. If Victor needed a break from the stresses and demands of running a fledgling business, he found it with Pseudo Brother. They biked and played racquetball together. Victor even spent time on the weekends helping Pseudo Brother with *his* home repair projects.

My "double-D's" didn't just stand for my bra size anymore. I felt Discarded and Dumped. Ever the "pleaser," though, I still doted on Victor because:

1. He was pursuing his dream.

2. He'd found a great friend to have fun with and find some relief to the mega-amounts of stress he was feeling (the reason he was so tired and not interested in any bedroom antics, or so he said).

3. He still made time for Alex by volunteering to coach his Bad News Bears version of a soccer team. I found that amazing because he knew nothing about soccer, but not knowing

something had never stopped Victor before. Practices and games were the only times besides meals when I saw him. At least we were all together in the same quarter-mile radius.

Victor was a fine, hard-working man and great dad. My needs, I decided, were selfish; so I bought larger clothes and became the best college professor, mom, and wife-on-call that I could be.

Deep down, however, I resented Pseudo Brother, nice as he was, because Victor clearly liked him better than he liked me. I tried to love Pseudo Brother as much as Victor did. How else would I ever see my husband if I didn't invite that man into our life and home?

And my miscalculations kept piling up.

If I had made a list of Victor's priorities at that time, they would have been:

1. Building his business

2. Spending time with Alex

3. Spending time with Pseudo Brother (and all related activities they shared)

4. Paying the bills

5. Eating good food

6. Watching the news without being disturbed

7. Sleeping

8. Telling anyone who would listen how to fix the problems in our country

9. Spending time with me

10. Fixing the Broken House

During the first year of our marriage, Victor probably wondered what the heck he had gotten himself into and who he had married. He probably wondered if I was even there for most of that year, given my struggle with alcohol—even though after I quit the second time, it was no struggle at all. Since that time, I had done everything I knew how to do to be everything he wanted me to be, to make up for my alcoholism, and to prove I was good at my core.

Now we were on different sides of the same closed door. We were approaching our tenth anniversary, and I felt like my husband had left me without telling me—he was gone but somehow still there. Had our marriage license somehow expired when he signed papers to own his own business and find a new best friend? How was I supposed to know who he needed me to be when he wouldn't even talk to me? Maybe his staff had sent me a memo and I'd never received it. I wasn't great at sorting and filing my paperwork.

I made a mental note to go through the mail and anything else that might give me a clue as to whether or not I had inadvertently lost my husband.

CHAPTER 18: PUSHMI-PULLYU

Even though I was a larger target, my husband didn't seem to see me. Maybe I needed a new look.

There probably comes a time in most marriages when the "until death do us part" vow seems either ill-advised or an invitation for Crime Stoppers. That time was coming in my marriage.

Hugh Lofting's Dr. Dolittle discovered an enigmatic creature on one of his marvelous adventures. This was the Pushmi-pullyu, a beast with two minds of its own. When both heads were aimed in the same direction, not much could stop it; but when opinions differed, trouble of the "stuck-in-the-mud" or the "rip-it-to-shreds" kind started brewing.

I discovered that our marriage was a Pushmi-pullyu beast through and through.

Victor and I were at our best when both of our heads and hindquarters were aimed in the same direction. Together, we had weathered many storms, including my alcoholism, parenthood, my graduate school, moving home, endless repairs to the Broken House, and his small business start-up.

By nature and choice, Victor led and I followed. That's what this fatherless, middle-child, I-aim-to-please Good Girl did as a matter of survival. I lived in fear that I would disappoint the people (men) that I wanted, no— needed to—please and become invisible to them. I made sure that "disappointment" and "Lorna" didn't travel in the same circles.

It was 1995 now. Time for another change. Victor's Law, that Every Three Years Something Big Happens, was immutable. His sales business was now so successful that he had just bought another old building to rehabilitate and then relocated his office out of the Broken House. He seemed attracted to older buildings in much the same way some men are attracted to older women, though, I imagine, for different reasons. Or maybe not. In the process, he hired more staff. My academic career was in overdrive, too, so career-wise, we were solid gold.

One change was definitely needed. Since my girth required me to shop in the Women's Plus department of Wal-Mart, I decided it was time to change my eating habits. Victor had gained a few extra pounds, too, but he was working them off with all of his extra-curricular activities with Pseudo Brother. Since dining out was the only activity we did as a family, I had to think carefully about my new eating plan. Victor already thought my food preferences were strange. Here are three of the stranger aspects of my old eating habits:

1. At some point during my youth, I'd decided I hated chocolate. My sisters loved me for that resolution, especially around Halloween, Christmas, and Easter. They got all my chocolate candy. To this day, I believe that avoiding chocolate kept my hair naturally golden blonde while my chocoholic sisters' hair turned darker over the years.

2. I disliked butter and high butter-fat ice-cream (except during my pregnant months when all bets were off).

3. I never liked fish or seafood of any kind. Who eats slimy, gross creatures that eat slimy gross creatures? I suppose a lot of people do, but I'm not a lot of people.

Now I decided to become a vegetarian. An animal-lover all my life, I don't know why I didn't think of that sooner. I was always queasy when it came to eating any meat that resembled body parts, like chicken wings, beef ribs, that poor pig with the apple stuck in its mouth. Beginning my change in stages, at first I ate only blobby meat like hamburgers and meatballs, not hunks of flesh that had bones and could, at least if I was living in a scary movie, move itself toward me. Eventually, however, my conscience and dignity shamed me into full-blown vegetarianism. How could I say with any credibility to my friendly server, "I'm a vegetarian, please don't put sausage in my spaghetti, but you can add extra meatballs"? Vegetarians and blondes don't need more jokes at their expense.

At least Victor, an epicurean adventurer and delighter in all that is tasty no matter where it was last spotted, was tolerant of my quirky new diet. But when ten-year-old Alex voluntarily joined me in my vegetarian stand,

Victor's tolerance morphed into apprehension, then to dismay. Our dining-out menu and venue options shrank considerably. For starters, Alex hated anything green, except Popsicles and lime Jell-O, so we became Italian. To Victor's credit and for the culinary challenge, he became quite a good vegetarian chef.

When I finally realized that substituting gooey cinnamon buns, pasta, and potatoes for meat wasn't the way to lose weight, I realigned my new vegetarian diet and started looking less like a Russian weightlifter and more like a shapelier pre-Alex me.

Ever so slowly, my self-esteem peeked up from the trenches into which it had fallen. I kept getting promoted and recognized at work. Victor showed his appreciation for my support of his entrepreneurial adventures by setting aside money for an entire kitchen/great room home-improvement project. Thanks to my weight loss efforts, I was getting smaller and with my career on track, I was getting bigger. Now was the time to assess my life with a new set of eyes. Pullyu eyes.

Victor was a reasonable man, especially after a couple of generous martinis, so my plan was simple. Every few days I would casually mention one of the few but major irritations that were fermenting in my mind, and ever so rationally I would offer a reasonable solution that would satisfy us both. He would finish his second martini, agree, and we'd turn on the news so I could be quiet and he could be informed.

My top three Victor-related frustrations were:

1. His office was more livable than our home. While I had grown to love our home because it was our home, I was ashamed of what it looked like. Victor chided me for never wanting to entertain clients at the house, but his office was much more inviting for guests than our home

was. That's because it was finished. I was embarrassed to invite anyone but immediate family members to the rooms in which we actually lived. Everything about the Broken House, inside and out, was in need of attention that had obviously fizzled out.

2. The Broken House wasn't the only thing suffering from lack of attention. I was a lonely wife who missed her husband. Victor had no time or energy for me in the way that I needed him. "Not tonight, dear, I'm too tired," was his line, not mine. But if Pseudo Brother called him up and asked him to get together, he was always raring to go, no matter when or where. I was jealous of his business and his friendship because he put them before me.

3. Our approaches to disciplining Alex were different. We needed a compromise position. Victor wasn't around Alex as much once Alex turned three and we moved home, so I became the parent who did almost everything for him. I knew his temperament better than his father did (or so I told myself). Although I tended to give Alex the benefit of the doubt when there was any doubt, Victor wasn't as lenient. He kept telling me, "I was a boy once. You weren't. I know what he's up to." He had a point, but so did I, "Alex isn't you," I finally replied. Victor didn't like that. I could never stand up for myself against him, but I stood up against him many times in defense of our son. Even though I was probably wrong to do so about half the time, I suffered Victor's wrath for not agreeing with him every single time.

These irritations were all solvable, so I put my Two-Martini Plan into action. My miscalculation was epic in comparison to any previous ones. What happened as a result of my Two-Martini Plan reminded me that there was a reason I was never a planner.

When the Pushmi-pullyu is going in different directions, its outward appearance still looks unruffled, but on closer inspection, you notice the uncomfortable straining. What is happening on the inside?

*****

I gently addressed my concerns over time and martinis. Victor was reasonable and listened as long as I didn't use *that tone*—it's the tone Husband hears as judgmental and accusatory but Wife delivers as an objective assessment of a factual circumstance that any judge and jury would find admissible, even impressive, in court. Yes, *that tone*. The problem was that Victor kept hearing a tone that I was deliberately not using.

Our communication issues needed more than a voice coach to fix. Victor felt that I was criticizing him for being a bad provider, husband, father, and maybe all-round bad human being. I felt that Victor didn't understand English.

Each time I raised a concern, Victor turned it around and blamed me for criticizing him. Being criticized and frustrated, I started crying, which, unfortunately led to *the tone* and toddler-like sentences ending in "so there!" or "that's just mean!" Then he started giving me *that look*—the one the Husband gives to the Wife (or vice versa) that says, *You're just making my case for me, I'll just wait for you to dig that hole you're in just a little deeper, go ahead, keep digging.* Victor had long perfected *that look* (probably because I gave him so many opportunities to practice it).

He was also a natural at confrontation. He loved a good argument, whereas I got all tongue-tied and confused and started sputtering like someone had watered down my high-octane gasoline.

I hated *that look* and the composed, aloof way he delivered it. My only option was to retreat in shame. After my self-imposed time-out, I came back to Victor and apologized. Always. He graciously accepted my apologies and bestowed upon me helpful hints about how best to avoid these marital blunders in the future by adjusting my behavior. He believed in the positive transformative power of his constructive criticism. My constructive criticism of him, it seemed, was less positively transformational.

Here are the outcomes of my planned action items to address my top three Victor-related frustrations:

1. His office was more livable than our home was. I clearly didn't, he said, comprehend what it took to run a successful business and how long it took to make a young business profitable. His office had to look professional and feel comfortable so he could impress his current (and future) clients. I also, he said, "conveniently" forgot all the "improvements" to the house and the routine benefits the business provided to us. Stop whining, he said, and be happy that I have a home with such grand "potential."

2. I was a lonely wife who missed her husband. His rebuttal was that I clearly didn't understand the enormous demands and stresses he faced every day as a small business owner. Everyone "wanted a piece of him"—clients, staff, colleagues, community members, professional organizations, et cetera. Our relationship was

founded on mutual values and support, not lust. Then he said, "Stop reading romantic novels."

3. <u>Our approach to disciplining Alex was different and we needed a compromise position.</u> And here, he contemptuously asserted that I clearly didn't understand children, especially boys. Alex wasn't as innocent as he pretended to be. Stop being so gullible.

The Pushmi-pullyu was stuck, its insides quivering. Everything returned to a quiet "normal," at least on the outside, with Victor always taking the lead. At least that's how I saw it. Maybe he would remember it differently, with me being the demanding, pushy one, but in that manipulative way where females, children, and hostage negotiators are trained to exploit situations to their advantage while pretending to be on your side.

In addition, I was providing the sure and steady bill-paying income, *not him*. While I did it happily and never lorded my stable job over his risky venture, he kept reminding me that "someday this business will take care of us." Maybe he was reassuring himself that I hadn't taken over the role of our family's primary "breadwinner."

Thus is the nature of the enigmatic Pushmi-pullyu: when the heads are facing different directions, how can they ever see eye to eye?

With all the pulling and pushing getting us nowhere, something shifted inside me. I didn't know if anything shifted inside of him. We were connected on the surface, but so deeply disconnected otherwise.

*****

261

Two things happened that changed me, and thus our marriage, forever. As I said, it was 1995 and change was in the air.

First, having given up on romantic novels, I began reading New Age books about exploring my Divine Inner Self, mostly hoping to find out if I had one. I started a daily journal because that's what Divine Selves do. My Divine Guts spilled out onto the pages with my private hopes, frustrations, and thoughts. I was writing without fear of criticism or censorship. The prefaces to all of the books I read about journaling assured me that these journals were sacred and no one would ever read them. It was basically guaranteed in black and white and in regular, not fine, print. Not being one to keep secrets (except for that whole alcoholism business), however, I told Victor about the journal. Sometimes I even wrote in it while he was in the room. Rather than hide it in a place so secret I might forget where I put it, I simply kept my Divine Journal in different Divine Places, all hidden from view, and trusted that journals were sacrosanct and that Victor would respect my Divine Privacy. Since he barely noticed me, I figured my Divine Journal was as invisible to him as I was.

Then I literally ran into Phil, my former college boyfriend—the hunk in the library, the man of my dreams who had made those dreams come true for six weeks before he broke up with me. While I wouldn't say I was obsessed with him, I sure thought about him from time to time to time to time, wondering if he remembered me. Something stirred in me when I thought about him and, if I was going to fantasize, Phil was going to be the center of the fantasy. Maybe I was a little obsessed with him, after all.

One afternoon, Phil was ascending while I was descending a stairway at LCC. (That's how I literally ran into him.) This serendipitous event sent me into a tornado-like tail-spin. I always figured that, since he resembled

Tom Selleck, Phil left a trail of broken hearts behind him. I was sure I was just one among a caboodle of anonymous broken-hearted females.

Amazingly, Phil recognized me. "Lorna, is that you?"

All I could muster was a nod. When I found my voice, we went down the stairs together and caught each other up on eight years' worth of our lives. I learned he was married and had a son Alex's age and an infant girl. He'd moved from Boston and now worked at a local company managing their information technology department. He said he had never forgotten me. I gave him the happy version of my life, and then we hugged each other and exchanged emails, "just to keep in touch on our birthdays." He had to go back to his meeting and I had to go back to my office.

We met twice later for very public and awkward lunches. I wanted to see him as a friend, but he always was and always would be so much more than that. We found it difficult not to touch each other when we were next to each other. Actually, just being near him got too hot for me to handle. Two lunches were enough to prove that our chemistry was too volatile to risk any more encounters. I didn't know it then, but I wouldn't see him again for a very long time. What I did know then was that my heart *ker-thumped* like a washer with an off-balanced load of twenty XXL flannel shirts. So did my libido. I was seriously giddy. That still-handsome man remembered me, noticed me, and still wanted me. Victor was close and well within my reach, but he didn't care to touch me; Phil was now close (in the same geographic area), but, alas, well out of my reach because we were both married with children.

So now my journal became my confessional and fantasy playground. There was one hunka-hunka-burning-love out there who had never forgotten me. I loved it! I was *somebody* to this man. I felt like I'd taken my first bite of sweet watermelon on a sweltering July afternoon. A paragraph later, of course, I struggled with guilt and remorse over each delicious thought or feeling. I was married and had Alex to think about. My heart and head were turning into a Pushmi-pullyu of their own. I wrote about that, too.

Knowing that anything I wrote in my journal was as confidential as what was whispered between a hit-man and the woman who hired him, I wrote my wild ramblings about Phil (past, present and...*sigh*...fantasy future) and my mind-numbing, spirit-crushing guilt over anything Phil-related. I had never felt so deliciously distraught.

Then, in a moment of Divine Inspiration, I stopped writing so feverishly about him. I felt like the fiery writing was making me more amorous for my untouchable man. If I stopped writing about Phil so much, I told myself, maybe I could focus on the deeper issue: what was missing in my marriage and life that made escaping from it so appealing? So I Divinely Wrote about that puzzlement. Which led me right back to Phil. I saw a pattern developing. I closed the journal and began reading more about finding my Inner Divine Self. I hoped I was more Divine than a guilty, compulsive, journal writer obsessively not thinking about my former lover. The Divine New Age Books, I was sure, held solutions to my challenges.

*****

Luckily for me in 1996, discord was brewing somewhere other than just in my marriage. The administration at my college was treating the faculty unfairly. Newly tenured, I was now fortunately immune from the former policy of firing untenured faculty the current president disliked for their political views or hair styles. Then Victor encouraged (cajoled) me to take an active, public role in fighting for a fair and equitable contract. He was completely supportive when I decided to do so, even though my instinct was to stay in the background and provide other, more natural, leaders with support in the form of research and/or speeches. I was always better in the chorus line than on center stage (even if I secretly longed to be the star everyone adored). But Victor loved taking on a good cause. He was a brilliant puppet master and master strategist. He could see the game the administration was playing and advised the faculty, through me, to switch from defense to offence. I became the articulate, intelligent, sweetheart voice of the faculty. Victor stayed behind the scenes, coaching me and at the same time letting everyone know that he was the brains behind this operation. Together as coach and assistant, we made an incredible and effective team.

My infatuation with Phil faded into the background. Suddenly I had a partner who cared about me—the professional, public me he wanted me to be, but part of me, nonetheless. Victor was proud that I was quoted in the newspaper, wrote erudite letters to the editor, and even inspired a few editorials. I was basking in the glow of his pride. His business was also increasingly successful. A new feature to his success, bonuses and profits, made a few vacations and home improvements possible. I felt like we were moving together and headed toward the same destination—a lifetime together.

I received yearly birthday emails from Phil and he received them from me. I loved and hated those emails. Sometimes, they were simple catch-me-ups, but sometimes conversations developed until it seemed like we were poised on the opposite ends of a rickety bridge and in danger of meeting in the middle. We had something special, something elemental, between us. I didn't want Phil out of my life. He'd gone away once and come back.

What were the odds? Were we meant to be together? But Phil had a family and so did I. We'd missed our chance to be together. My internal Pushmi-pullyu was hard at work not picking one direction.

If it's true that everyone has a special "one that got away," that was Phil. Victor knew about him. Early in our marriage, when my drinking was the only thing I was trying to hide from him, I had told Victor about Phil. He didn't seem to care. I guess I left out the part about Phil being my "one that got away." We were newlyweds and I thought it was best to focus on the "one that got to stay."

Phil and I kept our cherished distance. I wrote about my Divine Conflict in my Divine Journal, proving to myself how much I loved my husband and how confusing love can be.

Life was manageable until 1998. I should have known something big was going to happen. Three years had passed.

Victor read my Divine Journal. This gave us a textbook case of *Who Betrayed Whom?* He and I disagreed on the answer to that question.

*****

In retrospect, it seems to me that Victor must have figured I was up to no good because I seemed too happy. Knowing that Phil was on the same planet reminded me that I was a desirable woman, and that lifted my spirits. I used my new-found ego-boost to improve my looks and try to get my husband to notice me. All he noticed was that I was happier. Our relationship hadn't changed. He probably hadn't given any thought to my journaling and therapeutic reading of New Age self-help books.

My string of Victor-miscalculations kept getting longer and longer.

Phil aside, I was slowly discovering my Divine Self. Divine Lorna was lovely.

Victor's behavior slowly changed, too. He surprised me with a family vacation trip to the Caribbean. He bought me extravagant jewelry. I thought our relationship was experiencing a renaissance of sorts and I wrote hopeful entries in my journal.

Then, one summer day in the middle of the week, he asked me if I wanted to go for a ride before lunch. That was highly unusual because he was always extremely busy having business lunches. Although I felt a bit leery because the offer was so unexpected, I hopped into the car and we headed, literally, for the hills. We chatted about nothing important until we got to our destination, which was a dirt road in the middle of nowhere. He parked the car.

The secluded surroundings and his deep breathing might have been mistaken as a sign of romance, but that wasn't the vibe I got. Then he turned to me ask asked, point-blank, was I "seeing" Phil? He knew from fifteen years of marriage that I was not a person who appreciated being surprised. My heart races, head spins, and I generally go into a mild form of shock. But he interpreted my hesitation as a yes rather than "Lorna's brain just shut down." I sat there, dumbly staring at a tree as if it were the most fascinating creation since the invention of the Fisher-Price View-Master, while he carried the conversation with rhetorical questions starting with "Why?" and ending "Do you have any idea how much you've hurt me and Alex?" Whenever I started to speak and tried to explain the truth of the situation, he cut me off with his next question. I eventually figured out that this was less of a Q & A and more of just a big Q session. He already knew the answers, or thought he did. I was simply there to witness the pain I caused him. Again.

Not once did it occur to me to ask him, "How did you find out that I even saw Phil again?"

Now I know that either being psychic was a talent he never shared with me or he had ferreted out my Divinely Hidden Divine Journal and read its Divine Contents. Read them selectively. I didn't consider either possibility at the time, although if I'd had my wits about me I would have gone with the latter.

Unfortunately, my wits were nowhere to be found. I just took my verbal beating quietly as he likened me to a manipulative, malicious hussy, even though nearly all my life I'd fought so hard not be that person—pages and pages of my journal proved it, but I guess he'd skipped over those parts.

The scene was a rerun of the time when I confessed that I was an alcoholic. Victor announced that he would "keep me," but only under certain conditions. He must have watched a lot of *Let's Make a Deal* when he was growing up. He said I had to:

1. Stop "seeing" Phil, which must have meant I must stop visualizing him, because I wasn't actually seeing him.

2. Start attending church regularly with him as a family.

3. Arrange for marriage counseling on the grounds that I was an infidel who needed dehussification.

Unlike the ultimatum of 1984, in 1998, I told Victor I had to think about the ultimatum. That shocked the shorts off him.

My first priority now was to straighten out that whole "seeing" Phil misconception he had. I had seen Phil three times, three years ago, and had been in email contact with him twice a year—not exactly a torrid love affair or a cyber-sex addiction. If Victor had counted the number of times I "saw" Phil" in my mind, well, then, he might have had a case, but he made it sound like Phil and I were regulars at the Red Roof Inn.

The church condition seemed to come out of nowhere. It clobbered me over the head like the anvil falling on Wile E. Coyote. Victor knew I was in danger of breaking out in leprosy or hypocrisy if I attended church more than the obligatory Christmas Eve and Easter service, but now he said he wanted all of us to go every Sunday. He knew how to punish a wayward wife. But if I did this (and with good cheer), it would go a long way toward showing him I was committed to the marriage. That's what he said. At least I think that's what he said. Remember, I was kind of traumatized.

I also had to decide who I wanted more—my husband (real and remote) or Phil (fantasy and remote). Victor talked me into choosing him. After he was finished talking me into the indisputable fact that I was unfaithful in the worst way—in my heart and just as shameful as Jimmy Carter (his admission of "lusting in his heart," versus his presidency, which was decent enough). But Victor still didn't want to end his marriage to the alcoholic liar he'd married. I guess he was the forgiving sort, just like Roslyn.

What made him hang on? I gave that question a lot of thought.

1. He loved me that much. No. That wasn't it. The only non-sleeping action our bed saw was when I changed the sheets. Sex isn't the only way to express love, but I wasn't getting much in the warm-and-fuzzy department. Victor and I lived together and went places together. The same could be said of Felix Unger and Oscar Madison.

2. He loved the idea of me. That was a good possibility. Victor was quick to compliment me in public and criticize me in private. That was his special technique to motivate me toward becoming the person he always knew he wanted me to be. I was so fundamentally flawed with such great potential under his tutelage. He never came right out and said that, but I felt like I was one of the projects he had taken on, like becoming a millionaire or restoring the Broken House.

3. He wanted to keep the family together for Alex's sake. Another good explanation. Alex was only twelve years old. Victor emphasized how important two parents are to the successful upbringing of a child. I kept thinking my mom did a great job raising her three girls by herself, but I didn't dare bring that up because now Victor had issues with my two sisters. Since he knew they had never approved of him as a suitable husband for me, he constantly pointed out their quirks and the flaws in their marriages. And the list of gripes he had with me seemed to be growing daily.

4. He wanted to keep the family together for appearances. A very plausible explanation. Appearances were very important to Victor and his family. He was a successful businessman in a small community. What would his clients and potential clients think of him if his marriage fell apart? After bingo, gossip was the only sport in town. While he liked to be the subject of conversation, I bet he didn't want people speculating as to why I ran off with a married

man. It would look bad for Victor on too many levels.

5. He took his wedding vows more seriously than God did. I suppose that was possible. I just couldn't understand that kind of devotion to any structured religion.

Like the Broken House, I had so much unrealized potential. Victor could never pass up something unique that held future value. I suppose I qualified as unique. And, being Thursday's Child, I always did have "far to go...."

"You don't know what a real loving relationship is like," he told me. "Since you grew up without a father, you never saw how a husband and wife who love each other struggle through hard times, sometimes fight, but always remain friends."

"Okay. I guess you have a point," I said. "I never had any role model for 'normal' parents."

"Yes. You're using romance novels and movies to judge how a *real,* mature marriage should work. That's not real! Romance is a honeymoon thing, not a lifetime thing. At these stages in a marriage, couples are more like partners and friends." I'm paraphrasing here. Victor was more articulate, but I distinctly remember him saying the word "friends."

I didn't have a counter argument. Maybe it was guilt, logic, or fear of what would happen to Alex and me if we were on our own, but I chose to accept Victor's 1998 ultimatum...with the caveat that he had to understand that I wasn't "seeing" Phil. The new arrangement was that I had to break off all communication with Phil. I agreed on the condition that I could meet with Phil in person to tell him. I needed to do that. At least I would get to actually see Phil again for real one more time.

The deal was struck.

Meeting with Phil just to break things off was miserable for both of us.

"How did Victor know about our communications in the first place?" Phil asked. His eyes were so dark, so filled with the most alluring mixture of longing and concern for me.

"I wrote about you in my journal."

Silence punctuated by wide-eyed disbelief.

"Yeah," I admitted, "I shouldn't have written anything down about you. I know that was kind of stupid of me."

Phil had been a paratrooper in the Marines. He stood 6 feet, 3 inches, weighed maybe 250 pounds. He looked pretty imposing. I was a little afraid of him at that moment.

"He *read* your *journal*?" The incredulity in his voice was genuine, but I don't think the question was. I think the question he wanted to ask was *You actually wrote about us in a journal that you left lying around your house?* Or maybe *He had the balls to read your private journal?* It was hard to tell. I was a-flutter with a combination of fear and lust. I was very confused.

"Yes," I admitted again. "I feel really violated, but that wasn't the focus of any of our conversations." I went on to explain to him that, reluctantly, I had to stop emailing him and recommit myself to my marriage. "It's the right thing to do. For our families."

Phil, equally reluctantly, agreed.

He wanted to hug me as a parting gesture, but I wouldn't let him. I knew that if I let that man put his arms around me, I might just stay there with him forever. What were the chances that the man of my dreams would ever show up in my life a third time?

Although it was a sunny day, I felt like I needed my windshield wipers as I drove home. My vision was blurred by a torrential tear storm.

*****

Marriage counseling began and my Divine Writing and Reading Adventure ended. I donated a ton of New Age self-actualization books to my local library. I hoped they wouldn't ruin anyone else's life.

I can't reveal what transpired during the counseling sessions (privacy issues, blah, blah, blah), but Ms. Let's Explore That, our counselor, soon discovered that counseling a Pushmi-pullyu makes for an interesting walk in the park.

CHAPTER 19: PERCEPTION—IT IS ALL ABOUT HOW YOU LOOK AT IT

When he wasn't busy playing in the snow or in the water, Wolfer was teaching me a great deal about how to navigate life's bumpy road with grace and good humor.

I have a master's degree in counseling, so I was prepared for what we were facing. For a fee, the counselor, Ms. Let's Explore That, asks the Troubled Couple vague yet probing questions and assesses the Relationship Dynamic based on who answers and who doesn't answer and on body language rather than any words actually spoken. After several sessions together, the Troubled Couple sees Ms. Let's Explore That individually to identify each party's perspective and pinpoint what's wrong with

274

The Marriage, meaning the Person Not in the Room. This supposedly helps each party feel something resembling empathy for the other while it also boosts each party's self-esteem as it assures them that they are Good People in a Difficult Situation. That process varies in length and success. Finally, Ms. Let's Explore That sees the Hopefully-Not-As-Troubled Couple together, and they collectively decide if they want to save the marriage or skedaddle.

Ms. Let's Explore That immediately saw that our Relationship Dynamic was a classic one: Parent-Child, or in our case, Father-Little Girl. I was under the impression that Victor and I had a fairly equal partnership; but, well, I was also under the impression that automobile navigational systems always get you to where you want to go. Victor and I were both working as professionals and he always told others that we made a great team. Wasn't that proof enough that we were equal partners? Ms. Let's Explore That didn't see it my way.

Here's what she saw:

1. Victor did most of the talking and I did most of the listening. Unless I was specifically asked a question. I suppose she interpreted that as "children should be seen and not heard."

2. Whenever a decision had to be made (the next appointment, whether it was time to be seen individually, or if we should increase or decrease the number of our sessions), I deferred to Victor or Ms. Let's Explore That. I thought I was just being agreeable when I said, "Whatever works for you is fine with me." And it was. I had lived a lifetime of adjusting to other people's desires because that's what Good Girls do. Until now, being Miss Congeniality had

been good. Now it was bad because I was laying the burden of every decision on my poor husband's shoulders. The weight of all that control was apparently tedious and annoying. Didn't I have an opinion of my own? Well, actually, no—not about the next appointment. Other people's opinions suited me just fine. I was told (by Ms. Let's Explore That) that I needed to take responsibility for my own decisions and their consequences. Yeah, I thought. Yeah. That's what got me here. Good plan.

3. When things got tense, I cried. What Ms. Let's Explore That didn't know was that I cried whenever I experienced an intense emotion. Crying wasn't a sign of childish weakness in me or a means of manipulation. It was my passionate emotions spouting out of me like an over-pressurized fountain. My highly sensitive nature was sorely misunderstood and underappreciated by almost everyone in my life except my dogs.

4. I didn't have a father growing up. When she heard that Ms. Let's Explore That got all Freudian on me and suggested that I subconsciously sought out men who were ready, willing, and able to make decisions for me and keep me dependent. She was dead right there. I did not, however, and never would have penis envy.

5. I never defended myself when Victor made accusations of the "Lorna is a lying vixen" kind. Ms. Let's Explore That felt that my staring at my shoes and weeping was more child-like than

adult-like. When she asked me, "How does that make you feel?" I shrugged. Wasn't it obvious? How would it make you feel if your husband was a self-absorbed man who ignored you except to read only the most damning parts of your private journal and accuse you of sins you never committed? I wanted to ask that out loud, but I avoided the confrontation because it led to anger, which led to remorse, which led to guilt, which led to me apologizing just to stop all the distress. Dear Lord. I was a child!

Seeing us separately, Ms. Let's Explore That helped us to see that we were both responsible for our Couple-Troubles. That newsflash from an objective third-party was like my seeing piled-high presents on Christmas morning. I wasn't the only Couple-Troublemaker! I had secretly longed for another man and even contacted him; and, yes, I had allowed myself to be a child in my marriage. But Victor consistently chose to ignore me when I begged for his attention and he had also violated my trust by reading my private journal.

Our individual and separate counseling sessions lasted about four months. We saw Ms. Let's Explore That as a couple most weeks. During the early weeks, when she wanted to see us separately, she saw us each of us in the same week. Going to marriage counseling filled our social calendar

Finally Ms. Let's Explore That thought we were ready to live life without her. She had some conditions for both of us to agree to if we wanted our marriage to work. That was new. I wasn't the only one having to change! To save our marriage we *both* had to:

1. Behave as adults, not as Father and Little Girl.

2. Communicate regularly about issues in a nonjudgmental way. That meant we had to learn how to talk to each other so that we each heard what the other was actually saying, not what we thought the other meant. To do that, we had to start many sentences with, "I heard you say…" and listen to many sentences that began with, "Um, wrong…"

3. Forgive ourselves and each other for past transgressions, real and imagined.

4. Move forward with a clean slate, which meant that we could not bring up those forgiven past transgressions. Nor could I have any further contact with Phil. Victor and Ms. Let's Explore That were in complete agreement on the Phil issue. The birthday emails ceased.

Victor and I agreed that we could do this marriage homework. We held hands and affirmed our belief in each other and in our marriage. We even smiled at each other.

For about a month, we did our marriage homework. Then the "he" part of "we" stopped being so "we-ish."

*****

When I was going to AA, I heard about the phenomenon called the Dry Drunk. Dry Drunks are miserable but sober people who exhibit all the emotional instability and general disagreeable nature of raging alcoholics on a two-week bender. Just without the alcohol. Victor turned into a Dry Drunk. He kept saying mean-spirited things about me in public. In response to my attempts to start a light conversation, he often just grunted and walked away. While I was trying to reignite our comatose sex life, he ignored me while trumpeting his appreciation of other women's breasts or legs. I tried to talk to him about that, as Ms. Let's Explore That had instructed, but he told me I was imagining things and/or that I was being too sensitive. "Can't you take a joke?"

About three months after we left Ms. Let's Explore That's office hand in hand and smiling like a Happy Couple, I redoubled my efforts to be kind and thoughtful to my Miserable Husband. One thing that stuck with me from marriage counseling was that Ms. Let's Explore That had said, "We often treat house guests better than we treat our own spouses." I made sure I treated Victor at least as well as any house guest. I made him coffee in the morning and brought in his newspaper so he could start the day the way he liked. If it had snowed outside, I cleared the snow off his car. I left little love notes or cards in various places so he could be surprised and know that I was thinking of him.

None of this seemed to put a dent in his Dry Drunk Funk.

After about six months of being treated like Victor Enemy No. 1, I decided it was time for my own ultimatum. I reminded him of Ms. Let's Explore That's marriage homework. He was in our bedroom at the time, getting undressed for bed. I was frightened because I was about to say something that would surely lead to anger, confrontation, or both. Anger and conflict were as scary as flesh-eating bacteria to me, and what made it worse was the fact that Victor, the veritable Captain of All Debate Teams, would relish the challenge I was issuing.

I walked into the room and he, as usual, ignored me. After taking a deep breath, I said, "Have I done anything at all to make you feel that I haven't lived up to the agreement we made with Ms. Let's Explore That?"

"No," he said. "Nothing that I can think of offhand." He could have been replying to a telemarketer.

I took another deep breath. "I sense you're hanging on to your pain and acting like I'm still victimizing you. I'm not. If you're choosing to hold on to pain from the past, it's because it must be serving you in some way. If it wasn't, you'd let it go. Make a choice, Victor. Hang on to the pain or let go of it. If you choose to hang on, though, you'll be doing it alone because I refuse to be treated like this anymore."

I must have learned something from all that Divine Reading. But not enough.

Since I have always suffered from a confrontation phobia, I can only think one step ahead. I have one play, and that's it. After I make that play, I have no idea what might happen next, except that I will probably regret having said anything, freeze in terror, cry, retreat, and apologize. That is probably why I never was very good at chess, either.

I had no idea how Victor would react to my ultimatum: *shape up or I'm going to ship out*. I suppose I was so desperate that I didn't care. Something had to change. I sat on the bed, trembling while he stared down at me.

"You really hurt me and it's going to take some time to get over it," he said, sitting down next to me.

"Well, you really hurt me, too," I said. "And this punishment over the last few months hurts me even more because you promised you would work on mending our marriage, just like I have been. That's not how it feels. When I let go of the past, I let go—just like I promised. If you can't, you need to tell me now so we can stop torturing each other. I'm just trying to be an adult like Ms. Let's Explore That told me to be."

"It's going to take more time," he said.

"How much more time? I can't live like this. I deserve better. So do you."

He nodded his head in agreement. "You're right, I need to let go of the past like I promised."

I was happy I didn't have to pack my bags. I had no idea where I would have gone if he told me to scram.

So our relationship improved again. We took swing-dance lessons and went on more "business trips" to great destinations. It was the late 1990s now, and we even bought a little piece of Nirvana. It was lake-front property that I thought would be the site of our retirement home—a new, finished Unbroken Home where we would grow old together. Victor wanted to use the place right away, so we bought a luxurious camper, built a big deck around it, and called it done.

*****

Life was placid. I tucked Phil in a corner of my heart where he would be safe. I knew where to find him on the still-lonely nights when being Victor's wife meant being more like his sister. I came to accept that, though. Unless we were trying to be reproductive, sex was not part of our relationship. Since I was long past entertaining any idea of another child, Victor and I slept together only to get some rest.

Other than our unspoken celibacy, our relationship seemed solid. I supported him in his business expansions and he supported me as I grew professionally at the college. During those tumultuous years beginning with Victor's new business venture and culminating with our marriage détente that ended the millennium, Alex somehow became a teenager. I was with him for every "Student Citizen of the Month" award and book or science fair. I cajoled him to do his homework and taxied him to best friend's house for sleep-overs. I wish I could remember how he transformed from a little boy I had to bend over to hug, a boy with a little boy's voice. It must have been magic. Suddenly he was a young man who was my height and who no one mistook for me anymore when he answered our phone. While our differing parenting styles only became more obvious, we were able to work out compromises that felt fair to everyone but Alex. That made me figure we were doing the right thing.

*****

We really didn't need anything to complicate our lives, but on one otherwise unremarkable day—November 9, 2001—life got complicated...again.

During a morning meeting at the college, the conference room started spinning. No, we weren't in the midst of a tornado. I just looked around and felt like I was on a not-so-merry-go-round. I didn't give it much thought because college meetings with long-winded megalomaniacs have a way of messing with one's head. But this was different.

After the meeting, I went to the infirmary to have my blood pressure checked. It was low, but that was normal for me. Since the marriage counseling, I had taken more control of my life in more ways than merely speaking up when I had an opinion. I wanted to get my forty-something body in shape so it would last until I reached eighty-something. I jogged every day, lifted free weights, and had dropped several dress sizes. For the first time in my life, I was truly healthy, except for recurring migraines. My internal lady parts had become downright spiteful, too. Our relationship was never what you might call genial, so yanking them out due to dysmenorrhea and endometriosis at the age of forty-three was fine by me. At least I wouldn't have to worry about menopause making me (or Victor) cranky. We had enough cranky fodder as it was.

What is causing this dizziness? I kept asking myself as the floors and walls kept moving in different directions than I was traveling in, even when I wasn't moving. *I'm the healthiest I've ever been in my life. Is this what happens right before those athletes die while competing?* My predilection for melodrama was still alive and well.

All day, the whirling, swirling dizziness affected my ability to navigate the halls of LCC or even think clearly. I called my physician. Since it was Friday, I had to wait until Monday for an appointment.

During the weekend, I tried my best to ignore my incessant vertigo, but stumbling and bumping into furniture, walls, and family members became annoying for us all. I had never been that out of control, even when I was drinking jugs of vodka every day. When I was standing, the floor was moving; when I was lying down, the bed was spinning. The only time I could keep up with my constant motion machine of a brain was to keep moving. Which I did as much as possible. It was a highly kinetic weekend.

By Monday the dizziness felt worse. I was beginning to think something was really wrong with me. My physician—really my physician's assistant—gave me motion-sickness pills. They were useless. By Wednesday (my forty-fourth birthday), I was having trouble watching TV. The quick motion on the screen made me feel like I was falling or the top of my head was lifting off. Thinking I was having a stroke, Victor drove me to the ER. At that point I couldn't drive because the sight of cars moving past me made my head reel and my stomach lurch.

After the requisite six hours of waiting in the ER to resolve my emergency, followed by several blood tests, other diagnostics, and a CT scan, I was released with no diagnosis for the dizziness, but with the delightful new information that I had a tumor in the left frontal lobe of my brain. They told me to consult a neurologist. Happy birthday.

I thought a mortician might be a better place to start.

On our very somber ride back home, I said to Victor, "When I was a little kid, I was always afraid that I would die of a brain tumor. Now I have one. I must have been psychic."

"Let's not overreact," he said. "We don't know what kind of tumor it is yet and what can be done. Let's think positively." He was trying so hard to be the rational one, but I knew he was as panicked as I was. His pep talk lacked pep.

"Should we tell Alex?" I was already planning my funeral and seeing Alex in a tear-stained suit. He was fifteen and would be handsome and adorable, like Prince William at Diana's funeral.

Victor thought for a minute. "We should tell him that the physicians found something—a mass—but that they need to figure out what it is. And we need to assure him that everything will be okay. Okay?"

A mass? Was that like a "spot" on your lung or a "growth" on your liver? How many ways did doctors have to give you gift-wrapped crappy news?

"Okay," I said, "but you tell him. I don't think I can. We don't know that everything is going to be okay. I don't feel okay. Do you?"

"Don't worry," he said. "I'll handle it. I'll get the best of the best to take care of this. I won't let anything happen to you."

We told Alex. He was frightened but understood as little about *the mass* as we did, so he handled it like he handled all bad news, with cautious optimism and stoicism. I often wondered how old my son really was. He seemed so much more mature than me.

Our brief roles as Fairly Equal Adults in the Victor and Lorna Show now ended and we were recast as Mysteriously Afflicted Invalid and Heroic Health Advocate. Not that I minded. I definitely needed someone to drive Ms. Dizzy to physicians' appointments. And the idea of a brain tumor distracted me from asking pertinent medical questions or remembering pertinent answers. But having had all that practice years ago at pretending I was sober when I was totally loop-de-looped, I was still able to function remarkably well on a daily basis.

Indeed, I saw the irony here. While I was drinking, I used to spend every day trying to feel that woozy-dizzy way by drinking myself silly and then summoning every bit of energy I had so I could pretend that I was sober. Now that I had been sober for over seventeen years, I was feeling constantly drunk, buzzed, and like a permanent resident of Bed-Spin-City. At least I had a way of describing my dizziness to physicians so they would understand. I suspect that most physicians are people who have been dizzy-drunk at least once in their lives.

The dizziness baffled everyone and really annoyed me, but the brain tumor was my personal rainmaker. The tumor was:

1. Real. Not big, but visible on the fancy scanners. Therefore it was not just "in my head." Well, it was in my head, but not just in my imagination. Physicians couldn't see my dizziness, though, and started to wonder aloud about depression and anxiety, which only made me sad and worried.

2. Dramatic. Lots of people get dizzy for lots of reasons, but brain tumors are jaw-droppers. When you let it drop in the random conversation

that you have a brain tumor, people start saying nice things about you before you die.

3. Prophetic. When I was young, I convinced myself I would develop a brain tumor and die a theatrical Terms of Endearment death. Blame it on the mind-splitting migraines I developed at five years of age, my melodramatic nature, or some pretty awesome psychic ability, but I kind of "knew" my brain would turn on me, sooner or later.

The brain tumor was on my mind a great deal. I grew as attached to it as it was attached to me, so when the first neurologist we saw told us it was "nothing," I was insulted. He called it a meningioma, which is "just a pea-sized mass" that was lodged between my skull and the sheath that covers my brain. He'd just crack my head open, he added, and it would, "pop out and roll onto the floor." *Well, la-de-flipping-da.* Dr. Buzz Saw wasn't going anywhere near my precious tumor! I wanted another opinion from someone who took my tumor a bit more seriously than a flying vegetable.

Dr. Don't Worry became my permanent neurologist. He was professional, astute, personable, and believed in both my dizziness and my brain tumor. While he told me I should go see an actual neurosurgeon for the tumor, he diagnosed my dizziness as "basilar artery migraine" and gave me medications notorious for helping with this illness. Victor and Dr. Don't Worry spent lots of time arguing about my diagnosis while I listened and the room whizzed in circles around me. Victor, being a businessman and the world's expert on me, thought Dr. Don't Worry was wrong; Dr. Don't Worry, being a neurologist and having treated similar cases, felt he was on to something. I was the silent patient, patiently waiting to see who would win the argument. It was a draw.

Victor needed another opinion on the dizziness and I needed someone to tell me my brain tumor was dazzlingly ominous, so we went to two major medical centers in Boston.

After ruling out everything from AIDS to near-sightedness, the best medical minds in Boston decided I had Chronic Fatigue and Immune Dysfunction Syndrome, or CFIDS. The only thing I was fatigued about, though, was all the blood tests and diagnostic procedures involving spinning me around and blasting me with strobe lights. Back in the 1990s when Cher was diagnosed with feeling tired after all of her wig-tossing performances, the condition used to be called simply chronic fatigue syndrome. Physical fatigue and muscle achiness are the major symptoms, even among people without major wig and costume changes between live performances. Since then, slightly more has been discovered about the condition, such as the fatigue includes neurological as well as physical dimensions. Researchers believe the condition is caused by many different viruses that attack susceptible people like Cher and me and make our immune systems become melodramatic. The result is generally a chaotic and unpredictable symphony of symptoms that make physicians scratch their heads and refer you to some informative websites, but only after they have ruled out any other scary diseases that could kill you quicker than CFIDS, which could kill you as quickly and pleasantly as arthritis or incontinence.

But I had CFIDS-Plus. I had a *mass* to contend with, making me a more interesting medical case than Cher ever thought of being. CFIDS is boring because there are no diagnostic tests to point to and say, "Look! There it is! She definitely has it and this is proof." Neither are there any cures or accurate prognoses. Physicians hate diseases they can't cure. But I had something else they could see, conjecture about, and possibly cure (if it wasn't deadly).

Several more fancy imaging procedures revealed an anomaly in my basilar artery (one of the major arteries at the top of the spine supplying blood to the brain—major score here for Dr. Don't Worry). The neurosurgeons believed that my tumor was a meningioma, but they decided to scan me every six months to watch it and see if it moved or grew. They would decide if and when it should be removed. Maybe they would even tell me.

In the meantime, I didn't skip a beat as a successful college professor, mom, and marriage pal. I was able to drive short, familiar distances, even feed and dress myself. If I closed my eyes, I fell over, so I made sure not to close my eyes while teaching or driving—something I'd learned wasn't a good idea, anyway. For added excitement, I developed chronic nausea (from feeling like I was stuck in the spin cycle of an industrial Whirlpool washer) and a vigorous case of insomnia (from...oh, why not?).

What was a dizzy Lorna to do? I began writing funny stories about my childhood. That kind of writing was therapeutic and safe. It reminded me of the time when I was almost "too healthy," gave me something to laugh about, and (should Victor stumble across what I wrote), it wasn't anything that could get me into any trouble.

Like I needed more trouble.

*****

When I rescued a seven-month-old mixed-breed named Wolfer in the early 1990s, I thought his panting, groaning, and inability to stay still were because he was excited to have a loving home. I was wrong. What he had was severe, congenital, hip dysplasia. My vet

288

recommended that we put him down immediately to save him from suffering, but I couldn't do that. I was in love with him. With medications to ease the pain (his, not mine), the vet said he might live three to four years. I decided to give him the best life a disabled dog could have. But Wolfer had other plans. He didn't see himself as a disabled dog. He was just a dog. He ran and played despite my efforts to stop him from having fun. I finally stopped scolding him for playing and just let him whoop it up. We were both a lot happier and he lived (with the help of medications and ample doses of love) to be twelve years old.

What does Wolfer have to do with my dizziness? Wolfer taught me many lessons in his lifetime, but the relevant one here is about perception.

No one could see the three-ring circus happening inside my head except when I occasionally stumbled or bumped into a wall. Just like when I was drunk, I covered up my dizziness so well that I appeared normal to everyone around me. As a sociologist who had taught about "labels" and "stigma" for years, I knew what being defined as an "invalid" meant. Just look at the word: *in-valid*. When people see you as ill, they stop seeing "you" and only see the illness. That's what I did to Wolfer until Wolfer set me straight by refusing to act like a disabled dog. He was a dog that ran at break-neck speeds through tall grass, played hide and seek, and swam in any puddle, pond, or lake he could find. He was a dog with a tongue that lolled in sloppy satisfaction and a dog with smiling eyes. Sure, he had bad hips, but those hips didn't dampen Wolfer's spirit or define him.

I was determined not to define myself by an illness that was blanketed in mystery. There was no clear cause, treatment, or cure. If this disease had any self-respect, it would stop operating in the shadows. Until it did, I decided not to invest my limited energy in it.

To prove that I was essentially healthy with just a few health-related "issues," I insisted on working full time—taking sick days only for physician visits. Eventually, I adjusted my working conditions so I would have less time in the classroom. The subtle flickering of fluorescent lights and the constant motion of students panicked me because the stimulation overloaded my brain. *Why couldn't students just sit still in the dark as they absorbed my pearls of wisdom?* I developed online versions of my classes and took on administrative duties in lieu of teaching. Some of my colleagues got the impression that I was trying to upstage them, something a few of them feared anyway.

Unbeknownst to me, however, a small but powerful gang of faculty members was plotting my professional demise, should the brain tumor or falling down the stairs from dizziness not do me in first. I am (and was) smart enough to understand the axiom, *Keep your friends close and your enemies closer*, but having worked so hard to be Miss Congeniality, I wasn't savvy enough to know that I had enemies.

Regardless of how unpopular my move to part-time administrative duties was, I had to try this avenue. Teaching is what I loved to do, but teaching was making me sicker. To preserve my belief that I was healthy, I had to continue to work. To continue to work, I had to find something professionally challenging outside of the classroom.

As another part of my Healthy and Contrite Lorna Act, I joined Victor's small Methodist church choir. They needed a soprano. Actually, they needed more than one soprano, but I was a good start. I needed to prove that I was healthy enough to engage in social activities, and joining the choir fulfilled part of the deal I'd struck during marriage counseling. I loved to sing, and going to church with Victor showed him I remembered my recommitment to our marriage. Joining the ailing choir was also a way to show my appreciation for his herculean health advocacy efforts on my behalf.

So while I was busy focusing on Healthy Lorna with a few "issues," the people and professional colleagues around me, it seemed, saw an in-valid person. Victor saw a "responsibility" in need of a caretaker. He hugged me and held my hand, but that's the closest he got. Heck, I was dizzy, not contagious.

Family and friends saw what they imagined as my unimaginable suffering and felt bad for me. I appreciated that, but I also felt their pity. My mom said (more than once), "Lorna, of all the people I know, you are the one who needs your brain the most." I always laughed and said, "Mom, everyone needs their brain."

Alex didn't treat me like an in-valid. No, he withdrew. Maybe he was just at that age (seventeen) when boys disconnect from their mothers, but our relationship had always been unique. I was Mom, Advocate, Silly-Dancing Partner, Fellow Pet-Whisperer, and Safe Place. I believe he didn't want to think about his mom as ill, so he retreated to neutral, sterile ground. Of all the losses I experienced during that time, losing my often silly and always close relationship with Alex hurt the most. I bet he could say the same thing.

Along with the dizziness, I developed endometriosis, a precancerous condition in the female-plumbing area. I had a hysterectomy and started taking artificial hormones so I wasn't catapulted into early menopause. My Healthy Lorna crusade was losing steam.

In April, 2003, my Boston neurosurgeon informed me that he thought my innocent little meningioma was really a cancerous ganglioglioma. Could I come in for surgery next week? I was preparing for finals next week. I said no.

Although Victor was livid, I was certain that the *gang* of *liogliomas* would wait to kill me until after finals, so I scheduled the surgery for June. Did I mention that Victor was livid?

The way I saw it, he couldn't stay mad at me forever.

1. He'd forgive me if I died.

2. He'd forget about being mad if I made it through surgery and the outcome was positive.

3. I'd forget he was mad if I made it through the surgery and developed amnesia, Hollywood-style.

Keeping my healthy perspective was the toughest performance of my life...up to that point. But it wouldn't be long until my acting abilities would be tested even further.

CHAPTER 20: I BETTER NOT HAVE A SCREW LOOSE

Some women can pull off this look. I am not one of them. But bald isn't beautiful on me either.

I am a blonde, but I'm not one of those Dumb Blondes. I never have been. I knew I had a brain because I'd seen pictures of it on multiple MRI scans and felt it zinging around in my skull every waking minute. None of the Dumb Blonde jokes applied to me, except if "temporarily speechless" is what you mean by "dumb." I was the Dumb Blonde who had that wide-eyed stare and hopefully not too open mouth when confronted with anything unexpected or unpleasant. I was that Dumb Blonde a lot in my life—especially during the weeks that led up to my brain surgery.

Perhaps some examples will help clarify what I mean.

I had lobbied strenuously for another full-time sociologist at LCC for years. I redoubled my efforts because I was the only one and I was losing steam. Most sociology classes were taught by part-time faculty who had advanced degrees not in sociology but in "related" fields, like anything that ends in "-ology." It is hard enough for trained sociologists to teach the discipline and make it seem interesting, even harder for people who said they knew something about sociology but hadn't majored in it. The prevailing assumption on the part of my colleagues was that anyone who has lived in a society can teach sociology. With that logic, anyone occupying a body can teach anatomy and physiology. Like my empathy and sensitivity, my discipline was underappreciated and misunderstood.

While I was planning for my funeral on melancholy days and arranging for a service dog on more hopeful days, my colleagues at LCC hired a full-time non-sociologist sociology teacher without my approval. When I found out they had done something so integral to my professional work and standards without my input—even more so when I learned their maneuvering was unprecedented and irreversible—I turned into a Dumb Blonde.

After too many minutes of wide-eyed staring and heavy breathing, I finally found my words. "How could you do this...without my input? I'm the...I'm the...ah...expert in this, um, discipline."

"We knew you had a lot on your mind," they said in patronizing voices, "and we didn't want to bother you with another decision." They were looking at each other, not me.

"Huh." *Translation: How kindly paternalistic of you mostly female gang of academic thugs masquerading as my colleagues.* But I was dumbfounded...struck dumb...and still blonde.

The next Dumb Blonde moment was more ironic. I was sitting in my hairdresser's chair one day watching her shave off all my blonde hair. One of the pre-op instructions was to shave the left side of my head. Did people really shave only half of their head? I was forty-five and not interested in making any radical social, political, or personal statements with my appearance. I also knew I didn't have the charisma to start a fashion trend, so I decided no hair was better than half-hair. My hair style was somewhere between 1987 Princess Diana and 1997 Princess Diana. As I watched each clump of blonde hair fall to the floor, my dumbness deepened. My hairdresser chatted about how fast my hair would grow back, although others in the salon kept silent, glancing briefly but frequently at my balding head. Since "scalping" wasn't in the salon's pricing code, she didn't charge me for her work. She knew I was a loyal customer and I'd be back in a year or so. I pasted a thin smile on my face, hugged her, and left. Keeping myself calm and composed with a naked head was an act of sheer will. Nevertheless, when I got into my car, I locked the doors and sobbed for ten minutes. Never underestimate how attached a woman can be to her hair.

Victor and Alex kept our long ride to Boston lively with conversation. On my best days, when they talked, I rarely got a word in, but now I was grateful to be silent. Being a Dumb but Bald Blonde was okay by me. Arriving in Boston the night before the surgery, we went out for a meal, which I referred to as The Last Supper. No matter what the outcome of the surgery, I was never going to be the same again. Dead or alive, I would have a hole in my head and a part of my brain would be missing. My appetite wasn't up for much except ginger ale.

That night, I said goodbye to Alex like it was really *adieu*, which in French means "with God" and you'll probably never return. He wouldn't see me until after surgery. I didn't know if there would be an "after surgery" or what condition I would be in. He was so brave. I wish I could say the same for myself. Maybe having him console me gave him something to do other than feel his own fear. Yes, I'll go with that.

As Victor and I lay in bed, not sleeping, I tried to talk him into taking me home before morning. I had decided I really didn't want anyone messing with the brain that served me so well for over forty years. Some people might disagree with that assessment, but that's fine. I had grown quite attached to my quirky brain. Victor and I held each other and cried like babies who'd lost their pacifiers. It was the closest we had been in bed for years and it felt wonderful. I had always longed for that kind of closeness, but, well, not at that moment. Ironically, I was the one who wanted to get up and vamoose—usually it was Victor who got up and slept downstairs in his recliner, if he ever came to bed at all.

But we stayed in that hotel room and tossed and turned until it was time to go to the hospital.

I was a Stepford Wife Dumb Blonde the entire time I was being prepared for surgery. I answered every question calmly, did exactly as I was told, and was polite and friendly. I was the perfect pre-op patient. The only sign that I had any emotions at all was that I couldn't stop shaking. No matter how many layers of blankets they put on me, I trembled like I was having a 7.9 level earthquake inside me. I really hoped my body would stop shaking with the anesthesia; either that or I hoped the neurosurgeon was an expert marksman.

Being rolled into the surgical theater was surreal. I could see the eager medical students in the glassed-in observatory area above me. They were probably drooling to see my head being drilled. I watched the surgical assistants as they attached all manner of sticky things to me to monitor all manner of important things having to do with keeping me alive. Then I heard someone, probably Dr.

Braindrill, rev up what sounded like a chainsaw. It must have been the brain drill. (That's probably not the technical term for the surgical instrument that drills through a human skull, but "brain drill" works for me.) At the sound, I nearly jumped off the metal table and had such tremors that the *rat-a-tat-tat* of my bones on metal drowned out the *zzzzuuuunnnn-zzzzuuuunnnn* of the drill. Mercifully, the anesthesiologist injected his magical elixir and I was out in a matter of seconds.

*****

I woke up. That was the good news. Nurses started grilling me like I held State Secrets and I needed to spill the beans pronto. But having just been drilled, probed, cut up, and screwed back together, my brain wasn't working very well. When answers finally came to me, my mouth-bone seemed disconnected from my brain-bone.

Here's how the conversation went:

Nurses: What's your name?

Me: Um.

Nurses: Where are you?

Me: Ah.

Nurses: What year is it?

Me: 19... [It was 2003.]

Nurses: What's your name?

Me: Hmm. Lo-ah?

Nurses [collective sigh]: Cancel the call to Dr. Braindrill. Good Girl, Lorna! You're going to be just fine. Your family has waited a long time to see you. Do you feel like some visitors?

Me: Um....

One by one, Victor, Alex, Mom, Tina, Lisa, Victor's parents, and two of my friends came to assure themselves that I was alive and mumbling. I smiled, but I don't remember much else. The nurses kept asking me tricky questions about my name, the year, and even who was president. When I rolled my eyes and said with a bit of disgust, "Dubya," they chuckled and said, "Oh, she's going to be just fine."

Unlike all my other "female" surgeries on my lady parts, recovering from brain surgery was *easy*. My head didn't hurt, even without the pain medications. Even though I felt good enough to go home after the initial recovery period, they kept me in the hospital for four days. Dr. Braindrill wanted to make sure the titanium plate and four screws that sealed my gray matter away from all the other colorful matter in the outside world stayed put, thus preserving the shelf-life and freshness of my brain.

Unlike all my other surgeries, recovery from brain surgery was *long*. Dr. Braindrill told me to expect problems with communicating because the area of the brain he had drilled into and carved up was the language center. Plus, brain surgery creates brain trauma, which creates brain swelling, which makes you more stupid than normal for at least ten months post-surgery. Not only was I missing the *gang* of *liogliomas* in my brain, I was also missing my words. For example, I could feel the screws holding down the metal plate where part of my skull used to be, but could only point to them, since the word "screw" wouldn't come out of my mouth. Which was probably a good thing. When I managed to point and, after a minute or so, spit out a difficult word like "chair," I felt like I had a screw loose. I kept checking my skull to make sure everything was secure.

I still do.

Before we left the hospital, we received the news that my mass had not been tumor, which would have been cancerous. My ganglioglioma was just a calcified tangle of brain junk that I'd probably had since birth. The surgery hadn't been necessary. But, said Dr. Braindrill, his students learned a lot about how tricky it is to read an MRI. As my bandaged bald still-dizzy head left the hospital attached to the rest of me, I thought, *Glad to be of service to your medical education system.*

I spent the summer recuperating and pointing to objects because I couldn't come up with perplexing words like *book, plate,* or *clock.* I also nodded and shook my head a lot. My CFIDS-related dizziness worsened because I was less able to use my mental focus to keep the dizziness in the background. That's because I was busy using my mental focus to see a sock and try to say "sock." Oddly, I could engage in basic conversations with relative ease. It's just that people had to play fill-in-the-blanks with me when it came to identifying objects.

*****

First impressions being what they are—first—my new and hopefully temporary speech impediment, plus my Frankenstein-monster-ish head and hair style became quite problematic almost immediately. This was my first indication that Victor had fundamentally shifted his attitude about me and about us. Together, we had been dealing with CFIDS for three years. He was my advocate and protector, but without my noticing any change, he had begun worrying less about me and more about himself. While I was happy that I wasn't his "ward" any longer, we didn't talk about this change in our relationship. He just went ahead and changed it. I only noticed it well after it was underway and I was ill-equipped to change the flow of the new undercurrent.

We hosted a high school Swedish foreign student during the year of my surgery, which was also Alex's junior year in high school. The Swedish Meatball's host family in the U.S. had suddenly backed out at the last minute "for personal reasons." Being a small business owner in a small community, Victor was a man *in the know*. He must have heard that the Swedish Meatball's host family reneged. I wasn't privy to the details, but he mentioned that the family had misgivings about bringing a gorilla-like Swede into their home with two pubescent daughters. Now he wanted to swoop in and save the day, which is what he loved to do.

"Let's host this kid," he said.

"I don't know," I said. "We already have a lot to deal with without bringing a stranger into the mix."

"But Alex has always wanted a sibling," he said. "This experience will expose all of us to a different culture. As a sociologist, you should appreciate that."

I hated it when Victor was right. "Well," I said, "do you know anything about this kid?"

"Oh, yes! He's from Sweden. I've already spoken to the program coordinator about him, and they're so relieved that we're interested."

"You already said we're interested??"

"Well, I knew you would agree once I told you about this great opportunity." Classic Victor. Whether he'd suddenly forgotten my multiple health issues, which were exacerbated by stress, or whether he just thought that having a foreign student in the house would be fun for him remains a mystery to me.

The Swedish Meatball ended up being a big mystery. Even he didn't know why he was in America, except that his mother wanted him to go somewhere and America seemed like as good a place as any to be a delinquent.

This eighteen year-old boy was an obese, blond, wannabe rapper whose idea of lunch started with four sandwiches and ended sometime around dinner. In addition to trying to eat us out of house and home, he also caused a great deal of trouble at school. He was supposed to stay with us for a full school year, but he left in February after committing a criminal act involving bribery, two young boys, one penis, one ear, and one school bus. I can't do the math on that one. But I know it eventually equals being convicted of a sex crime, which would have negated the clause in his contract about acting as a noble ambassador representing his country in America. His mother reluctantly agreed to take him back, and the Swedish Meatball left to become a night club DJ in Stockholm. Or maybe he became a couch potato in his parents' living room, listening to his iPod and eating non-stop. My money is on the latter. Alex was grateful for his only-child status.

During the Swedish Meatball's stay, we got to know another exchange student, the Swedish Hottie. This was the guy most people visualize when they think of Swedish male models. Unfortunately, the Swedish Hottie's host family treated him like slave labor and refused to host his family when they traveled to America for his graduation. Again, Victor came to the rescue. He offered our lake retreat. It was a camper, but at least it was a roof over their heads. Including the Swedish Hottie, there were six in the family, so they needed to use our home for basic grooming during their two-week stay. They also wanted to spend time with us to show their appreciation for our hospitality and kindness toward their son during the year.

Under normal circumstances, this many people (no matter how nice they were) descending upon the Broken House would have caused me to panic. But they came two weeks after I had brain surgery. Had I been able to speak properly, I would have called 911 and asked to be rescued from a Broken House invasion. But what could I do? I was Dumb Cordial Glassy-Eyed Blonde, complete with a fashionable scarf over my carved-up head. Victor wanted to play Gracious Host. He never gave my addled brain a second thought.

So I muddled through being a host family as well as I could. Smiling was my major contribution to our hospitality. It was, in fact, hard to tell who was from the foreign country, me or the Swedes. Several years later, when we went to Sweden to visit them, they were pleasantly surprised at my command of the English language and happy to see my blonde hair. I fit right in.

*****

Determined not to let my health issues get in the way of my professional life, I contacted the college, assuring them I could resume work in September, which was just shy of three months after the surgery, on a half-time administrative basis only. Teaching was out of the question for me because articulate communication was out of the question. I figured a dizzy, brain-swelled person could easily pass for an effective administrator, but I didn't want to be remembered as Dr. Ditzy, the crazy professor who had to point at chalk for ten minutes before she could say "need chalk."

In August, the academic vice president called me in for a pre-semester planning meeting. I didn't want to go because my hair was only half an inch long and I was still having trouble speaking, but he assured me that I could just listen and "get caught up" with things that had happened over the summer that might affect my administrative duties. Since it was summer, I wore a fancy, Kentucky Derby-style hat to hide my scarred and fuzzy head and hoped no one would think that I had suddenly developed a smashing sense of style. And then, in the middle of the meeting, the VP asked me to briefly report on the status of my project.

What?

Rather than taking my imaginary mint julep and sashaying out of there on my high horse, I stumbled through a summary of my work to date. Or what I could recall of it.

"As you, um…know, um, we're in, ah, step, I mean, ah, stage B of the three stage or phase, um, plan. You know. The one…um…ah…people, the faculty…[by this time I was looking for words hopefully written on ceiling; unfortunately, the ceiling was bare]…said yes to—"

"Voted on?" Someone in the room was trying to end my suffering. Or theirs.

I slapped the table, "Yes! That's it!" I gave a wobbly a smile and braced myself for another attempt at reporting something when the VP interceded.

"So we are working on phase 2 of our three year plan. Is that correct, Lorna?"

"Uh huh."

"Very well. Next report."

I sat in silent shame for the rest of the meeting. Discomfort was visible on everyone's face, well, everyone whose head wasn't down or averted. Piglet from *Winnie the Pooh* would have been more articulate than I was that day.

When meeting ended, I fled. I didn't want to give anyone a chance to express in words what I'd seen in their faces or body language. I barely made it out of the building, in fact, before I started sobbing. There was one good outcome, though: the VP called me the next day to apologize for putting me on the spot. He also urged me to take more time if I needed it. I assured him that I could do my work, just not give public presentations for a while. But my articulation was still inadequate. One by one, other faculty members present at the meeting called me to tell me how brave they thought I was and how, on my worst days, I was smarter than anyone at the college. *How could these kind words make me feel so proud and so ashamed at the same time?*

But I made progress. Each month, I was losing fewer words, though I have never fully regained my ability to speak extemporaneously in my trademark easy, eloquent manner. I also developed a finger-to-brain coordination problem, something that proved exasperating when I tried to tackle online courses in the spring semester. I typed sort of backward more than forward and anything I typed was filled with spelling mistakes and silly keystroke errors. Everything I typed—comments to students, online lectures, emails, policy proposals, correspondence—had to be proofread at least five times. Victor began to complain about the excessive time I was spending on my work, but I couldn't admit that I was spending so much of my time correcting my own communication errors. Dr. Braindrill had said he'd only taken a small amount of healthy gray matter out of my brain to be sure he "got it all" in case there was anything suspicious.

Whatever he took, I needed it. I still have problems with typing. *If I tpye a sentnce an don;t bother ot corrcet it, ti loks like ths.*

After three years of constant dizziness and trying to hide it, I was dead tired. My body ached constantly. I finally came to believe I had CFIDS because I was always fatigued—both mentally and physically. My immune dysfunction was as clear as the dark circles under my eyes.

*****

But everyone was telling me I looked "great" in a buzz cut. Bless their hearts. They lied to my face just to make me feel better. I intend to return the favor at the first opportunity. Eventually of course, my hair grew back. It came back blonde and with that just-enough waviness to make it sassy. If my hair could make a comeback, I thought, then maybe I could, too.

Alas, the rest of my body wasn't so reliable. Some days I felt human; some days I was more like a zombie, assuming zombies felt morose and alienated in addition to being barely alive.

And Alex and Victor were as unpredictable as my health. In 2004, Alex was busy finishing up high school and preparing to fly the coop. He moved to a college three hours away (that's if I was driving; it was two hours if anyone else was). My son who had come to love the Broken House had come to terms with leaving it. Maybe this happens to all young people at eighteen, but I hear too many stories of thirty-year-olds still living with their parents to believe that. Maybe he didn't want to see his sick mom every day and pretend that she wasn't sick. Maybe he wanted to get away from the seemingly constant butting of heads between two very headstrong males living under one roof.

When Alex grew to be a young man, he emulated his independent-minded father. When they disagreed, which was often, I felt as if I were watching an *Animal Planet* program about two male rams locking horns over whatever male rams lock horns over. Never the bystander for long, I assumed my Middle-Child Arbiter role and interceded, but my voice of reason often fell on deaf rams' ears. Unfortunately, I didn't speak Ram.

Damage control was only possible when I could get them alone. I tried to convince Victor that Alex wasn't a hoodlum and to convince Alex that his father was only ensuring that his son's character was beyond reproach. Or something like that. They ended up okay with each other, but I got both barrels from both sides. Such is the lot of a Ram Whisperer. Some level of calm followed my interventions until the next episode of "Rams Gone

Rowdy" on *Animal Planet*. And so it was, forever and ever, amen.

With our nest newly emptied, Victor devoted more time to his business but still wanted Daily Invalid Updates. That, I think, unduly burdened him. I kept working part-time and did basic household chores, but I wasn't setting any land-speed records. He got more involved in community organizations and events and was just an all-around social animal. He encouraged me to "not push" myself so I wouldn't "pay dearly" for "overdoing it." I heard through friends that he spoke valiantly of me—his brilliant wife whose light was fading right before his eyes. How tragic for her. How tragic for him.

During the spring of 2005, I tried one more time to prove my illness wasn't going to define me. I applied for a Fulbright Fellowship and my first sabbatical leave from LCC in fourteen years. Technically, I was eligible to take a sabbatical every seven years, but until then, I had never considered taking one because I was the only full-time sociologist and I thought they needed me to teach. I wasn't sure what "they" needed now, especially since "they" went ahead and hired Pseudo Sociologist, who could teach my classes for one semester while I was broadening my intellectual and cultural horizons. But I was sure that I needed to challenge myself professionally as a way to reassure myself personally. So I applied for both the Fulbright and my first sabbatical leave.

The process of applying for a Fulbright is not for the academic faint of heart, but I did it. The fact that I still had the intellectual wherewithal to develop and write a proposal, then organize all the supporting documentation necessary for an application that would make applying for Medicaid seem like a vacation in Hawaii gave me confidence that I was Real Lorna, not Invalid (or In-Valid) Lorna.

I wanted to go to Finland to teach women's studies at one of their universities and study their health care system. Since I taught in both areas (women's issues and the sociology of health), that opportunity would significantly enhance my academic career. My grandmother had come from Finland, so I also had personal reasons to select that Fulbright position. Even if I couldn't speak to my distant relatives, I could smile and nod during conversations with them, I knew I excelled in the smiling and nodding school of communication. I had practiced it all my life.

I prepared my application for a Fulbright Fellowship while I performed my part-time administrative duties and taught an on-line course. Simultaneously, I applied for a sabbatical leave for the spring, 2006, semester.

The U.S. State Department awarded me the prestigious Fulbright Award in the fall of 2005. I was elated. But my elation was short-lived. LLC, the college I had poured by academic heart and soul into while healthy and ailing, decided to deny my sabbatical application. My elation turned into flabbergastion. At the same time I applied for my sabbatical, Pseudo Sociologist applied for a sabbatical to complete her Ph.D. coursework in *social work*, which is not the same thing as sociology. LCC couldn't have us both out at the same time, so they gave her the sabbatical. I had seniority and could have brought much-needed prestige to the college, but they chose her over me. As the VP of Academic Affairs explained privately to me, "Lorna, you're more valuable in the classroom."

"No kidding," I said as I walked out of his office.

I had no more fight left in me for the academic life...for that place. I realized that I had labored for way too long to hoist the sail on the LLC submarine. No wonder I was exhausted.

I contacted the State Department, explained the situation, and turned down the award.

After fifteen years of honorable service, I was done with LCC. But even negotiating early retirement turned out to be surprisingly difficult. The college lawyer wasn't convinced that I qualified. He finally understood when I explained my situation in this way: "Imagine that you just went out to a four-martini lunch. When you get back to your office, you're called before a tough judge to argue a very important case. You're able to rally all your mental resources to pull it off, but afterwards, you're exhausted. Well, that's how I feel every day. But *without the booze*."

In the summer of 2006, the college, my teachers' retirement system, and the Social Security Administration all agreed I wasn't fit to work. I entered the ranks of the permanently disabled.

All of my efforts to preserve my identity as a healthy person with just a few health "issues" were undone. I felt irreparably broken. Unfixable. So I did again what I had developed a habit of doing when things around me felt like they were coming undone: I reached up to my titanium plate and felt the screws in my head to make sure none of them had also come undone. I made sure I didn't have a screw loose.

For most of my life, I have lived according to an academic, rather than a normal, calendar year. How was I going to handle the fall 2006 semester commencing without me?

CHAPTER 21: I HAD TO LET GO BEFORE I GAVE UP

On the island of Oahu, there is a Buddhist Temple. Buddhists say the source of suffering is having expectations. Yup. Okay. That was my problem.

"They'll be dragging my scatterbrained, decrepit, old body out of the classroom in mid-lecture. The only reason they'll be able to do it will be because my arthritic fingers won't be able to hang on to the podium." That's what I used to laughingly tell my students and colleagues. I loved teaching that much.

Now I was forty-eight and prematurely retired.

To look at me, you'd think I was scamming the retirement system. I had all my limbs. I wasn't lugging around an oxygen tank. I wasn't talking to invisible people or listening as they told me to kill certain colleagues at the college. I started wishing I were disfigured, or at least had something visible that a medical specialist could point to and say, "See this? That's what is causing your dizziness, insomnia, irritable bowel, lack of mental focus, muscle aches, migraines, lethargy, and general housework aversion." That way, when people wondered why I wasn't working, I could just point to the lab report or the X-ray and shrug pathetically. But all my issues were invisible. Except the housework thing.

Retirement at the end of the spring, 2006, semester gave me the summer to contemplate being "disabled" without having to deal with being "retired." Professors don't typically work in the summer, at least not the sane or lazy ones. But I'd routinely worked nearly every summer day on updating my courses and other academic projects. Rarely did I work full days, but I devoted several hours a day to my beloved profession. It was a good way to avoid housework.

During the summer of 2006, an online writing group became my substitute professional activity. I couldn't justify preparing for classes I would never teach, so I resurrected the short, funny stories I had been writing since I became dizzy. The stories were my therapy as they reminded me of the lighthearted Lorna I didn't want to lose in all the confusion surrounding my marriage and health woes. I had a substantial collection of stories from my childhood to share with my family and friends. Everybody loved them, and now I needed to know if anyone other than people who loved me (the same people who told me I looked marvelous in a buzz cut) thought my writing had potential. So I joined the most legitimate-looking online writing group I could find—the one that didn't require an upfront fee to join, but did offer an upgraded membership that I really couldn't live without—and let aspiring writers tell me what they thought of my work. I got a lot of practice telling them what I thought of their work, too. I dove into this new adventure with the same zeal I'd always used to prepare for my courses. My new obsession gave me the perfect answer to the inevitable new retiree question, "What are you doing with all your wonderful free time?" *Didn't they understand I would rather be healthy and working than be dizzy and prematurely retired?*

I started to say, "I'm an aspiring writer." I was an actually more of an aspiring critic of other people's work and a constant editor of my own work. So I came up with, "I'm in the process of becoming."

"Becoming what?"

Only the truly inquiring minds would dare to ask. Most people would smile politely, nod knowingly, and back away slowly. They didn't know what I meant. But at least they nodded.

"If I knew," I would say, "then I would already have become it and could tell you. But I don't, so I know I'm still just becoming." For some reason the conversation always ended there. I figured they hadn't read many books by Buddhists or Dr. Seuss.

Victor supported my new adventure as long as he didn't have to listen to me read my work. His patience for my "hobby" lasted, at most, about five minutes. If I had been working on a best-seller with lucrative movie offers that would bring money or fame to him via me, then he might have taken my efforts more seriously. But I was writing about me.

Victor began spending incrementally less time at home, though he still called often to check up on me to see how I was feeling and to make sure I wasn't "overdoing it."

While he acted concerned, he was remote in every way that counted to me.

On weekends and many evenings, too, he loved to go to "our" place at the lake, which was a very nice "park model" camper with an attached deck. While he "invited" me often, the place felt more like *his* get-away than ours. We had a cadre of pets by that time: two dogs, two cats, and one cockatoo (Reggie, who didn't travel well). Victor was allergic to pet dander, so keeping the camper hypoallergenic made life easier for him, but leaving the pets at home meant I could only "visit" for short periods. I brought the dogs and Reggie down several times, but it was cramped and not very relaxing. Thus began, for what seemed to be practical reasons, a pattern of separate living accommodations in the summer.

That August, Victor had a business trip to Chicago. Much to my surprise, he invited me to join him. We had become increasingly distant and he had grown more concerned about my deteriorating health now that I was retired. We've all heard the stories of people who retired then expired.

I had never been to Chicago and wanted to spend some time away from the house, so I went with him and we had a delightful time, even though I had developed fairly chronic and agonizing backaches that even prodigious amounts of ibuprofen wouldn't relieve. I had given up my daily jogging routine about a year before because I developed flu-like symptoms for days after even a short jog—this is typical of chronic fatigue syndrome. My body didn't want to move faster than a slow walk, so I walked. My aging Wolfer appreciated the change of pace. The backaches were different from any I had ever experienced. They weren't just saying *Slow down*. They were saying, *Stop moving, you damn fool!*

Two days after we returned from Chicago, my lower back was vacillating between excruciating and agonizing pain. I finally listened to it and spent most of a Saturday afternoon lying down with a heating pad. But when I tried to get up, I couldn't move my legs without *kill-me-now* searing pain shooting through my back, up my spine, and out into the cosmos. "This is odd," I said before I gasped for air and after I pounded on the bed to avoid screaming.

As calmly as I could, I called for help. "Victor! Help! Oh my God! I'm paralyzed! I can't move! It hurts so much! Help me, help me, help me!"

Because I was using my "inside voice" (only an octave higher than my usual voice), I considered my call for help to be a calm request, not a raving lunatic-like scream. Of course, thanks to the pain, my recollection may not be entirely accurate.

Victor, thank God, bolted upstairs like a newlywed whose bride just shouted she was naked and ready to rumba. The minute he saw the panic on my face, he knew that the rumba was the last thing on my to-do list. When he tried to get me on my feet, I collapsed to the floor in agony.

Again, this was odd. I had seen plenty of women collapse in men's arms during my daytime TV days, but I never believed women actually did that kind of thing. But there I was, one of those women, doing that kind of thing. And it hurt! In Never-Let-a-Little-Thing-Like-Paralysis-Stop-Me fashion, however, I got downstairs and into the car so we could drive to the ER. This effort required the assistance of:

1. Victor

2. Alex

3. An office chair with casters that would roll on carpet

4. Clenching of teeth the likes of a rat terrier on your favorite pair of panties as I was bumped down the 143 stairs (it was really less than twenty, but it felt like more) to the first floor of our house, then out to the car.

We got as far as the car. As I tried to get off the chair and into the car, I began wondering what the woman in the magician's saw-the-lady-in-bits trick felt like if the trick went wrong. I bet she felt better than I did. Feeling like an agony-missile just pierced and detonated in my torso, I eased into the car; but I knew I wouldn't make the fifteen-to-twenty minute drive to the hospital. Passing out from the pain or dying from sitting were real possibilities. So is the fact that I'm exaggerating my level of pain. Dying from sitting is rare, but it happens if you sit in the wrong place (let's say a toilet) at the right time (let's say October 25, 1760). This was great news for whoever was in line for the throne after King George II of Great Britain.

Anyway, Victor called 911 and I got my first-ever ambulance ride. They offered me morphine, but I declined. It's not that I wanted to stay in excruciating pain. I just wanted to be able to accurately answer the diagnostic questions when I got to the hospital. Morphine might dull my senses and lead me to understate the severity of my anguish. I was having none of that.

Even though I was lying in a prone position, the ambulance ride was unspeakably unbearable. Every bump and turn sent shocks of pain up my spine and down my legs. I made a mental note to write my congressional representatives and ask about resurfacing every road in our county.

After all the ER tests and questions were completed, I gladly accepted as many doses of morphine as they offered. I may have asked for extra helpings—doggie-bags of the stuff, too, in case I needed more later.

The surgeon on call was a cardiac specialist who felt confident that what I had was a simple muscle spasm. *A simple muscle spasm?* Oh, I know the kind he meant—the kind you get when you wrench your back as you lurch off of the gurney while grabbing for the arrogant, uninterested ER physician's throat as he is writing down his obvious misdiagnosis. He released me late Saturday evening with a prescription for muscle relaxants and suggested lots of walking once I wasn't so woozy. The walking would help the constipation from the drugs. Win-win.

Sunday was a day of moaning and doped up dizziness. By Monday, my back pain was worse and my left leg was getting numb. Even though I lacked the experts' years of medical training, I knew that losing sensation in my leg wasn't going to help my walking, constipation, or stress levels. Something more ominous than a "simple muscle spasm" was happening in my aching lower back. I went to my doctor, who ordered an MRI. It showed that I had a partially blown L-4 disc.

Prior to the diagnosis, I had worried about depression when, for the first time since I could recall, a fall semester was starting without me. As it turned out, I worried needlessly. I was soon having emergency back surgery to prevent paralysis of my left leg. Missing college wasn't even on my radar. That was one blessing that was very well disguised.

*****

Of all the pre-operative experiences I've had—and I've had many, and I am counting my 23.5 hours of labor leading up to my C-section—that one was my worst. Since there was no local specialist qualified to diagnosis my back pain properly, it made perfect sense that there was no local specialist to repair the compressed disc causing all my pain.

I had to travel an hour and half to Glens Falls, New York, to find a surgeon to read my MRI pictures. He wanted to do surgery right away.

He explained the situation to me. There are four levels of severity when diagnosing and treating disc problems. Level One is the most minor and requires no intervention. Level Four is the most serious, requiring emergency surgery because paralysis and incontinence are almost always the outcome of waiting. "It looks to me like you are at Level Three. But any serious bump or jarring movement could move you up to a Level Four."

I wondered if the serious thumping of my heart against my chest was putting me at risk of jarring movement.

He had his assistant call the hospital to see if he could book a surgery that afternoon or the next day, which was a Friday. No go. We would have to wait until Monday. But we got the first surgical slot. I would have jumped up and down for joy, but I didn't want to be upgraded to Level Four. I was pretty sure it wasn't nearly as pleasant as being upgraded to First Class.

The surgeon gave me some good advice. "Try not to move between now and Monday. And take these for the pain. Those muscle relaxants they gave you are as effective as pissing on a forest fire."

I took the prescription for Oxy-Hard-Core and nodded in silent awe of the surgeon's effective use of a simile.

Not moving for a whole weekend was easy for my bowels. I can't say the same for the rest of me.

Monday morning started early and with a blinding migraine. Since I couldn't take any of my CFIDS symptom management medications before the surgery, I had my first medication-free migraine in years. I immediately knew my head wanted me to suffer. The only positive thing I can say about that monster headache is that it took my focus away from my unbearable back pain during the long car ride to the hospital.

At the hospital, Victor had to answer questions for me. Groans and sighs were all I could muster. I had to sign paperwork stating that I might die. Given that the agony I was suffering, dying was fine by me.

In the pre-op room, I begged for pain relief in the form of morphine and for something to calm my escalating nausea. I was writhing on the table from the pain in my back, head, and stomach. Then, my face started to sting as if I were being attacked by angry wasps. I kept slapping at my face and head. I think that's when the staff started to worry about me. Until then, they said, "We can't give you anything until the anesthesiologist speaks to you. He isn't in yet, but we've called him and he's on his way." I suppose that's the downside of being the first surgery of the day—snooze buttons, traffic, long lines at Starbucks.

When I began the facial self-flagellation, however, they must have sent a posse out to get the knock-out-team. Then a nurse came in and said, "We've got the okay. Your meds are right here. You'll start feeling better in a few seconds." The IV paraphernalia was already in my arm, so it was just a matter of injecting me with the feel-better juice.

Nothing. All I could do was cry when they asked me to rate my pain on a scale of 1 to 10. In retrospect, I'd say my pain level was "stick the laminated chart in my eye and pull it out of my ear." How many sad-faces would that be?

They checked with the anesthesiologist and hit me with another dose. Nada. Still writhing in pain, I begged them, "When are you going to give me something to help me?" Two hits of morphine and a drug to calm my nausea, and I felt nothing. This was no ordinary headache. It was Demonic Possession.

With a special dispensation from the pope and a Presidential Executive Order, I was given a third dose of morphine. Finally the woozy warm blanket of pain relief encircled me and I drifted off to sleep.

When I woke up, my surgery was over and I was recovering from having my L-4 disc repaired. My head felt normal—well, dizzy, but that was normal. My back, not so good. Although the surgeon declared the surgery a success, he said I wouldn't know if there was any permanent damage to my left leg for six to eight weeks, when I should be healed. But it might be up to a year because nerves have the nerve to make you wait a good long time to let you know if they have been repaired or not.

*****

In 2007, I had the good fortune to attend a lecture by Deepak Chopra, an endocrinologist, expert in mind-body medicine, spiritual scholar, and generally nice guy. His lecture was in Syracuse, New York, and a local newspaper was giving away free tickets to anyone who emailed him a question that he chose to answer in an interview prior to the event. I'd read many of his books in my efforts to cope with my health issues and was grappling with a question. *What's the difference between giving up and letting go?*

He chose my question, thus I attended his lecture for free.

Before I reveal his answer, some background is necessary.

My quest to be Healthy Lorna was failing miserably. The back surgery had put the kibosh on my illusion that I was "just fine." That left me with two options:

1. Give up. I wasn't experiencing a continual barrage of "temporary setbacks." I was a person who was falling apart at a fairly rapid and steady rate. Perhaps I should invest in a wheelchair and one of those Medic-Alert devices to hang around my neck in case I fell. And I would fall.

2. Uhhh....

I guess I just had one option.

*****

I saw a personal counselor to deal with my depression and periodic thoughts of suicide should a fall down the stairs or other health disaster not kill me humanely. By "humanely," I mean quickly and with as little warning as possible, like a sniper's bullet. I didn't really want to die; I just didn't want to live in a constant state of *in-valid-ism*.

I was slowly recovering from the back surgery, but a nasty and lingering staph infection set me back a few weeks. My left foot never regained full function, so my runway model days were over, given my tell-tale *tha-thunk tha-thunk* gait, especially when I was tired, which was just about always. Also, the muscles in my left leg began to disappear as the nerves from my spine stopped communicating to them. You would have thought they were an old married couple with dead batteries in their hearing aids. My right leg, thanks to great genes and lots of exercise, looked fit and trim, whereas my left leg looked like it belonged to an anorexic flamingo. Since modern medicine hasn't accomplished a successful full leg transplant yet, I had to get creative. I bought negative heel technology footwear that served the dual purpose of strengthening my leg muscles from the bottom up and protected me from anyone with a foot fetish due to their decidedly ugly appearance. After several months of wearing these unsightly but effective shoes, I figured only the most discerning leg-man could tell the difference between Former-Flamingo-Left-Leg and Sexy-Right-Leg. My "foot-flop" (yes, that's the technical term), was better, too, but I still avoided the runway unless an airplane was involved.

Besides seeing my personal counselor, I began reading a new category of self-help books. I was less interested in my Inner Divine Self now and more interested in finding inner peace. I realized that "issues" were just "problems" spelled with different letters. I wasn't the same Lorna I'd always been. I *was* different. But different didn't have to mean defunct. I just *thought* it did, and so did everyone around me, which only helped to convince me that I was as broken as the house that had become my self-imposed prison.

Reading books by Deepak Chopra and the Dalai Lama introduced me to Buddhism. They wrote about "letting go" (and they both also used lots of esoteric Sanskrit words that were both mysterious and difficult to pronounce). What I didn't understand was the difference between "letting go" and "giving up." And those were plain English words.

I was a lot of things, but "quitter" was never one of them, though maybe "stubborn" was. I've never been great at getting hints, so perhaps all these health problems were my body's way of slowing me down so I would have time to take a long, hard look at my life. *Maybe,* I said to myself, *I should explore this "letting go" business.* So I asked my buddy, Deepak.

He told me, via a newspaper article, that "giving up" implies you expect some outcome that you think you can control, but when it doesn't happen, you get frustrated. (Insert delightful chuckle at the silliness of that notion.) "Letting go" is a Buddhist practice in which you, moment by moment, drop all expectations of any particular outcome and just accept life and all its possibilities. Without judgment. (Insert nervous Lorna snort.)

It took me quite a while to process this distinction, but I finally understood. I needed to make friends with this new Lorna, the one with dizziness and all of the adventures that came with it. I had to drop any expectations of (a) returning to Former Not-Dizzy Lorna or (b) creating a New-and-Improved Lorna. I needed to embrace who I was every moment, accept that anything was possible in the next moment, and accept whatever that was, too.

Christians speak of "finding God." I found personal salvation in the simple instruction of "letting go." I still had the same life and the same symptoms, but felt so much more peaceful and calm. Everything I read about CFIDS that was confirmed by Dr. Don't Worry indicated that if my symptoms persisted longer than five years, my condition was likely to remain with me for life. I had now reached the five-year mark. I was fine with that because I was no longer enemies with my condition or myself.

I told Victor, "Everyone has something they live with and manage. This is my Something. I'm not wasting any more of my energy fighting it. I've made friends with it and it feels good."

"What do you mean? Do you feel better?" He was clearly confused.

"The symptoms are all still with me. I'm just not fighting them anymore. No more chasing 'miracle cures' to fix me. I accept myself this way and what happens, well, it happens. No more expectations. No more judgments. I feel more peaceful inside. Do you understand?"

"No. I don't know how you can just give up on your health like that."

Victor was categorically *not* fine with my new attitude. He could not tolerate a quitter, which is what he thought I was. But I didn't want a fifth and a sixth opinion from him about why I was wasn't "normal." In my heart, I was embracing Current Lorna as Normal Lorna, but Victor still wanted to know why I wasn't Former Lorna. He wanted me to be repaired, and, if possible, improved. In my opinion, I didn't need fixing anymore. With the tenacity of a pit-bull terrier on a mailman's trousers, my husband clung to a version of me that disappeared years ago or that would never exist. Maybe even one that never existed at all.

When I initially got dizzy all those years ago, we had shared the goal of fixing me—the idea of finding "the cure" had held us together. By moving along this new spiritual path, however, I was letting go of more than the self-destructive expectations that were exhausting me; I was also letting go of our common goal. I didn't intend to, but that's what happened. I was beginning to use singular possessive pronouns in reference to my health: *I. Me. Mine.* Victor wanted, and always thought he had, a *we/us* marriage. If I wasn't with him, I was invisible…or worse. I wasn't with him anymore and worse was about to happen.

I should have known that Victor would interpret my search for inner peace as a declaration of war against him. My string of miscalculations was turning into a rope, one that was getting uncomfortably taut.

*****

In 2007, I turned fifty years old.

Unlike most gerontophobic people, I was happy to be fifty and not dead. Sure, I had an extra hole in my head and a foot-flop, but I was around to talk about them. I gave myself a gift for the first time in my life: a bit of Buddhist wisdom. I thought my idea was inspirational and revolutionary. "From this day forward," I told Victor, "I will speak my truth with kindness and compassion."

I waited for a supportive "that's my Lorna" response, but he seemed to need some time to process my declaration. Finally he said, "What do you mean by 'your' truth?"

Emphasizing the "kindness" part, I said, "I'm an adult. I'm fifty years old! I'm finally giving myself permission to express my thoughts and feelings out loud, but always with compassion and kindness as my intention."

He still wasn't getting it. "Are you saying you haven't been honest with me all these years about your true feelings? And I suppose I'm to blame for you not feeling like you can say what's on your mind?"

"Well, no," I began. "I mean, yes. I mean, not always. Sometimes I don't say what's really on my mind because I don't want to upset anyone."

"Like you're doing now?"

"I didn't mean for this to upset you. I thought you'd be happy that I am acting like an adult, an equal partner. Finally...."

It was too late. Victor was scrubbing the cook top. He always resorted to cleaning kitchen surfaces when he was miffed at me. Our countertops were usually spotless.

Yes, my first act of speaking my truth-with-kindness flopped. In Victor's world, there was only one truth, and it wasn't mine. He took my announcement as an indictment of our relationship and his treatment of me. I was *talking about me*; he was hearing me *criticize him*. If I could figure out a way of expressing my feelings without using the words "I," "me," or any first person pronoun, I might have stood a chance at getting through to him. But I wasn't that linguistically innovative. Being kindly truthful with him was tricky.

As it turned out, kindness didn't matter, anyway. Victor didn't like his kind but candid wife. He avoided me by being more busy and more away from home. His allergies made him sleep in a recliner downstairs, so our bedroom was pretty much my bedroom. I periodically brought up our intimacy and communication "issues," but his only response was to tell me how I made him feel like a failure. My suggestions about trying counseling again—because it had helped so much the first time—fell flat.

I dove back into my books on Buddhism and found renewed inspiration to continue practicing loving-kindness. That just frustrated him more. The kinder I was, the more resentful he became. It was the Vicious Cycle of Kindness you rarely hear about in Buddhist teachings.

*****

Our relationship was always as cyclical as a revolving door in Grand Central Station. In early 2008, I thought we were turning the corner again. Victor liked to keep life, as he called it, "fresh," or, as I called it, "off balance" by changing things up when life got too predictable or surprising me by doing the opposite of what he said. I chalked it up to his Gemini nature.

This time the surprise came as our twenty-fifth wedding anniversary was approaching. We had purchased a time-share on Waikiki Beach, and now he suggested we take the honeymoon we had never really had. I was stunned. The man who made it his mission in life to stay away from me was proposing a two-week romantic get-away to Hawaii! I was completely on board and ready for some kind of Relationship Renaissance. I even suggested that we renew our wedding vows at the Buddhist temple that we had visited a couple of times on prior visits to Oahu. He seemed to like that idea. Given his newfound affection for our relationship, I pushed one step further.

"When we got married," I said, "I took your name as a sign of my commitment to you. How about as a symbol of your commitment to me and in honor of the next twenty-five years of marriage, you change your middle name to my maiden name, so we both have the same middle and last names?"

I had taken my maiden name as my middle name, and we had even given that middle name to Alex. Now all three of us would have the same middle and last names. It would be the onomastic (study of names) equivalent of wearing the same tee-shirt on vacation.

"That's a neat idea," he said. And that was all he said about my idea ever again. He continued, "But I was also thinking about the trip itself...."

I should have known that shoes come in pairs and that when one shoe falls, the other can't help but follow. But why does the other shoe always have to fall on your head with such a nasty *ker-thunk*? Victor named an assortment of people he wanted to invite on our "honeymoon."

Huh?

I said, "You want your Office Wife and her daughter, your computer tech guy and his family, Pseudo Brother and his family, your sister and her family, and maybe my mom to come with us? Victor, it's only a two-bedroom condo."

He was ready with an answer. "I was thinking we could stagger the visits so that not everyone would be there at once and save maybe two days at the end just for us."

Victor had concocted this entire scheme in advance. "It's a shame," he added, "to have this little piece of paradise and not share it with our family and friends."

I wanted to say, *No freaking way are we having a horde of people crash our supposedly romantic get-away. You go and have a blast. I'll stay home with the pets and save the cost of hiring a pet sitter.* But I didn't say that. It would have been honest, but not very kind. Instead, I said, "Still, that seems like a lot of people." I guess I was going for *reasonable* and *selfless*.

"Oh, they probably won't all be able to come," he said. "And it will be more fun with more people."

I wanted to say, *More fun for* you, *Mister Social Butterfly, but what about me? I guess your definition of fun doesn't include the any of the following letters: S, E, or X.* Instead I said, "Yeah, and the plane fare will probably be too expensive for most of them." Now I was going for *cooperative* and *practical.* Honest and kind just didn't play well with my husband when it was coming from me. Maybe the honesty never felt very kind to him.

The only person who chaperoned our honeymoon was my mom. My sisters paid for her airfare, and we covered her expenses while she was in Hawaii. I was thrilled that Mom got to go to Hawaii—this was a trip she never would have taken otherwise. Victor was delighted that his mother-in-law was able to provide an apparently much-needed distraction from me during our vacation. Being a gracious and generous host, Victor showed her a great time and treated her like a queen. I was treated like her daughter, the virgin princess.

As for renewing our wedding vows, my track record of having honeymoons-that-weren't remained unbroken. Normally, Victor would make elaborate arrangements for special events. His approach to our sacred event was flaccid. For the first time in his life that I knew of, he didn't plan something special in advance. We picked "our special day" the morning of the day, went up to the temple in comfortable tourist garb, and exchanged our informal, impromptu vows with each other. He didn't even offer me a single red rose. My mom videotaped the event, but the winds were fierce, so the video is a silent film (except the *whoosh* of wind) of two people whose lips are moving. Our words were forever swept away by the trade winds. As I would come to know soon, that was prophetic. Those words were just white noise.

Then we had lunch at Chili's.

*****

Victor turned fifty in May and embraced his sixth decade like it was the arrival of the Grim Reaper. He insisted that I not give him any kind of party—not even a small one with his family—and I was also forbidden to mention his age, in jest or otherwise. On the day after his birthday, however, I could tell he was upset with me. I asked him what was wrong.

"The people at the office took me out for lunch and had a birthday cake for me. You didn't do anything. I guess I know who really cares about me."

"But you said you absolutely, positively didn't want a party or any mention of your birthday...." The longer I lived with Victor, the more I seemed to miscalculate his motives and thoughts. Was it me or him?

"I didn't want a *big shindig*," he said now, "but you could have at least taken me out to dinner. You'd think after all these years of marriage, you'd know me by now."

"I'm sorry. You're right. How about dinner tonight?"

"No. I feel like going to the lake, and the camper hasn't been opened up yet, so you're not going to want to go." He was great at telling me what I wanted and didn't want.

"Okay. Sure," I said. "Maybe we can go out to dinner this weekend?"

"Maybe," he said as he left for work. Early. As usual.

Victor bought himself a gift, though: a 1970-something El Dorado convertible. It was white. Being a female, I remember specific automotive details like color. He knew that I can't ride in convertibles because the sensory stimulation made my dizziness worse. If this was a game of poker, he saw "my truth" and raised it with "his convertible." I don't know which one cost us more.

That summer was the worst summer for my health in the seven years since CFIDS and I were introduced. After a twelve-day migraine, I was desperate. Something had to give before I did. Praying came to mind. I wasn't on my knees, all angelic-like, though. I was pounding my thighs, pleading loudly though sobs of pure self-pity to Anyone Up There Who Would Listen. I wanted to cover all bases. Being friends with my condition was one thing, but my friend was beating me up. Badly.

I prayed for relief, just from the headache. Already having been through the first two stages of mourning my loss of everything precious to me, I was up to bargaining. I looked up to the cracked ceiling in the Broken House and said, "I vow on my soul to run toward anything that is positive and run away from anything that harms me if only You lift this pain away from me."

I knew, deep down, I was playing with matches in an oil refinery. But I also figured the chances of "just ask and ye shall receive" were pretty slim, even though you read about it all the time in the Bible—assuming you've read the Bible.

I learned that I should never underestimate the power of thigh-thumping, pity-partying, and vowing to Higher Powers.

CHAPTER 22: THE MIRACLE THAT HAD AN EXPIRATION DATE

Reggie and I had a lot in common: we startled easily, we loved to dance, we were dazzling on our good days and we had mysterious diseases that didn't allow us to reach our full potentials.

I wasn't quite finished with my hysterical version of praying when I noticed something, or, more precisely, *nothing*. My twelve-day, demonic migraine was gone. So were my dizziness and nausea. So were my dogs. The dogs always got nervous and cowered and hid during both thunderstorms and Lorna-Lunaticstorms. In their simple world, a storm was a storm.

I looked around, being careful to not move my head. Not wanting to disturb the good *juju*, I gingerly turned my whole upper body and saw my dogs cowering a safe distance from me—within visual but not flailing-appendage range. It was as if they knew something *National Enquirer*-worthy had just happened and didn't want to be in the vortex of an apocalyptic transformation spell. We all stayed in place like mannequins for about five minutes, after which I still felt *nothing*. Which meant I felt as healthy as I had seven years ago before my world started spinning.

"But I can't sit here forever," I said to the dogs. They seemed to agree, so I moved my head. No problem. I got up. No problem. I walked around. I was fine. In a bold move, I spun myself around. No dizziness. I'm not sure how many "thank yous" came out of me in the next several minutes, but I was in Olympic-Gold-Medal-for-Gratitude territory. For the first time in over seven years, I wasn't dizzy. I felt perfect, in fact. The dogs joined me in a frisky celebration dance. Once I got that out of my system and was still perfectly stable. I called Victor at work.

"Are you sitting down?" My voice was filled with giddiness.

"Yes." His voice was filled with uncertainty.

"I'm cured!" I was never great at keeping secrets…if you don't count the ten years I was a closet alcoholic.

"You're what?"

"I'm cured! I'm not dizzy. Not even a little. And my headache is gone." I told him the whole desperation, dealing-making, dog-disappearing story.

Silence.

"Are you still there?"

"Yes. I'm here." He sounded as if he was speaking to a crazy person or a telemarketer.

"Isn't this wonderful?"

"It might be a fluke."

"No! This is real! Really, really, real. For real, real. Aren't you happy?"

"I'll be happy if this lasts for a while."

"You'll know it's real when you see me! I'll join you down at the lake after work. We'll celebrate, okay?"

"I've got that guy coming to help dig a trench tonight."

"He won't be there all night, will he? Can't he work while we celebrate?"

"I'll need to supervise him. But I guess we can work something out."

"Great! The minute you see me, you'll know I'm cured. I promise!" I was bursting! with! exclamation! points!

I went down to our camp and danced on the deck while Victor supervised Trench Man. He supervised him for a very long time. How hard can it be to dig a straight trench with a backhoe? Victor was standing around pointing and Trench Man was operating his DYI-sized version of a backhoe meant to move gardens, not mountains. They kept looking over at me and saying things to each other, but I couldn't hear what they were saying. I was singing and they were clearly doing that man-to-man bonding/talking thing. Their furtive looks my way didn't bode well for either my solo vocals or my dance moves. I was glad I couldn't read lips.

"These two men obviously have no appreciation for artistic expression and excessive jubilance," I said to my dogs. Undaunted, I kept shimmying and singing my heart out. Not once did I feel as if my head would rotate off my shoulders. It was pure bliss.

Since I had time, I also devised plans for building a real home on that beautiful site. In my perfectly stable brain, I conjured up our eventual retirement home. It was cozy, energy-efficient, and completely finished. I thought Victor would be happy that I was finally taking a real interest in our lake property.

Wrong again.

When Trench Man finally left, Victor joined me on the deck. He had a glass of wine or a martini, maybe both, in preparation for talking with me. I was pure bubbles. Sitting still was hard for both of us. I told him the story again, twirling around for emphasis. I also shared my vision of our retirement home as we watched the dusk fall on the glass-like lake. Victor was unusually quiet.

"Whatcha thinkin'?" I playfully asked as I poked his arm. In love with life and full of energy, I wanted to make love to him on the deck.

"Aren't you getting a little ahead of yourself?" He was speaking to his drink.

"What do you mean? I love this lake. I was the one who wanted to buy this land for our retirement home. Now I feel like everything is possible is again. Look at me! I'm healthy!"

He continued to stare into his glass. Then he heaved a big sigh.

"What's the matter?" This guy sure knew how squelch a girl's exclamation points.

He finally said, "I don't know how I would handle it if you were really healthy."

I certainly wasn't expecting that.

He had gotten used to the role of caretaker; he may, in fact, have even gotten some sympathy-mileage out of it in the community. I think he liked having an "in-valid" wife, even if it was difficult at times. But enough of a bad thing was surely enough, wasn't it? He should be happy for me. For *us*.

I had already called Dr. Don't Worry and asked him how to wean myself off the medications I'd been on all these years and when he thought I could go back to work. His attitude was the same as Victor's: let's give this recovery some time to see if it's real. But he was a physician, and they're paid to be skeptical. They'd go out of business if all their patients got healthy.

Victor was my husband. Why wouldn't he want me to recover?

"I don't understand," I said. "What do you mean, you don't know how you'd handle it if I was healthy? What is there for you to *handle* if I'm healthy?" I was confused and tried to ask kindly, but I was hurt, too. My exclamation points lay on the deck like dead pine needles waiting to be swept away.

"Look," he said, "I don't want to be on this roller coaster with you. I never know how you're going to feel, so we can never plan anything. It's hard for me. If I get all excited and you're not really well, then it's just harder to recover from the inevitable disappointment." Although he glanced at me from time to time during this conversation, he never held eye contact.

"Maybe if you believe in me," I said, "it will help this be really real. I know I said I'm not trying to fix myself anymore, but I'm willing to accept this gift of wellness. Be happy for me. For *us*. Please?"

"I just can't." He got up. I think he took offense at my request for him to believe in me—as though I didn't think he believed in me, or something. A minute later, I could hear him cleaning the mini-kitchen in the camper. Without trying, I had pushed him over yet another cliff I didn't realize he was on.

Accustomed to that unwelcome feeling on my own property, I got up to leave. "I'm going back to the house," I called to him. "Are you coming?" My lust for life—and for him—had vanished along with my vision of our cozy retirement home on the beautiful lake.

"No. I've got some stuff to eat here. I'll call you tomorrow." He didn't even come outside to say this. He was still inside, scrubbing some kitchen surface.

"Okay. Have a good night. I love you."

"Thanks. Love you, too." He was still busy in the little kitchen.

I drove my undizzy self home and danced with Reggie, my cockatoo, before I went to bed. *Rye wuv roo*, Reggie reassured me in his cockatoo-garble as he nuzzled my neck before I put him in his cage. That "I love you" from a bird meant more to me than the one I got at the lake. It sure felt more genuine.

Try as I might to remain positive, the last thought I had before drifting off to sleep was, *I wonder if Victor is right to be skeptical.*

*****

My Miracle Cure lasted as long as the typical jinx fly (as it is aptly called): *two days.*

Victor kept checking on me. "Are you dizzy yet?"

His confidence in me was underwhelming, but I was determined not to let him get me down. Or dizzy. I kept spinning around like an ice skater practicing her short program. "Nope!"

On the third day, I woke up to that old familiar "bed-spin." It was faint, but it was there. As the day picked up, so did the volume on the dizziness dial. Yes, my Miracle Cure had expired.

I called Dr. Don't Worry. He explained that with CFIDS, symptoms are unpredictable. I guess disappearing symptoms are equally squirrelly. I didn't wait for Victor to call in for his Daily Dizzy Debriefing. I called him and told him I was back to normal, or abnormal, or whatever. Though he expressed proper disappointment for me, he at least didn't say, "I told you so." I appreciated his sympathy. Since it was Friday and we usually went out to dinner, he offered to take me out to a condolence dinner. I accepted.

He was very upbeat during the evening. I couldn't tell if he was trying to cheer me up or if he couldn't contain his own elation that life between us had resumed its old, familiar rhythm. It didn't matter. He was happy and I was dizzy. It was as if the last two days had never happened. But they had happened!

My Expired Miracle highlighted two undeniable facts. First, my husband was keen on keeping his dizzy-blonde wife dizzy and in-valid. Since I was committed to our marriage and loved him, I decided we were together to learn Valuable Life Lessons from each other. I had to learn compassion, forgiveness, and the joys of abstinence. What he had to learn remained a mystery to me, which suggested I also needed to work on understanding. Second, I had made a Real Deal with Someone Powerful Up There. Taking it back wasn't an option.

As if to poke a finger in an already sore eye, the Someone Up There started dropping hints as subtle as the H-bomb that I wasn't keeping up my end of The Deal. I was supposed to surround myself with only positive influences and get rid of all negative elements in my life; in return, I would find wellness. I got my taste of wellness. Now it was up to me to do some personal life "housecleaning." I hoped it wasn't as difficult, thankless and mind-numbing as regular housekeeping. And I was sure I wouldn't be able to find someone to do it for me for $15 an hour, either.

Just like regular housekeeping, I found excuses to ignore my personal "housekeeping." It seemed like a lot of work that would only end up causing a lot of trouble for someone whose name started with *L* and ended with *orna*.

I ignored my Sacred Pact and postponed my personal housecleaning for about a year. There were consequences, of course, but it was only with time, distance, and reflection that I could see the connection between my return to Dizzy Lorna and several new twists and turns in my life.

*****

The first turn was unexpected and tragic. Late in the summer of 2008, Reggie, my beloved cockatoo, died of some genetic nerve disease in his throat. He couldn't swallow, which meant he couldn't drink or eat. We had adopted him on Valentine's Day in 2005. That was the year that Alex went away to college, and our empty nest was feathered with an eight month old Triton cockatoo. Since neither Victor nor I knew anything about tropical birds, this decision seemed odd to our families. But Victor had always wanted a cockatoo and I thought that maybe this big white bird would make him happy. Reggie gave Victor a reason to want to come home. And Reggie gave me a reason to love being at home. I spent many hours every day caring for him and teaching him tricks, including how to speak in garbled cockatoo English. Reggie and I enjoyed the same kind of music, so we danced together. We laughed together, too. He matched his "Dr. Evil" laugh (*heh, heh, heh*) with my from-the-belly laugh. Reggie was more like a child/friend than he was a pet to me. To Victor, he was, like so many other things in his life, a treasured trophy.

Reggie was a bright light in my life, but he was also an incredible amount of work. Think of having a toddler hyped on sugar all day who poops anywhere he wants, and that was Reggie. He complicated my life and I loved him for it. He gave each day a purpose: to shower him, clean his cage, cook special meals for him, change his cage with various toys to keep him entertained, teach him new tricks and words, and practice our dance routine.

Early in 2008, I noticed he was losing weight and would only eat very soft food. Several visits to several vets yielded no specific diagnosis other than "spoiled brat." When we took him to a cockatoo specialist—yes, they exist and, yes, they are expensive—we got our unfortunate answer to his continued weight loss. In an effort to keep him with me for as long as possible, I hand fed him and gave him droppers of waters. The vet told us that when we found him on the bottom of his cage rather than on one of his many perches in his luxurious cage, he would be nearing the end. On the morning I found him huddled on the bottom of his cage, my heart sank. Reggie, a bird that should have lived long enough to give my eulogy and to be a burden to Alex in his old age, had to be euthanized at the very premature age of four.

His last words to me were a very weak, *Reggie...go...nigh...nigh*. I held him, rocked him, and sang to him all the way to the vet's office. He remained silent and stayed nuzzled in the crook of my arm until the vet lifted him away from me.

Without Reggie, life felt empty and humdrum, even though my aching back thanked me—no more bending over and cleaning up the cage—and I had no more worries about how I would take care of my precious Reggie should my life circumstances change. I still had two dogs and a cat, but felt like I had lost a child. I grieved more for that bird than I had for any loss I had ever suffered. But all I could see was my pain. I didn't notice that Reggie had set the stage to set me free from the Broken House.

*****

The next sign I chose to ignore didn't appear until a year later. Every year Victor's staff gave us a gift certificate to a spa or resort. Since he was an intense and demanding boss, I figured the gift was designed to relax the office staff as much as it was intended to relax us. In 2009, the gift was for a weekend at a B&B in Vermont. Since mid-September was close to our real twenty-fifth anniversary, I checked with Victor to make sure his calendar was clear before I made reservations. My mistake was expecting that he *wanted* to spend a weekend away with me. Since he wanted to leave Thursday and come back on Saturday, he conducted a lot of business while we were gone. I wanted to throw his Blackberry in the toilet. I dressed up in an attractive black dress for dinner, but he barely noticed. I was snapping pictures and asking resort staff to take pictures of us, but I had to ask him to take a picture of me. The dinner was very nice, but he spent more time talking with the wait staff than with me.

We left the B&B a day early because he'd forgotten he had a choral performance at some war reenactment celebration on Friday evening back at home. (In our area of New York, war reenactments are so popular that the cannons are always loaded in case some bunch of rag-tag uniformed men get a hankering to pretend-fight.) He didn't ask me, but, knowing how important it was to him, I offered to attend his vocal performance. Since many festive war events were planned, I even offered to drive separately so he could enjoy the whole shebang while I went home after his performance. He insisted we drive together, then he got angry when I wanted to leave early.

The rest of the weekend was uneventful. He went his way and I had a several-day migraine. Our twenty-fifth wedding anniversary came and went without fanfare.

*****

Between the fall of 2008 and summer of 2009 I dabbled in different approaches to save our relationship. I wasn't trying to push Victor away, I was trying to figure out how to make Victor happy with me. In the process of

339

getting happy with myself, I had to do something to get him on board with being happy with me and our relationship. But the more I threw the marriage life-preserver to him, the farther away he swam. It was as if he thought I was trying to hit him on the head with it and drown him. Didn't he know my aim was about as accurate as the assassin gunning for 007 in any James Bond film?

Having been through marriage counseling once and personal counseling for several years to deal with all the changes in my life, I begged Victor to try marriage counseling again. Since I was already seeing a counselor, my insurance plan would only pay if Victor initiated the new sessions. He never refused counseling, but he never called, either. Inaction is a kind of action. I didn't want to be a nagging wife, so I stopped asking if he called for an appointment after about fifty separate inquiries.

Since actions speak louder than words I rallied my inner resources and asked to attend social and business functions with Victor. I figured that if I was more a part of his world, he would feel closer to me. Wrong! Although I think he liked showing up in a crowded room with a shapely, pretty, blonde wife because of the attention we got, he always seemed edgy. People who knew me commented almost incredulously on how great and healthy I looked. While I thanked them, I also thought it was odd that they would be so flabbergasted that I was walking upright and breathing without an oxygen mask. Victor invariably asked me if I wanted to leave early. I invariably replied, "Only if you do." When we left early, I always heard him making excuses about how I could only take "so much" of this kind of stimulation before I "crashed."

Maybe I'm a dizzy blonde, but I'm not stupid. My efforts to connect with Victor nose-dived into the Bermuda Triangle of Relationships. If I was going to change my situation, *I* was going to have to change.

And that is where the real trouble began.

*****

Knowing that Victor couldn't understand how I "had given up" on my health, I educated myself on my dysfunctional immune system. Scientists believe that inflammation irritates the heck out of the body, and that's what causes the immune system to go into battle mode. Constant inflammation equals chronic inflammatory problems equals weakened immune system. I put myself on a very strict vegan diet and also eliminated all sugar, plus all processed foods, coffee, wheat gluten, and anything else delicious.

I lost weight, started sleeping better, and had more energy. I looked and felt better than I had in a long time. *And I was still dizzy.* But I was a foxy-looking dizzy blonde who had the energy and interest to do all kinds of things with her husband, in public and in private. This really annoyed Victor and really surprised me. Was his cantankerous mood caused by the fact that dining out was the only thing we ever did together, and now I was pretty much limited to a salad with oil and vinegar dressing, hold the croutons? Or was it because I wanted to attend all those business meetings with him and he had to explain why I wasn't in a wheel chair? Maybe he was afraid I was getting better, and because I was getting better, he and wouldn't know what to do with a healthy wife who spoke her truth with kindness and also wanted sex. Perhaps he was jealous because I was six months older than he was but wasn't overweight and looked ten years his junior.

I simply don't know. Victor's mood was such that asking him why he wasn't happy about his slimmer and vastly improved dizzy wife would have been the same as asking him why he was such a rotten husband. He was

341

angry with me when I told him I was making friends with my condition and simply letting go, which he heard as "giving up." Now he was angry with me for taking action to protect my compromised immune system from further damage. You know what? I think that man just wanted to be angry with me.

The more I paid attention to my life, the more I realized that I didn't know the man I had been married to for twenty-five years. But rather than taking this as a sign to pack my bags, I saw this as a challenge to rediscover him and to figure out what I could learn from the journey we were on together. My problem? I was so busy stoking the engine to keep the Love Train chugging forward, I didn't notice that he had purchased a one way ticket on an airline.

*****

The final twist was one I blundered into with the best of intentions. I simply wanted to expand my intellectual horizons. Being an academic, I should have stuck with Pulitzer Prize winning books, but I ventured into the magical world of podcasts and listened to two of them religiously. One was *Zencast*, which was about Buddhism. The other was *Theatre of the Mind*, a New Age program interviewing experts about metaphysical matters. *Zencast* helped calm me and reminded me that I had a choice in every moment to act in a conscious way. *What would the Buddha do?* I learned to ask myself that when I was confronted by another Victor-related rejection or conflict.

I tuned into *Theater of the Mind* when Kelley Howell was doing a series about the Mayans and 2012. The experts she interviewed explained how the Mayans lived by a natural calendar where the solstices and equinoxes were powerful days. The vernal (spring) equinox, these New Agers suggested, was especially powerful; it was the day when you "planted" your intention for what you wanted to "grow" in the year to come. Whether this was Mayan wisdom or New Age fantasy, it sounded neat to me. The sincere warnings to be very clear about what you wanted, because it *would* manifest, gave me pause, but I decided to ask for something I thought was beautiful, healing, and harmless. When I told Victor about the Mayans and my plans for a Mayan ritual experiment, he seemed interested and supportive. Either his second martini had seriously kicked in or he wasn't really listening.

At the spring, 2009, equinox, a dear friend and I stood together in my yard at the exact time of the equinox and I asked for "peace." I felt lighter and freer than I had in a long time. Being a novice, I didn't know that "peace" was a hugely vague request and could be interpreted by the universe in so many creative and, well, yes, turbulent, ways. Before you can regrow anything, you need to destroy what's in the way of the regrowth. Not being a farmer or a gardener, how was I supposed to know that? To make things even more interesting, destruction always starts with one small, seemingly insignificant event or flaw. Looking back, I get the image of documentaries chronicling levees failing and bridges falling. My insignificant event was asking for something so vague and ill-defined as "peace."

Once the "seed" was "planted," I was supposed to leave it alone until the summer solstice, at which time, I was supposed to begin work on tending to the growing "plant." As it turned out, my "peace seed" was growing in a garden of "war weeds" that summer. Victor was very unhappy. Not even martinis helped soften his edginess. The autumn equinox was the time to "harvest" and reap the rewards of what I had "planted." I sure didn't feel like I was harvesting any "peace."

*****

Cleaning up my personal house ended up with just what I feared: I uncovered something I didn't want to face. And now I had to deal with it. There was no sweeping that cosmic dust bunny under the rug.

CHAPTER 23: WAS I VOTED THE CLASS OF 1975'S GIRL MOST LIKELY TO BE DUMPED?

My Senior class picture, 1975

How can peace be so disturbing? I asked myself this question many times over the next several months. Did the universe misunderstand me? I thought I was clear when I simply asked for "peace." The universe is a vast place. Perhaps my request got lost in a black hole. Could it be that I wasn't ready for a peaceful life? No. I was ready. So what went awry? The most likely explanation? I was an inept metaphysical farmer.

Victor's business was booming. It should have been, given the number of hours he spent tending to it and to his clients. He spent as much time as he could at his lake retreat home. When the weather was bad or when he had to be home at the Broken House for other reasons, we managed a cordial, cautious relationship.

On and off, Victor wondered out loud about renovating his first office building—yes, he had a second one now—into a huge loft-style apartment for us where we could live in the winter and thus avoid the expense of heating our behemoth old Broken House. Part of this 15,000-square-foot former car dealership already had an average apartment in it, but creating a luxury loft would take mega-bucks, so the talk remained talk. During the summer of 2009, Victor became interested in turning the building into apartments as rental income. I wasn't keen on that idea because he was already so busy and had little time for relaxation. He took my less-than-enthusiastic response as another criticism of him, so I dropped my objections and repeated my new Buddhist mantra: *At their core, all souls are good.*

Then I decided to make Victor a queen-sized quilt for the lake camp bed. My logic was that if I wasn't there, my handiwork would be, reminding him of the best of me. I designed it especially for him. That summer, quilting became my meditation on love, commitment, compassion, and accepting things that I couldn't comprehend. The quilt design was "busy" with a kaleidoscope of different colors and shapes. It's a kind of fabric irony. I name all my quilts, and that one was called "Remember Me."

My pet menagerie that summer dwindled to just two dogs: Jazzy and Scrappy. My cat, Pudley, died from kidney failure at the not-so-ripe-old age of nine. Jazzy was very old and soon decided that life was too hard to live. On many days, I agreed with her. Early in October, we called Alex to come home to say goodbye to her since she was his dog. After he graduated from college in Albany, New York, he had stayed there and found a job. He called Albany a great "starter city." He had been reluctant to leave home, but he enjoyed his independence and never looked back.

After a sad weekend, we all took Jazzy to the vet for the final time. She was one of those dogs who asked so little of us and gave everything she could in return. My wellspring of unconditional love was running dangerously dry now that both Reggie and Jazzy had died. My cute but independent terrier-mix, Scrappy, was my only companion. He was never the lovey type like Jazzy was. Now sweet Jazzy was gone, leaving one less heart in the Broken House open to me. At Alex's request, we buried her at the Broken House, the place he would always consider home.

The weather turned cold that fall, so Victor reluctantly came home. One week after Jazzy died, he mentioned his commercial building, which contained partially finished apartments. Then he told me he was very unhappy and thought he needed some "space."

"Space?" I repeated. "This house is huge, we sleep separately, and you're rarely here. How much space do you need?" My voice was a bit higher than the tranquil Buddhist I was trying to become might use.

"I feel like I need my own space," he said, then looking away from me, he continued, "away from everyone to... sort some things out."

"By 'everyone' you mean *me*, right?" Now I was sniffling and wiping tears from my eyes. I lowered my aspiration to "adult Buddhist," but I think I missed that mark, too.

"There you go again, making this about you. It's not about you. It's about me. I need some time alone to figure some things out and that building is vacant. I can make it work. I need to make it work." He was pacing and looking for some kitchen surface to scrub.

"I'm sorry," I said. "I just don't understand. Plus it's not ready. It'll take months to be habitable." Knowing there was a mold issue in part of the building, I was concerned about his allergies.

But he said he'd been there and could have it ready quicker than I thought. I was living in the world where I thought my husband was merely going through a Discontented Phase, and I was working hard to Create a Contented Life With Me. And all this time, he was actively plotting a Contented Life Alone.

We talked through the weekend about "us," what used to be "us," and what could be but probably would never be "us" *because of me.* We went to his building and he enthusiastically showed me around his "new place." I walked through it in silent disbelief. I'm sure I looked like the people who tour the devastation that had been their home before the tornado or hurricane blew it to smithereens. Victor admitted that it might be months before he would move in…*if* he would move in. I didn't know it then, but he was trying to soften an inevitable blow, an upper cut to my jaw that would have me on the mat wondering why I was seeing stars inside my head. *Is there a nice way to punch someone's lights out?* If there is, I'm sure Victor was trying to find it.

Victor recoiled when I, again, asked for counseling and for him to accept the "new and improved" me. It seemed that whenever he heard my voice, he was overdubbing it with his *Lorna is criticizing me again, blah, blah, blah* tape.

On Monday, he suggested we call Alex.

"We should let him know we're having marital difficulties," my husband said.

Good idea. "I don't want to worry him, though. Do you?" I flashed back to our brain tumor talk and my concern about creating a family panic.

"No. We'll emphasize that we're trying to work things out."

Is that what he calls what he's doing? "Okay." Same flashback. Same lie to protect Alex. Same panic inside me. At least some things hadn't changed.

We sat with the speaker phone between us and Victor began.

"Hi, Lex. This is a tough conversation to have, but your mother and I are having some problems, so I've decided to move out this Saturday."

What?? Moving out this Saturday? He never said anything about Saturday!

All I remember of the rest of that conversation was that Alex was very understanding and sympathetic to both of us. He said he hoped that whatever happened, we would find happiness. He was always so mature and centered—except when he wasn't. But I didn't know about those times until a few years later.

I never spoke during that entire, critical discussion with our son. I didn't say a word. Again, I was the Dumb Blonde—the dumbfounded wife. Victor had ambushed me. He had been telling me a fairy tale that included words like "maybe," "in a while," "if I feel I need some space." And then he told me the truth in front of Alex. He had surprised his wife who he knew hated surprises.

After he hung up the phone, he said, "Well, I'm glad that's over. That was a tough one."

I just stared at him.

"What?" he said.

"You're moving out *this Saturday*? And you couldn't have told me *before* you told our son? I thought this was a *maybe-in-a-few-months* thing." I don't think I gave him a chance to respond, though, or if I did, I didn't hear it because I was in the middle of what most people would call "a conniption fit."

I kicked an empty laundry basket across the room, something he would later bring up as an example of my irrational behavior and one reason he no longer could live with me. It *was* irrational to kick an innocent laundry basket when I really wanted to kick his calm ass out of his precious recliner.

He told me to calm down. "You must've seen this coming," he said. "I haven't been happy for months, maybe years. I need time to figure some things out—to find out who I really am."

"'Figure some things out'? 'Find out who you really are'?" I was pacing and using air quotes—the Buddha wouldn't be pleased. "I don't know what that means," I said.

"Neither do I. I just know that when I'm around you lately, I feel like I'm doing everything wrong."

I might have said, *Well, join the club.* Maybe I just thought it really loudly. What I did was storm out of the living room and up to our bedroom, which was really my bedroom.

After an inordinate amount of heavy breathing on my part—which was the sexiest sounding thing to come out of that bedroom in ten years—I calmed down enough to go back downstairs to receive a civil lecture from him. He convinced me that his plan of moving out sooner rather than later was best for both of us in terms of our physical and emotional health. He used the following arguments:

1. He felt like an awful person around me. I made him feel that way.

2. He needed to get away from me to remember what it was like to be him.

3. He didn't feel marriage counseling would help.

I had nothing left inside me to counter any of his arguments. How could I argue with his feelings? I was surprised that he didn't pack up and get the hell away from me right now before I infected him with some flesh-eating disease.

Then he asked me, "Do you want to go out to dinner on Friday night, you know, before I officially leave?"

If our marriage had ever been a partnership, then I suppose that was the equivalent of the boss taking the employee he'd just fired out for a nice lunch—just to make sure the employee knew that being terminated was *nothing personal*. The employee—me—just hadn't performed up to his standards. The business was moving in a direction that didn't require my skill set of making the boss feel like a loser. *Was he going to give me a letter of reference, too?*

Since I didn't believe Victor would really leave and I was still stunned into Dumb Blondness, I hesitated in responding to the dinner invitation. As I write this, I have permanent amnesia about that week. The days passed. I wrote in a "gratitude journal" to help me focus on being positive, but entries for that week aren't helpful in reconstructing what happened. Here are some examples:

1. I walked Scrappy very early. The stars were bright, but no moon lit our way. My senses were keener even as I felt invisible, melting into the darkness, into a shadow. I'm a shadow and I feel safe. Quiet. Thank you for this quiet moment before I face the daylight chaos (10/19/09).

2. The gentle rainfall welcomed Scrappy and me on our pre-dawn walk. I'm grateful for my sense of hearing and for my awareness of the magical songs of nature (10/22/09).

3. If pain and disbelief fill me, then I am grateful for these unlikely friends. They keep me awake. My wish is that everyone who feels this kind of loss will find a way to feel whole, find comfort, feel loved (10/24/09, the evening Victor left).

Were we kind toward each other? Did I try to convince him to stay or ask him "why?" a million times? Was he away preparing his apartment?

I don't know what happened between Victor and me, but I know that I make a better poet than reporter.

I declined his dinner invitation. Crying nonstop has a way of ruining your appearance, no matter what they say about waterproof mascara. I told him no thanks when he came home from work on Friday. At least I think that's what I told him.

Victor was furious of course. By declining his invitation, he felt, I was rejecting him. But wait. Wasn't *he* leaving *me*? *Tomorrow!* I was living in a world where down was up and this was that. The only constant was that I was Mrs. Wrong and he felt like he was Mr. Couldn't-Do-Anything-Right. He marched up the stairs and packed his bags while I stood in the kitchen, hyperventilating. My husband was actually leaving me alone in the Broken House.

I remember what happened next as clearly as a recurring nightmare.

While we were in Hawaii for our Honeymoon-That-Wasn't early in 2008, we each purchased a gold band with an inlaid black opal to remind us of the Pacific Ocean and as a symbol of our renewed wedding vows. He had lost his ring during the summer of the same year, or so he said. I was still wearing mine. Now, while he was banging around upstairs, I took mine off and found a small box to put it in. When he came into the kitchen, all I could see in his face were anger and disappointment—double barrels aimed at my tender spots.

Assume that all portions of my part of the following dialogue are punctuated by tears, sniffling, and general discombobulation.

"So I guess that's that," he said.

"You're not really walking out of that door, are you?"

"Yes."

"If you're willing to stay here and work this out with me, I'll do anything to save our relationship. But if you walk out on me, Victor, it's a game-changer. I'm going to have to do my own thinking about what I want and who I am."

"Fine." He was firm and sure. He didn't realize that he had finally made a serious miscalculation of his own. He didn't believe me.

"If you're dead-set on leaving me," I said, "then I want to give you something. Buddhists say that when you give something away, it should be something you deeply care about. It makes the giving more meaningful to both parties. So I'm giving you this." I handed him the little box with my Hawaiian gold band in it.

He opened the box and looked at me with softer eyes.

"Every time you look at this," I said, "let the gold remind you of my hair and the blue remind you of my eyes." My actual speech was a bit choppier as I said it through sobs, but I meant it to be as tragically poetic (or poetically tragic) as it sounded.

He started to cry. I thought that maybe I had finally gotten through to him; that he saw *me*, not some pathetic invalid who made him feel awful.

Then he hugged me, tucked the box in his pants pocket, and walked out on me.

I felt like the most leaveable girl in the world. My dad had left me. All my boyfriends (except Dick, the blind-date, canoe-proposing maniac) had left me. My beloved pets had left me. My health had abandoned me. My son had distanced himself from me. Now my husband had just walked out on me. Someone could write a top-of-the-charts country-western song and call it "Leavable Lorna, she never met a soul she couldn't shoo-shoo-shoo away."

*****

What registered in my boggled mind about Victor's exit? Sounds. He closed the door harder than normal—somewhere between a *thunk* and a *wham*. I heard his footfalls stomp across our deck then crunch down the stone and dirt driveway to his car. Then car doors slammed. His engine revved as if he was getting ready for a drag race. The last sound I heard was his tires spitting up gravel from our driveway as he, indeed, raced away.

The now silent and empty Broken House closed in on me. The sounds of the door closing and his car driving away were still playing over in my mind. Every time I envisioned myself as an abandoned wife, I panicked. I felt like the contents of Alex's bucket of Lego parts still in his bedroom: once recognizable, intricate structures now reduced to countless disconnected pieces, buildings never again to be built.

I needed something else to focus on, so I worried about Victor. Where was he going to spend the night? The lake camp was closed and his new "apartment" was still in a shambles. I tried calling him, but he never picked up. I wondered what he thought of my twenty-seven voicemails.

Sometime that evening, I called Victor's parents to tell them he had just left me and I was worried about him. They said they would call him. Then I called my sister,

Tina. All she heard were my heavy gasping breaths and stuttering. I'm surprised she didn't hang up before I was finally able to tell her that Victor had left me. I never knew Tina to be a good actress or to censor herself, but she played the part of the consoling sister to perfection. She told me later she did a "happy dance" to celebrate my liberation after she hung up the phone. Her little sister was finally free from the man who made her blood boil (and not in a fun way).

Tina drove Mom to the Broken House and the Broken Lorna, and they listened together as I told them my story. Mom was genuinely concerned, but she didn't know what to say, except that she wished she could take away my pain; Tina deserved an Academy Award for holding her tongue and just repeating, "You'll be fine, Lorna. Things will get better, trust me."

Thus began the *official* phase of our *unofficial* separation, which had been going on long before I knew it. At least Victor had had the courage to make it official.

He left me. What did that mean in the cosmic sense? In the common sense? We never discussed the details of being apart: money, mortgage, or mail. How would I ask him about the details? How long should a dumped wife wait before she called her estranged husband? I didn't know anything about "separation etiquette."

*****

In the days and weeks that followed, like Greta Garbo, I wanted to be alone. I needed to sort out my feelings. Well, first, I needed to identify them. My family and the two close friends I told didn't understand my refusals for company or when I repeatedly declined invitations to their homes.

Besides being dizzy, nauseous, and sleep-deprived, intense emotions kept surfacing at random times. I just didn't want anyone to witness what seemed like multiple personality disorder. Here is a list of the most acute emotions that overtook me, the ones I needed to corral, tame, or release into the wild:

1. Abandonment. When I told the story of my marriage falling apart, the phrase, "he left me," was critical. I needed people to know that I was the one who tried to make it work and that he deserted me. I understood that he had left me for what in his mind and heart were valid reasons. I wasn't perfect. Although I tried to be objective and put myself in his place, I could see the situation from the only vantage point I had. Mine. But I couldn't believe that I was completely at fault, so I assumed he that he gave up on "us" for reasons he wasn't willing to tell me.

2. Humiliation. I was embarrassed to be a cliché— a woman in her early fifties whose husband had left her to go "find himself" (translation: midlife crisis; evidence: convertible). I was also ashamed that, after all my efforts at loving kindness and support, I had failed so miserably. How could I have gotten everything so wrong?

3. Confusion. Victor never gave me a straight answer about what made him so unhappy. I had always tried to please him and everything always backfired. Why? If it was me, then what was it about me? If it was him, then what was it about him? Why couldn't I get any answers? His idea of our relationship moving forward also confused me. He wanted us to live apart

forever and get together every once in a while for dinner, just as friends. He would live "the bachelor life" in an apartment or at the lake and I would live "the abandoned wife life" in the Broken House waiting for his call.

4. Fear. Although all my reading and self-development work in Buddhism trained me to rid myself of fear, I had to face the stark reality of being financially responsible for my future. I was permanently disabled, and the chances of me working again were about the same as the chances of Victor realizing that I was the perfect woman.

All my self-reflection led in a direction I didn't anticipate. I suppose I should have expected that the surprises in my life weren't over—my life has been one curve ball after another.

*****

I ignored one of the biggest *aha!* moments I had when I was exploring Buddhist teachings. Try to avoid asking "why." That is one question that only wastes precious energy because:

1. Asking why something happened to you doesn't change the fact that it happened. A more skillful use of one's energy is to focus on how best to deal with what happened. It's the difference between living in the past and living in the moment.

2. "Why" is an impossible question to answer. There are so many variables that coalesce to form any event. How do I know with any

assurance the truth about why something happened, especially when the truth is such a slippery thing?

While my head was full of Buddhist wisdom, my heart was a slow learner. The end of my marriage devastated me. I kept hearing myself asking, *Why does this hurt so much?* I wasn't madly in love with Victor. We had some wonderful times together and had a Miracle Child, but we also had some very trying times, as when his words and actions left me feeling like a flawed little girl who needed constant fixing.

But there I was, months after he left, wailing into my mom's shoulder, asking, "What is wrong with me? Why am I so unlovable?"

"*I* love you, Lorna," she said. She was crying, too. My mom rarely cried.

Then it hit me. Like an intricate domino spiral that goes into a backward-falling motion as one tile topples onto the next, my mom's word's "*I* love you, Lorna," brought me swirling back into my past and the key that unlocked the biggest "why" of all: why had I lost myself by living a life of pleasing others at the expense of pleasing me?

Enter my phantom father....

CHAPTER 24: SECRETS ARE LIKE PUPPIES (THEY'RE DIFFICULT TO CONFINE)

When all you have of your father are photographs and papers with his name on them, he is a two-dimensional character in a three-dimensional world. No wonder I was so confused about him.

My parents' marriage endured a little more than six years. I obtained information about my father by asking questions (mostly asking my mom when I was old enough to be seen *and* heard) or by uncovering things I wasn't supposed to see. My father was all of the following things to me at different points in my life: stranger, hero, angel, devil, victim, and flawed human being.

But he was never a father.

The people who knew him—if anyone ever really knew him—and knew about what happened to him didn't want to talk about him "in polite company." I guess "polite company" included children, specifically, my sisters and me. Was it because the people who knew were trying to protect us? Was it because they were trying to protect themselves from reliving their own pain or shame? Was it easier to erase him than to acknowledge him?

Does it even matter?

My father wasn't the only secret in our family, but he was the best-kept one. He was such a well-kept secret, in fact, that I wasn't fully aware that I had once had a father until I was almost ten years old. Before then, I believed that fathers didn't really exist except on television. The TV fathers were, of course, handsome, wise, and kind, even when doling out much-needed punishment to their children for their childish shenanigans. I didn't have a father, though, and I didn't feel I needed one because I was the last little girl you'd find involved in any kind of shenanigan.

Growing up with a mystery father affected me more than I could ever have imagined. I can't say whether the secrets my family kept from me served me or not when I was young. What I can say is that, once the secrets were revealed, the truth about my father explained a lot about me. Which helped explain why I felt so lost.

*****

I have so few memories of my father that I can claim as my own that I can count them on the fingers of one hand.

1. I remember crawling into the bathroom while he was sitting on "the john." He told me to go away.

2. I remember sitting on his big lap and we were playing the game "hot and cold" with a piece of plastic fence from a farm set. We were both laughing. His laugh came deep from his belly and went all the way up to his crinkled eyes.

3. I remember sitting beside him in his pick-up truck. Tina was sitting on his lap and he was letting her drive, or at least hold her hands on the steering wheel. I was awestruck that my five-year-old sister was driving that big truck up our twisting driveway. He told us not to tell Mommy, which made me wonder if Tina's driving or Daddy trusting us not to tell was the best part of that truck ride.

4. Finally, I remember once when he was very angry about something. I knew he was angry because he was yelling and I could feel the fury in the air. It felt hot and shaky. I thought I heard him say that he was going to shoot a rabbit. Then my mom started crying and yelling at him to stop. I didn't understand why she got so upset over a rabbit. When he slammed the door to the trailer, I think some glass broke.

Daddy died when I was four. I call him "Daddy" because that's who he is when I remember him.
What did he leave behind?

1. Three little girls. Lisa (who had just turned two), me (age four), and Tina (who was just about to turn six and was sick with some kind of trouble that made her pale, thin, and important).

2. My twenty-nine-year-old mother, who became the official head of the household, when all she ever wanted to be was the best wife and mother known to mankind.

3. A small life insurance policy, unpaid bills, not much cash, and the trailer we were living in. Mom sold the trailer and used the money she had to bury him and buy a brand new Ford Fairlane 500. It was black with a gray vinyl interior. Mom called it "Nellie."

4. His family, which didn't support my mom or us girls, either financially or emotionally. Since my grandpa was a dentist and lived in a real house, I figured he was rich and would help us. But I don't think he believed in charity. Maybe he wanted to build our character, as if losing Daddy wasn't enough to teach us how be characters.

Being the commander of our all-female troop, my mom made an executive decision not to tell us anything about Daddy's death except that he was in Heaven. That seemed like a fine place for him to be, so I didn't worry much about him or how he got there. I was four years old, remember, and more concerned about snack time than the details about how people got from Here to There. When I recited "Our Father Who art in Heaven...," I thought I was talking to my daddy, and figured I could ask him for stuff like a pony or my very own angel that I could see.

Daddy's departure to Heaven wasn't very well-timed. Tina's trouble kept getting worse, making her thinner, paler, and even more important. I finally figured out that she had some kind of disease, but Mom never wanted to discuss it with me, and Tina sure wasn't talking. Lisa was going to remain a terrible two-year-old for at least another year—maybe more. Plus, Lisa had what's now called "an artist's temperament" but was known then as a bad case of individuality. She was quirky and prone to bronchitis. So Mom had her hands full.

My little-girl heart sensed that Mom needed a child she didn't have to worry about, so I decided to be her full-time A+ Good Girl—obedient, smart, funny, and never, ever a trouble-maker. Lucky for Mom and me, I had the personality to pull it off. I became the family peace-maker. My sisters fought a lot, but only when they were healthy and feeling feisty. They looked different on the outside, but they were the same type of sister on the inside: conspicuous, irrefutable (especially during board or card games), and unwilling to concede anything to each other. As Mom's objective reporter, I stayed out of the line of fire, which made me real popular with my sisters. I felt bad when they got punished, so I would cry for them, and that frustrated everyone. Empathy was woefully underappreciated in my family.

As time went on, details of Daddy's death leaked out.

When President Kennedy's funeral was televised in November, 1963, I remember Mom watching and crying. We never watched TV during the daytime, and Mom never cried, which made President Kennedy's funeral quite memorable. Plus, we got to stay home from school. Triple memorable. But I was confused because Mom was crying, and I thought the TV was showing Daddy's funeral. *But why would all those people on TV know about my daddy?* "Mommy," I asked, "are all those people crying because Daddy's in Heaven?"

"No, Dear," she said. "That is President Kennedy. He was an important man and he is in Heaven now, too." She dabbed her tears as she looked at the TV, not me.

"How did he get to Heaven, Mommy?"

363

"Oh, Lorna. You should not ask those questions."

"I'm sorry, Mommy. I just wondered if he got there like Daddy did."

Now she turned away from the TV and stared at me, almost as if she had never really seen me before. "No, Dear," she said after a minute. "Your father died in an accident. Yes. It was an accident."

"Oh," I said. I was trying to be calm, but my six-year-old mind was churning. *An accident? Did he trip? I bump into things all the time. Am I going to end up in Heaven real soon, too?* "What kind of accident, Mommy?"

"Lorna, please stop asking so many questions. Can you not see that I am busy?"

I could always tell when Mom had had enough of my curiosity because she would tell me to shut up, but in a polite way.

But when it came to questions involving my own impending doom, patience was not my virtue. If Daddy had been accident-prone and ended up in Heaven, I wanted to know what I needed to do to stay on earth. I wasn't going to get any more details from Mom, however, at least not while she was crying about this other man who had somehow ended up in Heaven, so I just tried to be extra-cautious. Then I forgot about it. Lunch or dinner probably distracted me.

My feelings about fathers changed. I finally decided I had actually had one once. That was new. Now I needed to sort out how I felt about him. Since he had died in an accident, I felt sorry for him. He would be with us if he could, but—*oops!* something happened, and he now had to dutifully watch his family from Heaven. He and God, I decided, were buddies. I felt safe, even though I didn't know much about either guardian. On the rare occasion when I got into shenanigans, I was sure one or both of my powerful-but-mysterious protectors would swoop down and save me, just like *Mighty Mouse*, my all-time favorite hero. I just hoped Daddy had learned to avoid accidents in Heaven.

When I was about seven, I asked again about what kind of accident took Daddy to Heaven. We weren't allowed to watch much TV back in the early-1960s, but *Lassie, Bonanza,* and *Dr. Kildare* gave me all kinds of ideas about how a person could accidentally get to Heaven. I wanted to know if Daddy had lost a fight with a bear, fallen down a well, gotten in a tussle with some whooped up ranchers, or had something wrong with his internal organs that caused great concern, lots of tests, and furtive looks between nurses and doctors. So I asked.

"Your father died in an automobile accident, Lorna."

Mom said this in a way that signaled the end, not the beginning, of a discussion. She used that same look and tone when she told us to get dressed for school. At least it was more information than I'd had before, but it still didn't allay my fears. My family rode around in automobiles. How dangerous were they? Did they just decide to explode sometimes, like on *The Man from U.N.C.L.E.?* Is that what had happened? My imagination ran amok until, again, I forgot about it. Being seven years old had its advantages in these circumstances—you're easily distracted by the sound of the Good Humor Man's bell as his truck turns the corner onto your block.

*****

I was ten years old when at last I got the full story. I suppose Mom felt that that her girls were old enough to handle the truth. Daddy had killed himself. He had shot himself between the eyes with a rifle and been found in his pickup truck on a road between Somewhere and Nowhere on March 18, 1962. He'd been drinking. Since he was in an automobile, I gave Mom credit for not quite technically lying about the whole story.

That news was a game-changer for me. My drunken father had killed himself the day after St. Patrick's Day. I demoted him from superhero to a weak, selfish drunk who ditched his family. I was glad he was dead and dropped my God-as Daddy's-Buddy theory. He had never been watching over me or protecting me. *He had abandoned me.* Before, I had occasionally thought about him; now I made it a point to hate him every day. But I tried not to show it. Mom still needed me to be her Dependably Good Girl— and Good Girls didn't go around harboring ill will toward people, especially their dead fathers.

I knew I was hiding my true feelings from Mom, but she had hidden some true facts from me. She always insisted on honesty from me, but she wasn't honest about a pretty important detail in our family history. Even as young as I was, I understood her reasons—suicide isn't something people brag about. One thing I learned was that lying or withholding the truth to protect those you love was apparently okay. That's what people must do sometimes. That revelation changed my life.

Were there more truths that Mom was still hiding? I was too young to develop a suspicious nature, so I capitalized on my curious nature and just became more observant. If there was something to find, I'd find it.

And I did—or at least a little more of the truth came out.

Whether it was thanks to being able to count my years in double digits or the hormones that come along with that privilege, I was able to muster the courage and confidence to ask Mom more questions about her not-so-dearly departed husband. I could tell she wasn't comfortable answering my questions, but she answered them. She even offered information that I didn't know to ask about. I was making real progress in learning about the side of my family I never considered my family. I learned six secrets:

1. Grandpa was an alcoholic. I thought he was just a jolly dentist and an important man in his community. A lot of people thought that. Daddy had drunk a lot, too, so he was probably an alcoholic. Once my secret about alcoholism came out, Mom listed about a dozen of Daddy's relatives who were heavy drinkers. It's a miracle any of them made it to church on Sunday morning since they were all such devout Methodists.

2. Daddy was abused physically and emotionally by his father, my grandpa. For reasons unknown to my mom, but that would be made clearer well after Daddy's death, he was the whipping-boy for his father's drunken rages. Daddy was labeled the Black Sheep of the family and often considered more of a chore hand than any of the other nine children in his family. He had a twin sister. She got birthday parties, complete with her name on the cake and presents. But there was no cake or presents for the little boy that grew up to be my Daddy. When the family went on a day-trip or the rare vacation, he would have to stay home to tend to the house. Mom told me, "He always craved love, but he never knew how to give love because he never received it when he was growing up."

3. Neither Grandma nor any of Daddy's siblings ever intervened in the beatings. No one ever stood up for him. He was alone in that large family with a drunken tyrant at the helm. Grandma, being so in love with the Lord, probably hid somewhere

praying while her son was being brutalized. My aunts and uncles probably were also hiding, fearing they might be their father's next victims.

4. Daddy didn't finish high school. He joined the army, but he was dishonorably discharged less than three years into his tour of service. He didn't tell why and apparently no one ever asked.

5. Daddy was unpredictable. He couldn't hold a steady job. While they were married, he would disappear for days and Mom never knew where he was. Sometimes he would bring a paycheck home; sometimes he would say he'd spent the money helping a friend or buying rounds of drinks at a bar. (I bet he was quite popular at bars.)

6. Mom married him because she felt sorry for him, not because she loved him. He told her those stories about his childhood, and she wanted to create a loving family for him. She did her best. It just didn't turn out so well.

I didn't like what I was hearing about my father, but what I was learning was transformative. My resentment and hostility for him melted away. Now I felt sorry for him, and I turned my bitterness toward his family. In my eyes, he was a victim of abuse and neglect at the hands of his parents while his siblings just let it happen.

I also learned something about myself. I'd been wrong about him. *What else was I wrong about?*

*****

After I got over my little-girl dream of becoming a nurse to "help people" (having realized I was scared to death of needles and old people's toenails), I wanted desperately to be an actress. I loved the idea of adopting a dramatic *femme fragile* persona and acting out death scenes that would leave my audience openly weeping—even the women. *Love Story* was my inspiration. I *was* Ali McGraw in that death-bed scene.

My acting talent was something I probably inherited along with migraines from Mom's side of the family (plus alcoholism from Daddy's side). Acting seemed to be woven into my genes. When it came to keeping secrets, spies and teens who've done pinky-swears would crack under the CIA's "enhanced interrogation techniques" well before any of the adults in my family would. My secret was that I could act. On the surface, I was sweet, demure, and charmingly witty, whereas inside, I was lost and afraid of being abandoned or of being overlooked, so I made it my goal to be whoever anyone wanted me to be. I was, in essence, a reflection, shiny and waiting for someone to animate me.

Even though he was absent for almost all of my life, my father, or his absence, profoundly affected me. I just didn't know it. Yet. Finding out about his suicide and his troubled childhood was just the beginning. I was still a girl hearing stories about a ghost—a man who existed only in my imagination. Pictures of him were so few that they could have been of some stranger my mom once knew.

Then on an otherwise ordinary summer day when I was fifteen years old, everything changed. My ghost father became *real*, and his reality let loose an internal maelstrom of emotional debris that had accumulated because he'd vanished. My teenage hormones probably didn't help my tumultuous mood.

Until the summer of 1972, thoughts of my father's suicide, his cruel father, his cowardly family, and my glaring imperfection at being so wrong about him would randomly surface, but I just stuffed all this down as best I could. Feeling like a fatalistic semi-orphan, I believed my life had been ruined by adults who had never considered the consequences of their actions to the unborn or barely born. I wasn't quite sure how they'd ruined my life, but I felt quite sure that family scandal rarely skipped a generation. I felt destined to suffer the shame. I was sure something awful would descend on me, like becoming cross-eyed, getting hemorrhoids, or developing an alarmingly poor fashion sense. I just couldn't manage managing *it*; so *it* continued to accumulate.

On an unremarkable weekend day, *it* surfaced. I never saw *it* coming. If I had, I would have ducked.

Mom was doing her annual rearranging of our junk in Mémé and Pépé's attic. Our trailer barely had room for Mom and the three of us girls, so our non-essential items were stored in their attic, which made sense because we stored the trailer right next to their house.

As usual, Mom somehow managed to be in two places at once. She was in the attic with my sisters, telling them which boxes to carry down to the trailer, and at the same time she was in the trailer with me, supervising which piles to place things in: Throw Away Later or Throw Away Never. Mom and her mother had lived through the Nazi occupation of Paris, so this exercise in rearranging our various artifacts provided "proof of life." Neither of them could ever throw *anything* away.

I wasn't thrilled to spend a Saturday sorting, but keeping adults happy—as opposed to making them angry— always seemed like a wise choice to me. My low expectations for the day couldn't have been more wrong.

Tucked in a stationary box I mindlessly opened were relics of my father's death: his obituary in a yellowed newspaper clipping, condolence cards and notes, the prayer card from his funeral, and two little dog-eared pieces of paper that brought him right back to life. These were invoice sheets with his name and "Plumbing and Heating Contractor" as the header. Both had sloppy notes written in long-hand in the area where he would have detailed the billing for labor and parts. In pencil. With misspellings.

The first one I read was his suicide note. It was not dated.

> *My Darling [Mom's first name], I love you*
> *and the children, that is why I want you to*
> *have someone else who can make you*
> *happy. I love you all with all my heart. Good*
> *bye. Bob.*

(When I started writing this book, my mother requested that her name and our last name not be revealed because she is still, after fifty years, embarrassed that her husband killed himself. "After I'm dead," she told me, "then you can use my name. Then I won't care.")

The second note was more formal. It was dated April 15, 1962, about one month *after* he killed himself. On the line meant for the name of the customer, he wrote, *Last Will and Testament.* His final wishes were as follows (I give them verbatim):

> *I [his full legal name] being of sound body*
> *and mind leave all my earthly possessions to*
> *my Wife Mrs. [his full legal name].*

He signed it with his full legal name and dated it April 15, 1962. Did he get the date on the note wrong or the date of his own death wrong?

Neither his death nor his life had been real to me until that minute when I held his suicide note and his will— two documents I never knew existed—in my hands. That was as physically close as I would ever get to my father. He was both dead and alive *for real* at the same moment. I was holding the proof.

These papers had my daddy's handwriting on them. I had never seen his handwriting. For the first time in my life I faced mourning for a real person. My father. Who shot himself in the head with a rifle. Who had sloppy handwriting and poor English skills.

Those two notes threw a wet blanket on my red-hot certainty about my father's character flaws, and the resulting smoke obscured my vision of what it now meant to be the daughter of that dead man. He had never been my superhero, my enemy, or even someone needing my pity. He had been a troubled man who did what he thought was best under tragic circumstances. He was human. He was my father. He was my daddy.

I had never grieved before, not even for a pet, so this was a big grief project for a beginner. Not only was I now suddenly grieving over the long-ago death of my father, but I was grieving over the demise of myself as a smart girl who never got things wrong. I, apparently, was human, too.

I wondered, *How long will this grief-thing take?* It was summer. I didn't have the distraction of homework or tests, so I dedicated myself to being completely miserable. It was a time of writing heart-wrenching poems, engaging in melodramatic bouts of silent tears, indulging in atrocious moodiness. The misery lasted about a month. Well, except for the soppy poetry writing. That lasted for years.

Luckily, I found an upside to grief. Other people's misfortunes, as any soap opera or reality TV show junkie knows, are alluring. People are just dying to know the sordid details. My father's life and death gave me plenty of "chatter cash." I just had to learn how to spend it wisely.

As the middle child, I was an attention-junkie. My grief was good grief—it earned me attention. I gained sympathy from friends to whom I told my sorry tale, always swearing them to secrecy. Secrets being too hot to hold, my confidences spread to various adults, who started to admire me for being courageous as well as sweet and smart. Their lingering gazes, barely noticeable nods, and pitying smiles told it all. My grief also became a way to manage my hyper-sexed boyfriend's constant desire for sex. I became the grief-stricken girlfriend who needed compassionate cuddling, not persistent groping.

Although I still had innumerable questions that needed answers so I could deal with the death of my father and the demise of my perfect self, I had no one to help me answer them. Mom had a rule to never discuss self-identity, sex, or suicide. My sister Tina was impatient and testy on a good day, and Lisa was sympathetic but easily distracted. My boyfriend listened to me for a while, but then he suggested that sex was the best medicine for what ailed me. Mémé and Pépé were old and didn't believe in feelings. Even the family cat was aloof.

I decided that dead fathers created a lot of trouble for their kids.

*****

After I saw my father's suicide note and sketchy will, I talked with Mom about my feelings and, of course, asked her more questions. Gradually, I learned about four more secrets.

7. Mom was relieved when she learned that Daddy was dead. Now she didn't have to worry about where he was and what he was doing. I had always pictured her as sad and distraught at the news of his death. "No, not really," she told me. "Being married to him was very stressful." Mom was never one to sugarcoat things.

8. He could be violent. Mom told me he had never hit her or any of us, but there were times when he came close to it. My daddy got angry a lot and

ended up dead. Once. But that was enough to convince me that bad things happen around anger. I always thought I was a timid little peace-maker by nature or birth order. Now I realize that I'm holding on to a child's belief that bad things follow anger like "u" follows "q" in every truly English word. No exceptions. It's creepy but true. Although I'm well into adulthood, that little-girl fear of anger stains me like ink stains cotton. *Is it any wonder I aim to please and am quick to apologize just to smooth ruffled feathers?*

9. Daddy had another family in a town about fifty miles from where we lived. Mom remembered a veiled woman who stayed in the back of the church at Daddy's funeral. People remarked at how upset she was. She left just as the mass was ending. Mom didn't give it much thought, however. She knew her husband had vanished for days on end and thought he had to be doing *something*. In the mid-1990s, that woman's daughter phoned my mom in search of her "real" father. That means I have a half-sister. When I contacted her via mail and telephone, I tried to empathize with her and gave her as much information about our father as I knew, but she wanted more. She wanted a relationship with me and my sisters. Unlike the TV portrayals of joyful reunions between illegitimate siblings, I didn't want anything to do with her.

10. In early 2010, while my mom mentioned that she had never received veteran's benefits even though Daddy served in the U.S. Army, I took it upon myself to find out why. For my mom, Daddy's "Don't ask," about his discharge spoken fifty-seven years ago was enough for her. But after so

many other secrets, I wanted that mystery solved too. Mom guessed he had "carried on" with an officer's wife and gotten kicked out. My sisters and I thought he got drunk and beat up the wrong person. Either way, he was discharged dishonorably. His discharge papers revealed two codes: COFG AR—615—365 and AR—600—443. The first was general: "for the convenience of the government." The second was specific and surprising. It was under rules regarding the U.S. military's long-standing aversion to homosexuality among the rank and file. Even back in the early 1950s, the military had a "Don't Ask, Don't Tell" policy. I thought it was President Clinton who came up with that policy, but after triple checking the code, I had to face the fact that my strong, six-foot-four-inch-tall father, who Mom said "loved the ladies," was *gay*. I must have gotten my acting talents from him. Or maybe he was just experimenting one time with a man who was gay and got caught. Back then, one time was all it took to either face an inquiry or sign papers admitting to your guilt and accept a dishonorable discharge. Then he came home and married the first woman who agreed to be his wife. The rest is twisted history.

Maybe this wasn't a secret, but I came to realize that "respectable" people don't "do" suicide. They don't speak about it or support the family members left to pick up the pieces. At gatherings of my father's family, I always felt like a stranger. I wasn't connected to anyone there because no one ever spoke his name. They erased him so effectively that, for a while, I thought they were just inviting us as their Christian act of charity for the day. It was the *Adopt a Blonde Girl for the Day and Save Your Soul* Program.

As I reflect on my maniacal need to please others at the expense of myself, my conflict-aversion behaviors, my boy-craziness, and the alcoholism that arose from these roots, I see more clearly the trajectory of my life story. I was a lost, scared soul, looking for someone to define me. Once someone gave me a role to play, I had the aptitude to play it to the hilt—sometimes because of, sometimes in spite of alcohol. Award-winning Actress Lorna needed a director. I was constantly searching for the perfect director (usually a man), figuring that being someone else's reflection would make me shine.

And here's the Biggest Secret of All: Although I didn't know it yet, I didn't need anyone to make me shine. I was just afraid to step away from the camera and be my own director.

What I didn't learn until relatively recently was that *I could shine on my own.* So many secrets had been kept from me by the person I trusted the most: my mother. With all this not-knowing, is it any wonder that I was so unsure about myself?

And I didn't know that there were still things that I didn't know.

*****

My father's death wasn't the only mystery in my childhood. It was a big one, but not the only one. My older sister Tina had something wrong with her—and not just normal big-sister, bossy-pants issues. There was something that was making her both grumpy and pale.

After our father died, our mother moved us to Glenbrook, Connecticut—eight hours away from her parents, her only real support system. We moved to an

Italian neighborhood, which seemed quite sophisticated compared to the hillbilly neighborhood we'd just left. Being blonde made me as much of a novelty in my surroundings as having all my teeth did in my former one.

Daddy's twin sister and her family lived in Glenbrook and (in a moment of temporary compassion) had offered to help us. Mom was ashamed of being a widow by suicide and wanted to live where no one knew the circumstances of her widowhood. Being a single mother in the early 1960s raised enough eyebrows. If she was going to be judged, at least it would be mostly by strangers, including her in-laws.

But another factor influenced her decision. Tina was ill with a mysterious disease involving her tummy. She was growing thinner by the day, not wanting to eat and suffering when she did eat. I just couldn't imagine a fate worse than food being an enemy and making someone suffer like my sister did. Mom told me that when Daddy was alive, they had taken Tina to both the local hospital and one in Canada, where the doctors spoke a different language and maybe knew a different cure. The doctors weren't sure, I learned, but they thought either Tina was a little kid with a grown-up ulcer or she was faking it. It's hard to fake skin that is the color of Elmer's glue, so everyone believed she had a bona fide serious case of something—just like the poor people on *Dr. Kildaire*.

Mom never discussed the move with us girls. Children didn't have opinions back then, at least none that mattered to adults. What mattered to Mom was that she had me, her good and healthy girl to rely on when she was busy taking Tina to doctors and, eventually to hospitals. I wasn't told why she was taking Tina to these places or what would happen to my sister if she didn't go to these places. My job was to trust that everything would be okay as long as I did what Mom asked me to do. So that's what I did.

Mom left Lisa and me alone a lot, or so it seemed. I guess I don't remember all the times Mom was home with us, however, because those times weren't traumatic, thus not memorable. My aunt's offer to help us petered out not long after we arrived. Besides, her Italian husband seemed a bit too interested in his beautiful and recently widowed sister-in-law. My aunt was jealous. She told my mom that *we girls* were a bad influence on *her boys*, as if Lisa and I were young vixens tempting her "innocent" older Italian wise guys into unthinkable acts of tomfoolery. So Mom had to trust her two young daughters to stay alone and stay out of trouble while she was away on a medical mystery with her oldest daughter. I was only seven years old, and though I tried to be good and responsible while on duty, common sense wasn't my forte. Knowing this, she made up some pretty strict rules for when she was away:

1. Be quiet.

2. Never use the phone unless it was the prearranged time when she would call to check on us.

3. Stay on the property—preferably inside.

4. Don't let anyone, even friends, inside the apartment.

5. Eat only the food Mom prepared for us.

6. If we were in desperate trouble, go to Signore e Signora Upstairs (the ancient Italian couple who lived in the upstairs part of the house they owned while renting the downstairs part to us). But we had to be desperate to go to them. Lonely didn't count. Open wounds did.

Lisa and I became inseparable. I was her idol, which went a long way toward satisfying my Middle Child need for attention. Everything I did, she did; everything I liked, she liked. It drove everyone but us nuts. We had lots of time to bond. Having been alone most of the day, we used to sit on the stoop outside our apartment in the early evening, just waiting to see Mom's car drive up the street.

"I bet the tenth car will be her," I would say to Lisa.

"Okay. But you count better. You do it." Lisa trusted me with her life and with counting.

It was never the tenth car. So then I would say, "I bet it's the fifth black car. You keep track of the colors."

"Sure! We're a great team, Lorn!"

When we got sick of that game, I would engage Lisa in some weighty philosophical discussion, like the pros and cons of the red-skinned hot dogs versus the brown-skinned ones.

All these mental gymnastics were distractions. I was trying not to think about the unthinkable, which I managed to think about anyway. *What if Mommy never comes home?* I only knew how to take Mom's prepackaged lunches out of the refrigerator and serve them. *Could I fend for Lisa and me on my own? Who would I call if I wasn't supposed to use the phone?* I didn't even know how to dial the phone.

By the time I'd worked myself into worrying that Lisa and I would have to hop a railroad car, hoping it would lead us to somewhere safe; Mom's car would invariably appear. *We won't be abandoned today. Whew.*

All was right with the world. Or so I thought...

Although it felt to me like we lived in Connecticut forever, we really only lived there for four years.

From my perspective, Tina had both a sour and a sweet deal. She seemed to be really sick and miserable a lot of the time—that was the sour part of the deal. But she got lots of attention and never got in trouble for being miserable—that was the sweet part of the deal. I didn't know what was making her sick and miserable, but whatever it was, it was big. She got special treatment all the time. When she was at the hospital, she had Mom's undivided attention and all the doctors and nurses at her disposal, too. I imagined her like the Queen of Sheba with servants all around her, tending to her every wish. When she was home, she had her own special food to eat at her own special times, whereas Lisa and I had to eat whatever Mom fixed for us and we weren't allowed to eat between meals. When Tina was grumpy, Mom told us to be nice to her because she wasn't feeling well. When we were grumpy, Mom told us to get over it. On the other hand, Tina couldn't play very often and missed a lot of fun times Lisa and I had. I think she covered up her jealousy of the closeness Lisa and I developed by making fun of us and pretending that our games were stupid. But I didn't figure that one out until just a few years ago.

I always wanted to know why she wasn't feeling well. "That does not concern you," Mom always said. But it did concern me. If I was going to compete for Mom's attention, I didn't stand a chance if I didn't know what I was up against. Plus all the fuss around my sister didn't look good for her. I watched *Dr. Kildare*. I could add two plus two and get "tragic outcome."

When I was nine, Mémé came for a "visit" just before Mom and Tina left for the hospital again. Because we had adult supervision, I figured that Mom wasn't coming back the same day. I asked Mémé if she knew what was happening. Apparently Mémé wasn't part of the *Cone of Silence*. She told me.

"Tina having operation," she said. "Anyway, she very sick in the stummy." (This was Mémé's word for stomach. Her English wasn't very good.)

An *operation*. "Wow," I said. "I didn't know she was that sick." I immediately felt guilty about the Queen of

380

Sheba imagery. I also felt bad about all the times I'd been jealous because Mom spent time with her in the hospital. Tina might have had nurses to take care of her every day, but she didn't have Mom every day; Lisa and I had Mom more often than she did. I was such a selfish little sister.

"*Oui*," said Mémé. "She could die. Anyway, we pray for her."

I'm sure Mémé thought she was being helpful, but I just felt worse with every morsel of broken English she dropped at my feet. My eyes got big and watery at the same time. I didn't have any direct experience with death at the time (not yet understanding about what really happened to my father), and now my grandmother had told me my older sister might die.

"It's not that bad, is it?"

"*Oui*. Very bad. Anyway...." Good old Mémé. She could tell the truth when she wanted to.

I went to Tina's bed and picked up her favorite stuffed animal, a big floppy black dog, and hugged that dog all day and even cried myself to sleep holding it. I may have drooled on it, too. I was a sloppy griever back then.

When we finally got word from Mom that Tina had survived the surgery on her stomach and that she would recover normally, I was enormously relieved. Our little family was little enough. I didn't want it to get any smaller. To show Tina how much I loved her, I asked Mémé to tell Mom to tell Tina about how I went to sleep crying with her floppy dog in my arms. I hoped nothing would get lost in the translation.

When Tina came home after several weeks, she greeted me with, "You cried all over my favorite stuffed animal? If you ruined it, I'll kill you!"

Yay! Tina was back! Maybe they'd forgotten to surgically remove some of her grumpiness, but my big sister was back to stay. That's all that mattered to me.

*****

And so, one by one, family secrets were revealed to me. What I learned helped me to make sense of my little world and of Little Me. I felt small, but not because of my physique (I took up plenty of space) or because of my talents (I knew I was smart and could charm any audience). My sense of triviality stemmed from the irony that I was integral to my family's dynamic, yet I was also clueless about the truth behind that dynamic. And today I wonder...if I hadn't been so persistently curious, when would I have uncovered these secrets? What other secrets were out there?

My life, I was sure, would be an adventure filled with secrets—mine and other people's—and the consequences of holding on to and letting go of those secrets.

CHAPTER 25: I WASN'T JUST TWIDDLING MY THUMBS

I went from living with a husband, son, two dogs, two cats and one cockatoo to just Scrappy and me. While it wasn't easy, we seemed to have weathered the attrition with no visible scars and quite shiny hair.

By the time I considered writing this memoir, I was beginning to understand how I had become such a cliché—a woman in her fifties whose husband of twenty-six years had walked out on her to "find himself." My life had been built on my belief that if only I were "good enough," bad things wouldn't happen to me. Bad things happened to me, though, so I must not have been good enough. I wasn't ready to abandon this fundamental belief and admit that I might need to find *myself*. I was still obsessed with finding the real Victor.

It occurred to me that Albert Einstein was a genius. He's known mostly for his witty quotes and sobering theories that few people understand. A lot of people could have saved a lot of money on psychotherapy if they'd just taken as gospel the definition of insanity that is usually attributed to Einstein: "doing the same thing over and over again and expecting different results."

When I say "a lot of people" here, I'm referring to one person. Me.

*****

Victor and I worked out a system of communication to manage our bills and other necessary couples-type issues like mail and being polite strangers versus hostile strangers. We became very cordial acquaintances who managed our daily affairs through phone calls and occasional meetings at the Broken House. I thought it was odd, but very courteous, that he asked permission to enter his own home. As long as our conversations stayed on a strictly business level, things between us were fine. But if I ventured into the Land of Feelings, I tripped an alarm that signaled either his hasty exit or a difficult conversation filled with my specific *help-me-understand* questions and his evasions and non-answers. I even wrote down his answers in an attempt to piece them together later, as if they were clues and I was Nancy Drew. I wanted to ask him, "If you're trying to find yourself, like, say, you'd find the keys you always misplace, why don't you tell me where you're looking so maybe I can help you?" But he might have interpreted that as sarcasm. Which, yes, it was.

I kept getting that familiar feeling that he was keeping some buried-down-deep secret from me, but no matter how persistent I was at digging for answers, he was keeping that one buried.

After about two weeks of living alone, I noticed some interesting developments:

1. I was calmer.

2. I was losing weight—a significant amount of weight—which was making me look officially "small-boned."

3. I was sleeping better.

4. I liked my independence, especially when it came to not watching the news and eating when and what I wanted. (This connection to my newfound calming thinness was not lost on me.)

5. I still didn't understand exactly why Victor had left, but I was also beginning to see how much pain he was in and coming to realize he deserved happiness, too. That "overly-sensitive," or empathetic, nature of mine came in handy when the compassion was directed at the people who were driven most crazy by it.

Never predictable, Victor suggested that we try marriage counseling. Since I'd been advocating marriage counseling for months, I felt obliged to go along, even though we were now, technically, in *post-marriage* counseling.

I'm bound by the sanctity of counselor-client confidentiality not to reveal the details of what transpired during the three months (mid-November, 2009, through mid-February, 2010) when we saw our previous marriage counselor, Ms. Let's Explore That. I feel safe revealing these completely biased recollections:

1. Victor and I were equally confused, but for different reasons. He wanted out of our marriage, but was conflicted about those blasted

wedding vows. His solution to that moral conundrum was that he still wanted me in his life, but only in a very limited way. As a friend? As someone to have dinner with every so often? For appearances? I wanted a straight answer from him about what "finding himself" meant so I could decide if I wanted what he found. The only straight answers I got from him involved faults he saw in me that made him feel flawed. I stopped asking for clarification because it was too confusing.

2. We loved each other in that I've-Grown-Accustomed-to-Your-Face—and-Secrets kind of way. But we weren't in love with each other. As it turned out, love didn't matter to Victor. Getting the hell away from me mattered.

3. The first round of post-marriage counseling didn't work as well for Victor as it did for me. I was much better at forgiving and letting go than he was. I had given him too big a pile of things to forgive, and during one particularly difficult session he reminded me of all them. By the end of it, I was convinced I was solely responsible for my father's suicide. I wasn't interested in answers about Victor's discontent any longer. He was clearly in pain, wanted a scapegoat, and I was bleating all over the floor. Albert was right about repetitive action and insanity.

Ms. Let's Explore That and Victor agreed the next step was a formal separation. They seemed so sure, who was I to argue? They suggested something called a "compassionate divorce," which is psychologist-speak for avoiding the high financial and emotional costs of the contentious, litigious legal system. It was like magic, only based on trust instead of smoke and mirrors. Well, perhaps a bit of both. All we had to do was negotiate the terms of "forever until divorce does us part" without lawyers to help us. At least that's what I did. Victor retained a lawyer. If you can't trust your husband who is divorcing you, I guess it wasn't much of a divorce to begin with.

Everyone who cared about me told me to hire the sharkiest lawyer I could find and take what was rightfully mine, which was half of everything we owned, including Victor's business and the six properties "we" or the business owned. Victor and Ms. Let's Explore That assured me that a local mediation service was fair, reasonable, and quick. That sounded good to me. It sounded *supercalifragilisticexpialidocious* to Victor.

To satisfy my supporters (who usually had nothing good to say about lawyers), I met with a lawyer. Tina went with me for moral support and to remind me of what transpired because I went into my typical "freeze" response in the face of danger. The lawyer explained to me that half of everything we owned, including Victor's business and all properties, was mine (I already knew that from Internet research). For a retainer of $1,500 and an estimated $5,000–$20,000 more (depending on how complicated things got), he would be happy to handle my negotiations.

Victor is a very complicated fellow, and so were his finances. I saw myself five years in the future still bickering with him while in a hospital bed and hooked up to feeding tubes and IV drips. Mediation it was. Like a magic show, I had to suspend my beliefs about a lot of things if I was going to make it through this show.

Victor wanted me to keep the Broken House. Like Alex, I'd grown attached to it during the twenty years I had lived there. But the house, it seemed, didn't want me. It was too big and too unfinished for me to care for by myself. Almost to the day Victor left, the furnace had decided to act like a cantankerous burro, working only when it felt like it. I called Furnace Repair Guy constantly. He probably thought I was attracted to the smell of fuel oil in a man's greasy hands and hair. I think he developed a crush on me. After ten years of celibacy, I was ready to petition the Vatican for a new Sacrament (let's call it Revirginization), and so I wasn't about to jeopardize my chances for a Papal decree with Over-Heated Furnace Repair Guy.

No. I needed to keep my life pure and simple. I also needed a fresh start in a home I could manage.

Being budget-challenged, I drew up my Excel spread-sheet and did my best to guess what my monthly expenses in a pretend home would be. All I wanted was the financial wherewithal to live on my own for the rest of my life. I left everything "we" owned jointly to him. I wanted money to get into a modest home, monthly support to pay a mortgage and his life insurance benefits I would collect when he met his Maker.

I then presented Victor with a settlement offer I had come up with on my own. The mediator thought it was the deal of the century for Victor. I was letting him have his business and all shared properties. But Victor just had to bargain me down on the monthly support amount; he was a business man, after all. We finally came to terms and were legally separated on Good Friday, April 2, 2010.

*****

Besides crying, feeling sorry for myself, and dressing only in pull-on flannel or fleece garments, I somehow knew I had a life that needed living. *What kind of life?* I had no idea. People can tolerate a miserable, sniveling, pitiful, helpless (does this cover it?) victim for only so long. I knew even my family would get sick of being around me if I didn't rise above this *husband-dumped-me* persona. Like previous challenges in my life, I had to overcome this one, too. Plus, I was on a budget. Puffs tissues with lotion were expensive.

What did I do during the six months from the day Victor left to the day we signed the separation agreement?

1. During the summer before Victor left, I had boldly registered for a weekend Buddhist retreat. Since I was a lonely Buddhist in my Be-a-Christian-or-Die community, I wanted to meet people who were on the same spiritual path as I was. The retreat was scheduled for the week after Victor left. Although I didn't know that would be an issue when I registered, I went anyway, hoping for lots of compassion and loving kindness. It was a silent retreat, however, so I didn't get a chance to bond with many people, even though I exchanged many deep, knowing looks and had an abundance of time for much-needed self-reflection.

2. On my birthday, I received a surprise email from Phil—my former hot-as-molten-lava flame and the man I'd had to give up when I recommitted to Victor after our first marriage counseling endeavor. He said he had overheard someone talking about my separation. I was stunned. Victor and I had agreed to keep the news confidential—immediate family only. Which I did. His "immediate family" apparently included his staff at work. I don't know who went home and told how many other residents of *Whoville* or who they swore to secrecy, but small towns being what they are, the break-up

of the Power Couple was *Miracle-Gro* for the grapevine.

3. Once Phil heard the rumor, he wanted to know if it was true. He was also concerned about my welfare, so he broke the no contact rule and emailed me. I wrote back and verified the facts. Since I wasn't sure what was happening with Victor, I needed to keep Phil out of the picture. I didn't want anything complicating an already confusing situation. He understood. Out of my life he went again with the assurance that, if I needed him, he was only an email or phone call away. He was still married and I didn't want to be the catalyst of the kind of hurt in his relationship that I was experiencing in mine.

4. I completed the quilt that I had started for Victor. I was determined to give it to him as his Christmas gift. My family and friends thought I was crazy and said I should keep it, but they didn't understand what the quilt symbolized. Since I was giving up all rights to the lake property—my "piece of heaven"—I wanted a piece of me at the lake. Plus, I like to finish what I start.

5. I hosted our family's New Year's gift exchange (our compromise to Christmas), which was the last family gathering in the Broken House. It was a doozy. We're supposed to write a poem or say something reflective about the year. That year, I decided to have everyone dance with me to my 2010 theme song, "Unbreakable," by Bon Jovi. Even Alex boogied along with the rest of my hip and happy family. (I had told him in advance, "This song is a power song about me,

not a slam-song about your father." He understood completely.)

6. Before Victor left, I had wanted to audit a writing class at LSU, (not LCC, where I used to teach, but the local university). I had never taken a writing class beyond freshman English. I didn't let getting dumped stop me from auditing an expository writing class that began in the spring, 2010, semester. I was the only non-traditional (i.e., old) student in the class. The professor loved my writing, but was brutally constructive in his suggestions for editing. My essays always needed editing—usually deleting unnecessary lingo. He told me not to bother taking another class. He said I should be writing for publications, but when I asked him, "Do you know anyone interested in publishing my work?" he didn't. At least he boosted my confidence.

7. I cooled off the Furnace Repair Guy.

8. After one of many this-marriage-sucks-because-of-you counseling sessions in early January, 2010, I picked the first realtor's office I saw on the street and bravely went in. The only realtor there to help me was a kind, compassionate, savvy woman who had plenty of tissues in her office. First, I explained my situation, then we began hunting for a small, reasonably priced home that required no maintenance. She was kind enough to withhold the fact that such a dwelling is imaginary. We searched for a while, and found one that met two of the three criteria (maintenance-free, ha!) in time for me to put a

real budget together for my final negotiations with Victor.

9. I sorted through the entire Broken House for the few material items I wanted to take with me, knowing that in my fresh start I didn't need the weight of "stuff" from the past to clutter my new space. I sorted and packed and left things behind that I thought I could never part with. I took anything that was mine (not ours), plus small items like lamps and a couple of dressers. Victor requested that I leave "just a few pictures to remember our past life." I took about a third of the pictures and some precious mementos of Alex's childhood. Victor probably thought I would strip the place clean. He went back to a still-fully-furnished house with dishes, flatware, linens, and all.

10. I volunteered at the local animal shelter and the public library to help them write grants. Feeling productive and needed by someone other than my family was essential to my sense of self. I needed to prove I could still function in the real world, mostly because I had to function in the real world.

In March, 2010, I made an offer that was accepted on a sweet little condo that was perfect for Scrappy the dog and me. Maybe it didn't have granite kitchen countertops or a circular staircase, but each room had ceilings and all the electrical outlets were covered. I couldn't wait to move in into my new home. As it happened, I would have to wait a long time.

I hadn't planned to apply for a mortgage after the mortgage crisis leading to the Wall Street Bail-out. A year before, bankers had been begging to give you a mortgage.

All you needed to have as collateral were a pulse and the ability to sign an X on the dotted line. But getting a mortgage on my modest new home proved vastly more difficult. I had my own solid credit history and, with Victor's monthly payments, qualified for the mortgage. I also had a credit history entangled with Victor's. But my name was also on the mortgage of the Broken House and two other properties I no longer owned, and one credit card with a balance, too. While the terms of our separation stated *he* was supposed to refinance those properties in *his name only* and pay off the card, cash flow wasn't flowing fast enough to make all of that happen quickly enough to satisfy the Mortgage Gods, who saw me on paper as a "risk."

Victor, being in the business community, found a mortgage broker known for being "creative." Mortgage Wizard assured me that my mortgage would close by the beginning of May, 2010. Since another term of our separation was that I had to pay Victor rent to stay in the Broken House until I moved out, I became a renter in the home that had been mine for the past twenty years. But it was only for a month, I thought, so I sucked it up and paid Victor the rent I owed him for April.

As April wore on, I could see that Mortgage Wizard's act was as genuine as the Wizard of Oz, or, actually, the man behind the curtain. Closing my mortgage was pushed back to the middle of May, and he needed volumes more documentation from Victor and me. Believing that he was telling me the truth (naïve mortgage dolt that I was) and not wanting to rent my former home for another month (dignified cheapskate that I was), I decided to move out May 1. My younger sister and her husband own a vacation home about an hour away in the mountains. They offered it to me rent-free for as long as I needed it. We all thought it would only be a couple of weeks, and I needed a little R&R after a decade of illness and relationship turmoil I'd been through, so a two-week "vacation" in the mountains seemed perfectly timed. My older sister and her husband have a large covered trailer into which we moved all my earthly possessions, save the few things I took with me on my "vacation." My "stuff" was hauled to their house and I hauled Scrappy and myself to the mountains.

As I walked through the Broken House one last time, I was uncharacteristically dry-eyed. I had said my good-byes so many times, the final farewell seemed anti-climactic. The only room in which I cried was Alex's. And there I sobbed as I remembered the days when I had bathed Alex and sung him to sleep; I could still hear his peals of laughter and feel his too-tight hugs. I grieved the loss of my son who didn't know how to love his mother up close anymore. I cried for him and the pain he'd locked inside himself because he hated change and change was all around him. I cried for myself and my irrational desire to understand Victor's motives for leaving me. I cried for Victor and how hard it would be for him to come back to that big, empty house.

Then I stopped crying and thought about rehydrating.

*****

My two-week "vacation" in the mountains was great. I had good cell-phone coverage, but no Internet. TV reception was as good as it was in the 1800s. I got quite chummy with the local librarian, who let me borrow more than the normal quota of videos and DVDs. I read, wrote, took Scrappy for walks, and spent a great deal of time pestering Mortgage Wizard.

During this time, I also called Phil to let him know I was officially single and doing fine. He was relieved and had a story of his own to tell me. His marriage had been on the skids for several years, but he was holding it together for the sake of his children (the youngest would be going off to college that fall). He knew that once the kids were gone, his marriage would be gone, too. I suggested marriage counseling. Well, gee, it had worked so well for me both times. When we spoke again, he told me his wife wasn't interested in counseling. He said he wanted to see me, just to talk. I agreed, but made it clear I wasn't the "other woman" kind of gal. We saw each other and the same sparks that had ignited thirty years ago lit up an already bright day. We talked a long while and many times after that. He soon left his wife and their formal separation followed.

Two weeks of "vacation" stretched into four weeks, which distended into six weeks. Taking care of my mail and bills, seeing my family and friends, and making appointments with medical doctors became nightmares since I had a two-hour round trip facing me every time I left my temporary home. By mid-June, my younger sister and her family needed their lodge back. Summer was here and her kids were out of school. The sellers of my condo were also getting nervous. They gave me an ultimatum: "Close by June 30, or we're pulling the contract."

As the universe gave me a reminder that was hard to ignore, I forgot my Buddhist teaching about not to worry about the future. On June 10, 2010, I was almost struck by lightning. For the second time.

But you already know about that.

EPILOGUE

All is well in my world. It always was. I just didn't know it. And it always will be. Now I know it.

When Phil separated from his wife, he moved into my little condo with me and Scrappy. I never expected him to be in my life again, let alone living with me. Had I known he would be part of my picture when I was looking for homes, I would've chosen a place with room for a wood shop—one of his many talents and passions. But the condo was a perfect place for both of us. We each needed to let go of the remnants of our pasts and simplify our lives.

We spoke at length about our separate pasts and our future together, something the Buddhist in me warned against but the human in me required. We agreed that our ex-spouses had found it easy to blame one or both of us for breaking up our marriages. I can understand that. What are the chances that an accidental meeting in a library when we were in our early twenties would end up with thirty years of finding each other again and again until we stopped losing each other? If it hadn't happened to me, I wouldn't believe it, either.

Neither of us regrets the paths we chose, nor the lives that came from those choices. Still, we are keenly aware that we were given something few people in this life get: *another chance*. It seems that now we're both ready to be in each other's lives for good. When I imagined Phil during my lonely years, I created Fantasy Phil—a two-dimensional sexy hero. My imagination pales in the face of Real Phil, who is a multi-dimensional perfect-for-me man. He's kind, funny, smart, thoughtful, and generous. This man actually whistles while he works, reminding me of only one other man in my life who did that—my beloved Pépé. He's also very handy around the house, finishing every project he starts. Whether I stay just as I am or change day by day, he loves me. And he, too, loves dogs.

*****

I'm in my mid-fifties and I'm still asking, "How was I supposed to know things would turn out like this?" My only answer is: *I was never meant to know*. There was a time when that answer would have scared the bejeebers out of me. Not anymore.

For the first time in my life, I'm perfectly fine being lost. Being *me*. I may not know what lies in wait around the corner, but I finally know that I can handle whatever it is. Rather than relying on others to tell me what I should do, think, or feel, all I have to do is trust my voice…now that I have found it.

And to think, all it took for me to transform myself from *actress into director of* my life was finally realizing that lightning, alcoholism, childhood tragedy, health crises, and getting dumped after twenty-six years of marriage have never stopped me from looking forward to what's next.

And I've got this feeling that whatever is next is going to be good. Maybe it will even be worth writing about.

ACKNOWLEDGEMENTS

Every person in my life—past and present, dead or alive—is, in some way, responsible for helping to make this book—my dream—a reality. Whether your part was large or small, you impacted me, thus you influenced my life, my story, and how I chose to tell it. For that I thank you, whether you wish to be thanked or not.

There are, however, specific people who were integral in bringing this book out of my head and into your hands. Since you know I have a fondness for lists, why stop now?

1. To Barbara Ardinger, Ph.D., my editor: I'm not sure how you are able to shape my words to say what I mean rather than what I wrote, but you can, and I am forever in your debt. That we share a love of the English language, life-long learning, words, puns, and a sassy sense of humor made working with you both fun and educational on so many levels.

2. To Emily Castine and Phillip Gugliotti: You both took time from your uncommonly busy schedules to read my not-ready-for-prime-time manuscript and gave me constructive feedback on how to make it readier-for-prime-time. You both did this not because you *had to* (like my family sort of had to) but because you *wanted to*. It was a big job and deserves a big thank-you of your choosing. We'll talk later, okay?

3. To my many, many blogger buddies at WordPress.com: You read snippets of my stories over many months and told me they were good.

You encouraged me to write this book and gave me tips on how to publish it. You even are helping me to market it. I can't name all of you, so naming any of you doesn't seem fair. Just know that I know who you are and I am so very grateful for your support—past, present and future.

4. To Alex, Mom, Tina, Lisa, the rest of my family and my friends who have served as proofreaders (Alex, Mom, Tina, and Lisa) and very tolerant listeners as I have blathered on about little else other than this book for way too long: I appreciate your support of me and this seemingly interminable endeavor more than you could possibly know. During those long years when I felt knocked down by my dizziness and lethargy, you longed to have something else to ask me about other than my health. Well, here's a lesson! Be careful what you wish for.

5. To Scrappy: I'm sorry for ignoring you. Does it help that I plan to write a book about all of my animal companions over the years? I thought not.

6. Finally, to my Phil: Without your computer savvy, this book might never have actually looked like a book. You mastered Photoshop so you could do the cover. You figured out the uploading-conversion-hocus-pocus. You fixed the furnace when it broke. You made me laugh when I started to panic. You read the first draft and laughed. You also said, "Really?" A lot. You believe in me and this book. For all of this and so much more, *I thank my lucky stars for the gift of you.*

ABOUT THE AUTHOR

Lorna Lee

In her former life as a sociology professor, Lorna published many academic and research papers. Creative writing is a new path taken since her premature disability retirement in 2006 due to Chronic Fatigue and Immune Dysfunction Syndrome. In 2010, she was a finalist in the Memoir genre of the *Writer's Digest Annual Writing Contest* with her short story, "Monkey Business." This memoir is her first book-length publication. Somewhere in her mom's closet is a single edition of original poems about a frog, a ghost, and a kitten. The booklet was illustrated by Lisa (her younger sister) and compiled for her mother's birthday when Lorna was about seven years old. In case anyone is searching for it, the cover was made from green construction paper.

Lorna currently lives with the man of her dreams and the dog of her dreams in the home of her dreams: a cozy, finished, and decidedly unbroken home. She keeps herself busy writing, quilting, walking, and blogging. To find out more about Lorna and her current shenanigans, visit her blog, lornasvoice.com.

SUGGESTED BOOK CLUB DISCUSSION QUESTIONS

- Novels require plots to move the story along. Memoirs are held together by one or more themes. What theme(s) do you think the author used in telling this portion of her life story? Give specific examples from the book.
- What surprised you about the author's life story or how she told her story? Give specific examples. Why were you surprised?
- What lesson(s) did you take away from the author's life story? Did it/they have more to do with what happened to her or how she told her story? Explain, using details from the story.
- Did your impression of the author change over the course of reading the book? If so, in what way and why? If not, what quality or qualities remained consistent throughout your experience with this author?
- If you were to tell your life story, did this memoir influence either how you would tell it or what you would include? Be specific in your answer.

Made in the USA
Lexington, KY
27 June 2013